Aunt Phil's Trunk
Volume Five

Bringing Alaska's history alive!

By
Phyllis Downing Carlson
Laurel Downing Bill

Aunt Phil's Trunk LLC
Anchorage, Alaska

www.auntphilstrunk.com

Cover photograph of the northern lights over Kodiak Island in May 2015 by Melissa Baines Graphic Design & Photography of Kodiak, Alaska.

Other front cover photo credits from top left: Street merchants, Alaska State Library, Pipeline Impact Collection, ASL-P17-9124; strings of pipe, Alaska State Library, Trans-Alaska Pipeline Construction Collection, ASL-P2-5-56; helicopter, Alaska State Troopers. Center photo, Anchorage Fourth Avenue earthquake, Alaska State Library, U.S. Army Signal Corps, ASL-P175-186. Lower left: Walter Hickel, Alaska State Library, Portrait File, ASL-P01-4686; MV Wickersham, Alaska State Library, Herbert J. "Red" Lockert Collection, ASL-P452-169; X-ray pipe weld, Alaska State Library, Pipeline Impact Collection, ASL-P17-8052.

Back cover photo credits from left: Oil platform Cook Inlet, Alaska State Library, Alaska Division of Tourism Collection, ASL-P22-06-069; Howard Rock, University of Alaska Fairbanks, Alfred R. Ketzler Collection, UAF-1992-202-9; Cowboys in Fairbanks, Alaska State Library, Pipeline Impact Collection, ASL-P17-8218.

International Standard Book Number 978-1-940479-26-2
Library of Congress Control Number 2016908361

Printed and bound in the United States of America.

First Printing 2015
First Printing Second Edition 2018

DEDICATION

I dedicate Volume Five to the memory of my paternal aunt, Phyllis Downing Carlson. She was one of Alaska's most respected historians, and without her lifelong interest, and then researching and writing about Alaska, this series would never exist.

I also want to dedicate the work to Aunt Phil's stepchildren, grandchildren, great-grandchildren and their families; to my brothers and sisters, their families and all our cousins. And I dedicate the work to my husband, Donald; son Ryan and his wife, Kaboo; daughter Kim and her husband, Bruce Sherry; and daughter Amie and her husband, Toby Barnes. Thank you so much for believing in me.

Lastly, I dedicate this collection of historical stories to my grandchildren, Sophia Isobel and Maya Josephine Sherry; Aiden Kou and Fischer Nhia Bill; and Toben Alexander, Conner Vincent and Zachary Victor Barnes. May you and future generations be the keepers of our history.

ACKNOWLEDGMENTS

I extend a heartfelt thank you to Robert DeBerry, formerly of Anchorage, for his excellent attention to detail as he readied for publication the majority of the historical photographs that appear in this volume of *Aunt Phil's Trunk*. I also am grateful to Nancy Pounds of Anchorage for slaving away with her eagle eyes to carefully proofread the pages.

My family deserves medals, as well, for putting up with me as I chased down just the right photographs to go with the stories, pored through research and sat hunched over my computer for hours writing the stories that fill the pages of *Aunt Phil's Trunk Volume Five*.

I love each and every one of you!

INTRODUCTION

The stories that fill this fifth volume of *Aunt Phil's Trunk* pay homage to people, places and events that helped shape Alaska's first 25 years of statehood. While it does not cover every story of the era, it highlights some of the major and minor tales between 1959 and 1984.

Those early Alaska statehood years were a roller-coaster ride that took the infant state from the poorhouse to the penthouse. Oil discoveries on its North Slope brought riches beyond any of its residents' dreams. Billions of barrels in black gold surpassed the golden riches clawed out of its creeks and mountains during the gold-rush era.

The new state traveled a rocky road on its journey from rags to riches. When it officially became a state on Jan. 3, 1959, it had a population of about 200,000 people. Its newly elected governor and legislature had to create a government to cover 586,412 square miles – one-fifth the size of the entire Lower 48 – from scratch, since the federal government had run the show since 1867, following America's purchase of Alaska from the Russians. The United States designated the vast land a possession at that time, run at first by the War Department. It became a territory in 1912.

"We were the only organized territory precluded by federal law from selection of any lands, from the management whatsoever of its natural resources, from creating a territory-wide judicial system, or a local government system, with the exception of the creation of certain first-class cities," said William A. Egan, Alaska's first elected governor, in an article for *The Anchorage Times* on Jan. 3, 1984. "We had no voting rights in Congress, yet we paid all federal taxes."

Alaskans entered the new era with optimism, but they also knew they had a lot of work to do. They faced challenges in health care, housing, communications and an inflated cost of living. Howard Weaver, then managing editor of the *Anchorage Daily News*, described it best in a special publication titled "The Flag Unfurled," dated Jan. 3, 1984, which highlighted Alaska's first 25 years of statehood.

"... children died because the best medical care was a seven-hour plane ride away in Seattle. The worrisome initials were TB, not PCB, and tuberculosis consumed Alaskans at a fierce rate. Village housing would have needed considerable improvement to deserve a 'sub-standard' rating, and inflation and the cost of living regularly galloped past national rates. Long-distance communication was either expensive or absent."

In light of all the challenges facing Alaska, Weaver asked the question: Why do all those photos of early statehood days show so many smiling faces? He concluded what most Alaskans instinctively know – living in Alaska may be challenging, but it's fun.

"The secret of Alaska is that verbs matter more than nouns," he wrote. "It isn't the parade that's important, it's the parading."

Which is why it's not surprising to those who call Alaska home that the early movers and shakers of statehood jumped into the deep end of the pool and soon were attempting to better the lives of Alaskans. They built the infrastructure for self-governance, including creating a judicial system, a local government system and a land and resource management system. The Alaska Marine Highway System developed during this time, too. By early 1964, new ferries connected the people of Southeast Alaska and transformed their lives.

Alaskans accomplished much during the first five years of statehood. The next five brought the lowest of lows and the highest of highs to the fledgling state.

The lowest point occurred on March 27, 1964, at 5:36 p.m. The largest earthquake ever to hit the North American continent struck Southcentral Alaska with a jolt that measured 9.2 on the Moment Magnitude Scale and lasted nearly five minutes.

That Good Friday quake devastated communities from Prince William Sound to Kodiak Island, killing 114 people in Alaska. The seismic sea wave that fanned out into the Pacific killed another four people in Oregon and 12 in California.

Alaska's people were down but not out following this horrendous event, which caused $400 million in damage – more than $3 billion in 2015 dollars. They rolled up their sleeves and dug in for the hard

Anchorage Museum at Rasmuson Center. Ward W. Wells Collection. AMRC-wws-4176-19

The largest earthquake in North American history, registering 9.2 on the Moment Magnitude Scale, brought Alaska's residents to their knees on March 27, 1964. This view, looking west down Fourth Avenue in Anchorage, shows how the street dropped during the 4 minutes and 38 seconds of violent shaking.

The tall building in the background is the Anchorage Westward Hotel. Other businesses shown include Anchorage Arcade, Scandinavian Club Bar, Mac's Foto, Frisco Bar & Cafe, D & D Bar and Cafe and Koslosky's Store for Men.

work of rebuilding their towns, roads and bridges. Federal aid helped ease some of the financial burden caused by so much destruction.

Then, in March 1968, Alaskans learned the solution to future financial worries might be just around the corner. Atlantic Richfield Co. announced that one of its exploratory wells hit black gold on Alaska's North Slope. In partnership with Humble Oil Co., Atlantic Richfield's test well showed a flow of a couple thousand barrels of oil a day pouring from its Prudhoe Bay site.

Another well drilled the following summer confirmed that the largest pool of crude discovered in America lay beneath the wind-swept tundra of Prudhoe Bay. Experts estimated it held about 10 billion barrels of recoverable reserves.

In 1969, the state leased land to many oil companies for drilling in Prudhoe Bay, which added almost $1 billion to its coffers. But the state faced a major roadblock to the building of a pipeline to carry crude from those leases to tidewater. Alaska Natives claimed much of the land across Alaska belonged to them, so the issue of who owned what land needed to be settled.

Again, Alaskans hunkered down and got to work during the next four years to settle the land issue. On Dec. 18, 1971, President Richard M. Nixon signed the Alaska Native Claims Settlement Act into law. It was the largest Native land claims settlement in U.S. history.

With the land claims issue settled, construction began on the 800-mile-long trans-Alaska oil pipeline to carry crude from Prudhoe Bay to a marine terminal at the ice-free port of Valdez. The first barrel of oil flowed down the engineering marvel in 1977 and started royalty dollars flowing into the state treasury at a rate of about $70 a second.

Those pipeline-building years brought a huge rush of people to Alaska, as well. By 1980, Alaska's population had doubled to about 400,000. The people who headed north to take advantage of new opportunities were not all associated with the oil industry, however. Immigrants from Asia, South America, Russia and many other places carved out niches in the Last Frontier. They came alone or to join family members and often started out as dishwashers, maids and laborers until they learned enough English to move up the labor ladder or establish businesses of their own.

Jobs from coal extraction, mineral development, commercial fishing and a burgeoning tourism industry also began to grow. As the first quarter-century of statehood came to a close, its first governor saw nothing but opportunities on the horizon for its next 25 years.

"I see as much progress, as much growth, in the next 25 years, if not more, than the first 25 years of statehood," Egan said in 1984.

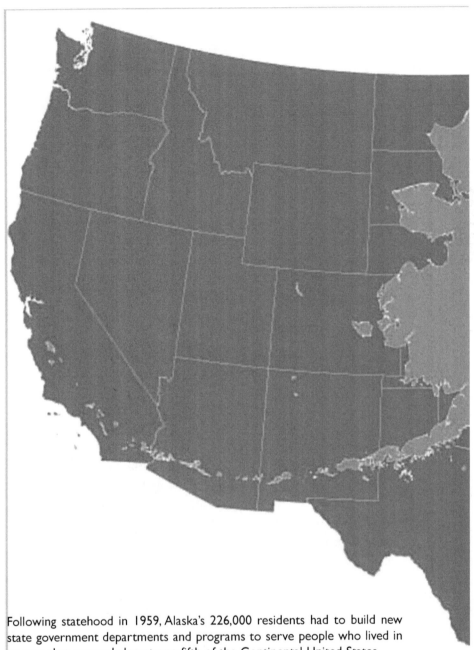

Following statehood in 1959, Alaska's 226,000 residents had to build new state government departments and programs to serve people who lived in an area that covered almost one-fifth of the Continental United States.

Alaska

TABLE OF CONTENTS

TABLE OF CONTENTS

THE BIG YEAR

1

THE PEOPLE'S GOVERNOR

Alaska's first elected governor had a wild ride through the early statehood years. He and the first state Legislature created a government from scratch, opened up Southeast Alaska with the Marine Highway System and rebuilt Alaska following the destruction wrought by the largest earthquake ever to hit North America.

How did Alaska-born William A. Egan get the tools needed to lead the 49th state through those uncharted waters? A look back at his early life may give some clues.

Egan entered the world on Oct. 8, 1914, in Valdez, the sixth child of miner William Edgar Egan and his wife, Cora Allen. The family arrived in the little saltwater town on Prince William Sound in 1903, following copper mining in Montana and mining for gold in Juneau, according to an article by June Allen, titled "Oct. 8: William A. Egan Day," which appeared in *SitNews* on Oct. 8, 2003.

During Egan's childhood, Valdez grew into one of Alaska's largest Southcentral communities – bigger than Seward and Cordova. Surrounded by gold-bearing mountains, the prospects for the Egans seemed limitless – until disaster struck.

An avalanche tumbled down a mountainside in 1920 as Egan's father and three other mining company employees were shoveling out a tramline on Shoup Glacier, about seven miles out of town. Piles of snow buried the men.

When Alaska's first elected governor was born in Valdez in 1914, the little town in Prince William Sound was well-established with several businesses.

Rescuers managed to dig three of them out alive. But when they reached Egan's father, he was dead. The miner left his wife with seven children to care for on her own.

Cora Egan managed to eke out a living for herself and her children. She rented rooms, took in laundry, nursed people when needed and even worked part time as a jail matron.

Young Bill chipped in, too. By 10 years old, he was attending school and working in a local cannery to help support the struggling family, Allen wrote.

Since there were no restrictions on driver's ages at the time, the lad also learned to drive and began shuttling tourists around his picturesque town during summers. By 14, Egan was driving dump trucks for the Alaska Road Commission.

He also learned to fly and caught the attention of Robert "Bob" Campbell Reeve, who arrived in Valdez in 1932 and became one of

Alaska's most well-known aviators. Reeve witnessed Egan's first solo flight and signed him up as a "bombardier" to drop supplies at mining camps. The young pilot later worked as Reeve's mechanic, according to late historian Elizabeth Tower.

Egan enjoyed school and was a good student. He graduated salutatorian from Valdez High School in 1932. That honor meant he had to give a speech at graduation. A skilled writer, he crafted a good address, but he panicked halfway through its presentation and froze. Class valedictorian George Ashby finished the speech for him.

Following Egan's graduation, his godfather, Anthony Dimond, ran as a Democrat and won the position as the territory's nonvoting delegate to the U.S. House of Representatives. Dimond – a local lawyer, two-time mayor and member of the Alaska Territorial Senate – sent copies of the Congressional Record back to Valdez for his constituents to read.

His godson eagerly perused the documents and absorbed the nuances of politics with a passion. He had a gift for remembering facts and names and retrieving them when needed. He became known for debating issues at the Pinzon Bar, as well as engaging in political debates with another Valdez boy, George Sullivan,

When Anthony J. Dimond became the territory's nonvoting delegate to the U.S. House of Representatives in the 1930s, he sent copies of the Congressional Record back to Valdez, where his godson, William A. Egan, read them with great interest.

who later became the mayor of Anchorage. Witnesses said that Sullivan's mother often coached young George in order to counteract the arguments Egan, seven years his senior, presented.

Egan also became interested in the grocery business in the 1930s. He and a friend bought a grocery store and butcher shop in Valdez. Then, in 1937, Egan began pursuing another interest when a young lady from Kansas arrived in town.

Desdia Neva McKittrick, one of three new teachers at the Valdez school that year, caught his attention. She turned down the grocer's offers for dates at first, but she warmed up to him when she learned of his "kind and considerate" nature, she once told an interviewer.

The couple married in 1940, the same year Egan won election to the Territorial House of Representatives. The freshman Democrat introduced a statehood referendum in 1941, which the Territorial Senate rejected.

When World War II erupted, Egan joined the U.S. Army. After the war ended, he returned to the House in 1946 and reintroduced the statehood proposal. He also became mayor of Valdez that year.

He and Neva welcomed a son, Dennis, in 1947. Dennis followed in his father's footsteps to become a state senator and also served as the mayor of Juneau.

Egan spent three more terms in the House, from 1947-1953, and then was elected to the Territorial Senate. He continued to suffer from his fear of public speaking, however. He often practiced in front of a mirror to lessen the stress. A witness later said that during one of his speeches in the Legislature, even Republicans could be heard to mutter, "Come on, Bill, you can do it!"

Even if public speaking was not his strong suit, members of both houses respected him. They knew he was steadfast, dependable and had Alaska's best interest at heart.

So when the 1955 Territorial Legislature decided to follow the precedent Tennessee had set in 1796 – drafting a constitution and electing congressmen as if it was already a state – they chose Egan as chairman of the Alaska Constitutional Convention.

Egan presided over the 75-day convention at the University of

William A. Egan, pictured in the center on stage, was chosen chairman and presided over the Alaska Constitutional Convention at the University of Alaska Fairbanks from November 1955 to February 1956.

Alaska at Fairbanks and became known as the father of the state's constitution. The document that evolved was signed by members of the convention on Feb. 3, 1956, and approved by Alaska voters on April 24 by a vote of 17,447 to 7,180, newspapers reported.

Voters also chose Egan and Ernest Gruening as their first U.S. senators and Ralph Rivers as their representative. Alaska's new congressional delegation left Alaska in December that year and drove across the country to Washington, D.C. They averaged 300 miles a day, and when they finally reached the nation's capitol, they presented Alaska's Constitution to Congress.

The Alaska delegation pounded the halls of Congress for a year and a half trying to convince lawmakers that Alaska should be made a state. Egan later confessed that he thought the statehood bill was dead the day before the critical vote in May 1958.

"That night the Alaska delegation and their friends made 91 phone calls, and the outlook was not favorable," Egan said in a 1978 interview for the *Anchorage Daily News*.

1. Level and rolling land with good drainage.
2. A good road system with prospects of better.
3. Alaska Railroad and airport facilities that can be enlarged.
4. Ideal weather conditions for health and flying.
5. Plenty of land, property values low.
6. Safe distance from military target, in case of nuclear warfare.
7. Big Lake and Mt. McKinley recreational areas, Matanuska Valley farm products and Anchorage culture only a short distance away.

Big Lake's residents showed much enthusiasm for their Capital City idea, but it went nowhere. And people across the state continued to complain about the difficulties of getting to and from Juneau.

So how did Juneau become Alaska's capital in the first place? Russians had chosen Sitka as the seat of government at the time Alaska became a possession of the United States in 1867. The first Organic Act of 1884 officially established "the temporary seat of government" there, as well. The first five governors appointed to America's new possession, most of which were military men, used the long Russian building adjoining the parade grounds for their offices.

The discovery of gold deposits in the 1880s in the area that became Juneau caused that town to grow in population, influence and accommodations. A need also grew to settle boundary disputes, contracts, payments and other legal matters that necessitated travel to Sitka to see a judge.

Only two ships a month sailed between Juneau and Sitka. So if attorneys had issues that needed resolving, they had to hope they could conclude their business quickly or they had to wait two weeks to catch a boat back home.

Lawyers in Juneau began pressuring Congress to pass a bill that would move Alaska's seat of government to Juneau, stating the town now was the largest city in Alaska, had become an established mining town and had a promising future. Juneau also featured great communications. It took a few weeks for mail to travel from Washington, D.C., to Juneau, but months to reach more northerly sites, according to historians.

Gov. John Brady did not want to leave his home in Sitka to move to Juneau after the Civil Code was adopted in 1900. This photo shows his garden at Old Castle Sitka.

Their efforts succeeded. President William McKinley signed the Alaska Bill, or Civil Code, into law on June 6, 1900. The 600-page document was the longest bill ever passed by Congress at the time and it stated, in part:

"… The temporary seat of government of said district is hereby established at Juneau: Provided that the seat of government shall remain in Sitka until suitable grounds and buildings thereon shall be obtained by purchase or otherwise at Juneau."

The language providing for the delay in the move was aimed at discouraging Juneau property owners from jacking up the price of their land. But as soon as the Civil Code became law, the District Court and the U.S. Marshal moved to Juneau. Two years later, the Collector of Customs transferred his seals, sealing wax and papers.

Moving the seat of government to Juneau wasn't a big deal for most of Juneau's residents and merchants. It basically meant that the governor and surveyor-general's offices would relocate.

But that did not happen for six more years. Then-governor John

THE BIG YEAR

Brady did not want to leave Sitka and his home. He had his hand in business ventures there, including a sawmill, and decided to stay put until his term expired and continued to promote resources in his neck of the woods, according to a 1984 article about Brady written by Alaska historian Stephen Haycox.

However, when people began complaining to Washington that Brady was consorting with a con man named H.D. "Harry" Reynolds, who was bilking people out of money for a railroad out of Valdez, the Interior Department terminated Brady's tenure and appointed Wilford B. Hoggatt to the office of governor on March 2, 1906. The U.S. Senate confirmed Hoggatt, who had mining interests in Juneau, on March 21.

Hoggatt immediately established an office in Juneau, accepted Brady's clerk's resignation and had all Brady's records packed up and shipped to Juneau. In September, the surveyor-general boarded a steamer with 40 tons of paperwork and traveled to Juneau. That completed the transfer of Alaska's "seat of government."

Juneau officially became Alaska's first and only capital in 1912 when Alaska became a territory of the United States. Elections held

University of Alaska Fairbanks, Nome dog mushing photographs. UAF-1984-192-17

Lawmakers from Nome mushed dog teams for months to get to Valdez, where they then continued on by ship to Juneau to attend the territory's first legislative session in 1913.

The first Alaska Territorial Legislature met on March 3, 1913, in the Juneau Elks Hall.

that year provided senators and representatives for the new territorial Legislature. Legislators from Nome, Ruby, Fairbanks, Seward, Valdez, Skagway, Sitka, Wrangell, Ketchikan, Fox, Knik, Iditarod, Candle and Katalla traveled to join legislators of Juneau and Douglas for the first legislative session held in March 1913.

Grumbling about the difficulty of traveling to the capital from these locations began immediately. Charles D. Jones and Elwood Bruner of Nome left town on the last southbound steamship in October in order to get to Juneau in time for the session. And they had not yet been elected to office. Luckily, the men won their seats that November.

Four more candidates from Nome waited for the election, and when they won their bids to join the territory's first legislators, hitched up dog teams and headed toward Fairbanks on Jan. 7. Conrad Freeding, Frank Aldrich, J.C. Kennedy and Tom Gaffney stopped en route at Ruby and picked up Dan Sutherland, Ruby's representative, according to a story written by June Allen titled "Alaska's First Legislature, 1913" that appeared in *SitNews* on Jan. 18, 2003.

The five men mushed on to Fairbanks. There they rested a bit and then continued on to Valdez, where some sources say they met Henry Roden of Iditarod and Milo Kelly of Knik. The men boarded the steamer *Northwestern*, bound for Juneau, in mid-February.

Alaska's first legislative session, consisting of eight senators and 15 of 16 elected representatives, met in the Elks Hall for their first gathering on March 3, 1913. The federal government paid them $15 per day (about $360 in today's dollars) and .15 per mile, which came to $600-$700 for the Nome fellows who traveled by dog teams (around $16,700 in 2015 dollars), Allen wrote.

This first territorial Legislature quickly brought up the question of moving the capital. The body of 23 members – J.J. Mullaly of Fairbanks had left Alaska before the November election and never returned to claim his seat – debated the issue when they introduced a bill to ask Congress for a federal building.

Col. B.F. Millard of Valdez proposed his town for the new site,

Alaska's new governor, Wilford B. Hoggart, set up offices in the Presbyterian Mission Building in Juneau in 1906, seen here as it was being torn down in 1929 to make way for the new Capitol Building.

but Juneau legislators protested that it would be too expensive and politically foolish to move the capital.

"Juneau is not Alaska," Millard retorted. But the issue was allowed to die. The legislators adopted a budget that totaled $68,000 (more than $1.6 million today) for that first year of operation, according to newspaper articles.

The territory's Legislature met in rented halls for the next 18 years before they moved into the Capitol Building, completed in 1931. Two issues had delayed its construction: World War I, and the owner of the property wanted twice as much as the government wanted to pay for the land. Juneau residents took the matter into their own hands and raised the balance of the purchase price to get the project going in 1929.

The capital move came up again during the 1955 Constitutional Convention held at the University of Alaska in Fairbanks that November. Most delegates wanted to avoid the issue. But those who wanted the capital to remain in Juneau hoped the final draft of the constitution would make it the permanent capital. Those who wanted the capital moved to Western Alaska wanted nothing that gave Juneau constitutional status as the state capital, according to historians.

When the convention finished its job in February 1956, the constitution adopted for establishing statehood included Article XV – Schedule of Transitional Measures, Section 20: "The capital of the state of Alaska shall be at Juneau."

Following Alaska's official entry as the 49th state on Jan. 3, 1959, a petition immediately began circulating to move the capital. On Aug. 9, 1960, voters turned down Initiative Proposal No. 1 to move the capital from Juneau to the Cook Inlet Railbelt area with 18,856 voting yes and 23,972 voting no.

Undaunted, those who wanted the capital moved regrouped and got enough signatures to place another initiative on the ballot two years later. It called for relocating the capital "… in Western Alaska, to a site not within 30 miles of Anchorage." The November 1962 general election resulted in the same outcome as before – voters rejected the proposal by a vote of 26,542 for and 32,325 against.

The state Capitol Building, seen here at 120 E. Fourth St. in Juneau, was completed in 1931. Note the bronze brown bear sculpture by R.T. "Skip" Wallen in front of the building. It was commissioned by the Silver Anniversary Committee of Juneau to celebrate the first 25 years of Alaska Statehood 1959-1984. It's called Windfall Fisherman.

The third time was the charm for the capital movers' group, which had been supported and cheered on by Robert "Bob" Atwood, editor and publisher of the *Anchorage Daily Times*. Voters approved Initiative Proposal No. 1 to relocate the capital to a Western Alaska site at least 30 miles from Anchorage in August 1974 with a vote of 46,659 yeas to 35,325 nays.

This initiative provided for a selection committee to pick three sites for consideration by the voters. Two years later, Alaska voters had to decide between Mount Yenlo, near Skwentna; Larson Lake, near Talkeetna; and Willow, located on the Parks Highway between Anchorage and Fairbanks – and 900 miles northwest of Juneau. Alaska law said if one site got one vote more than the other two, the capital must begin moving there in less than four years.

Voters chose Willow in the fall of 1976. Turns out that Juneau engineers and architects had compiled a 37-page report that recommended Willow, as well, 14 years earlier. That report advocated a 6,400-acre tract for a new capital city a few miles from Willow, with separate transportation and industrial sites and an airport.

The report stated the site had "... outstanding advantages. It is separate and apart from other developed areas which might give rise to conflicts ... has no permafrost or other sub-soil difficulties ... is on high and gently sloping ground requiring a minimum of clearing, grubbing and draining to be prepared for development."

The writers concluded that a completely new city for 9,500 people located on 1,420 acres would cost $262,700,000 for everything, including 3,035 single homes. That October 1962 analysis was short-lived, however, when voters rejected moving the capital to Western Alaska.

But by 1976, construction of the trans-Alaska oil pipeline was peaking and thousands of workers from the Lower 48 were calling Alaska home. Many of them felt that Willow was more accessible to the majority of the state's residents.

Jay Hammond, who had been elected Alaska's governor in 1974,

appointed a nine-member planning committee in June 1977 to plan the new capital site. Among its members were the mayors of Juneau and the Matanuska-Susitna Borough, mandated through a

Arliss Sturgulewski, acting chairwoman of the Capital Site Planning Commission, leads fellow commissioners Ron Larson and Lee Coffman, left, through the weeds of Willow after voters approved to move the state capital to that area.

bill passed by the Legislature. Other members included Arliss Sturgulewski, at the time a member of the Anchorage Municipal Assembly and a member of the original Capital Site Selection Committee; George Morrison, vice president of Alaska Mutual Savings Bank; Susan Overby, an active participant in Anchorage civic projects; Ken Carson, a contractor and former Fairbanks city councilman; Charles Behlke, chairman of the engineering department at the University of Alaska; Lee Coffman, president of the Juneau branch of Alaska Federal Savings and Loan; and Alaska Federation of Natives President Byron Mallott of Yakutat.

This commission faced the politically sensitive task of planning for a new capital city at Willow. They were to draft plans and cost estimates for a city of 30,000 people that was to be in operation by 1980, and present the plan and blueprints to the state Legislature by March 1978.

Willow residents were filled with joy. They invited everyone to a two-day midsummer festival during the 1977 Fourth of July holiday. They called it the First Annual Capital City Picnic, and it included a big bonfire, picnic, foot race and marshmallow roast that Sunday and Monday. The community also wanted Alaskans to look at the area where Alaska's new capital would be located.

Many people considered moving the capital a boondoggle.

"Willow was picked primarily because the folks in Los Anchorage – who really wanted the capital to themselves – felt that they needed to pay lip service to their friends in Squarebanks and pretend that a new capital – located between the two, but actually a lot closer to Anchorage – should be built in a brand new city," wrote Dave Kiffer in an article titled "We're Off On The Road To Alaska's Capital!" for *SitNews* on Aug. 31, 2009.

By 1978, estimates for the capital move bandied about in the press caused voters to think that perhaps they may have been a bit hasty to put down Juneau as their capital in the 1974 election. They approved an initiative that required the voters to approve any bond associated with costs to move the capital. They then rejected $966 million in general obligation bonds to build the new capital at Willow.

Anchorage Times photo

Helicopters became a common site as surveyors visited Willow.

Alaska voters again voted down a bond to move the capital from Juneau to Willow in 1982, when the bondable costs associated with the move came to $2.8 billion.

"Voters (or at least all those folks from Oklahoma and Texas who were pretending to be permanent) agreed [with the move]," Kiffer wrote. "But when it came to actually spending the money to carve Alaska's Brasilia out of the mosquito infested swamp in 1982, voters said 'wait just a darned cotton picking minute.'"

Eleven years later, a group headed by Alaska Rep. Pat Carney of Wasilla filed a petition for an initiative to move the capital to Wasilla, one of the fastest-growing regions of the state. The Wasilla City Council appropriated $40,000 to gather 26,000 signatures to place the question on the ballot.

That caused the Fiscally Responsible Alaskans Needing Knowledge Committee to get involved. It proposed an initiative that stated no money could be spent to move the capital until a commission appointed by the governor presented a bondable cost figure to voters and that voters had to approve the costs of such a move.

Voters made their wishes known in November 1994. They approved the FRANK initiative by a whopping 77 percent and rejected the initiative to move the capital to Wasilla, according to newspaper reports.

Proponents for moving the capital tried again in 2001. Lt. Gov.

Fran Ulmer certified an initiative to require the Alaska Legislature hold its sessions in the Matanuska-Susitna Borough and to repeal all provisions of the 1994 FRANK law.

"Three-fourths of the state's people live within a tank-full of gas of the valley," Uwe Kalenka said in an interview published by *The New York Times* in May 2002. Kalenka, a mini-mall manager from Anchorage, was one of the leaders of Alaskans for Efficient Government, the citizens' group that collected the signatures.

"They could travel by road to get their legislative business done in as little as a day – no boats, no planes, no weather delays, no expensive three-day overnight stays, no hassle," Kalenka said. "And it won't cost all that much to make the switch because there's not all that much to be done."

Those who wanted to keep the state Legislature in Juneau, headed by Win Gruening of the Alaska Committee, said the relocation forces were trying to "slip in through the back door," with their initiative to only move the Legislature.

University of Alaska Fairbanks, George A. Morlander Collection, UAF-1997-108-1

Juneau, seen here circa 1960, remains the capital of Alaska to this day.

"If the Legislature were to be moved, it would be only a matter of time before the rest of the government would go," said Gruening, whose family has a long history in Alaska politics. "And that would be a disaster for Juneau. Government accounts for close to 40 percent of the city's economy. You eliminate that and you don't solve a problem. You create one, because one of the three largest population centers in the state would be devastated, and at the same time the state would have wasted millions it doesn't have on a pure folly."

Voters soundly defeated this initiative on Nov. 5, 2002, by a 2 to 1 margin.

Improvement of communications through satellite offices and Internet access may have put a lid on future attempts to move Alaska's capital. Declining oil production and revenue also may reinforce what Gov. Bill Egan said in 1959.

"I don't think we can afford to foot the bill."

Which is why the issue of moving the capital died in the new state Legislature that year. The representatives of the state's first Legislature had bigger issues on their plate – like how to build new departments and programs needed to transfer from federal to state leadership.

3

FIRST STATE LEGISLATURE

Three weeks after President Dwight D. Eisenhower signed the statehood proclamation, the first Alaska State Legislature met in Juneau while Gov. William A. Egan recuperated from abdominal surgery in Seattle. Acting Gov. Hugh Wade welcomed the new representatives. One of the first orders of business following the opening gavel on Jan. 26, 1959, was to set legislators' terms.

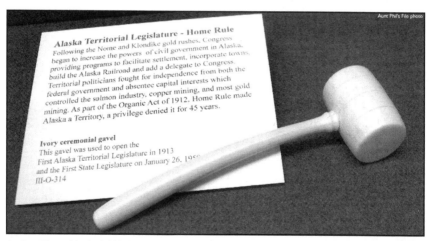

Aunt Phil's File photo

Alaska Territorial Legislature - Home Rule
Following the Nome and Klondike gold rushes, Congress began to increase the powers of civil government in Alaska, providing programs to facilitate settlement, incorporate towns, build the Alaska Railroad and add a delegate to Congress. Territorial politicians fought for independence from both the federal government and absentee capital interests which controlled the salmon industry, copper mining, and most gold mining. As part of the Organic Act of 1912, Home Rule made Alaska a Territory, a privilege denied it for 45 years.

Ivory ceremonial gavel
This gavel was used to open the First Alaska Territorial Legislature in 1913 and the First State Legislature on January 26, 1959.
III-O-314

Acting Gov. Hugh J. Wade rapped this ivory gavel – used to open every territorial Legislature – to call to order the first session of the first Alaska State Legislature on Jan. 26, 1959. Created by an unknown Eskimo carver, the gavel head is made from the tusk of a mammoth, a creature extinct in Alaska's Arctic and sub-Arctic regions for about 35,000 years. The mallet's 8-inch handle is carved from a walrus tusk.

Members of the first Alaska Senate included Senate President William E. Beltz, D-Unalakleet; James Nolan, D-Wrangell; Frank Peratrovich, D-Klawock; Walter O. "Bo" Smith, D-Ketchikan; Howard C. Bradshaw, D-Sitka; Thomas B. Stewart, D-Juneau; Ralph E. Moody, D-Anchorage; Irene E. Ryan, D-Anchorage; Balfour J. "Bob" Logan, D-Cordova; Joseph Earl Cooper, D-Anchorage; Irwin L. Metcalf, D-Seward; Alfred A. Owen, D-Uganik Bay; George B. McNabb Jr., D-Fairbanks; Robert J. McNeally, D-Fairbanks; Jack E. Weise, R-Bethel; John B. Coghill, R-Nenana; Hubert A. Gilbert, D-Fairbanks; Lester Bronson, D-Nome; Eben Hopson, D-Barrow; and John A. McNees, D-Nome.

All 60 members were carry-overs from the territorial Legislature, elected on Nov. 25, 1958. Senate Bill 70 set all representatives' terms, and senators serving short terms, to expire on Jan. 22, 1961. All terms for senators with long terms were set to expire on Jan. 27, 1963.

Alaska's legislators then rolled up their sleeves and began the task of creating dozens of bills to build the infrastructure necessary to run the nation's newest state. And they began their business amid forecasts by doomsayers that Alaska never could survive as a state and never would be economically viable. In fact, one state legislator was quoted as saying, "the honeymoon is over," during one of the Legislature's first meetings.

The job of equipping the huge frozen backcountry with the political machinery for self-government was a daunting task – especially considering the size of Alaska.

People were split into numerous local factions over where highways should be built, how boroughs should be set up and how the state would take over responsibilities that the federal government had always taken care of before statehood, according to newspaper articles of the time.

Alaska's problems may have been similar to those faced by previous states, as it strived to find funds to pay for increasingly costly schools, highways and services. But those other states grew up with the nation over a long period of time – Alaska had to catch up fast.

Members of the first Alaska House of Representatives included: Speaker of the House Warren A. Taylor, D-Fairbanks; Charles M. Jones, D-Craig; Oral E. Freeman, D-Ketchikan; James R. "J. Ray" Roady, D-Ketchikan; John E. Longworth, R-Petersburg; Frank E. Cashel, D-Sitka; Andrew Hope, D-Sitka; Douglas Gray, D-Douglas; Dora M. Sweeney, D-Juneau; Morgan W. Reed, D-Skagway; Harold Z. Hansen, D-Cordova; Bruce Kendall, R-Valdez; James J. Hurley, D-Palmer; Helen M. Fischer, D-Anchorage; James E. Fisher, D-Anchorage; John S. Hellenthal, D-Anchorage; Earl D. Hillstrand, D-Anchorage; Peter J. Kalamarides, D-Anchorage; Edward R. "Russ" Meekins, D-Anchorage; James E. Norene, D-Anchorage; John L. Rader, D-Anchorage; William M. Erwin, D-Seward; Allen L. Petersen, D-Kenai; Peter M. Deveau, D-Kodiak; Henry L. Haag, D-Kodiak; Charles J. Franz, D-Port Moller; Jay S. Hammond, I-Naknek; James Hoffman, R-Bethel; Donald Harris, R-McGrath; Grant H. Pearson, D-McKinley Park; Frank X. Chapados, D-Fairbanks; Joseph R. "Bob" Giersdorf, D-Fairbanks; Richard J. Greuel, D-Fairbanks; Robert E. Sheldon, D-Fairbanks; Warren A. Taylor, D-Fairbanks; R.S. McCombe, D-Chicken; John Nusunginya, D-Barrow; John E. Curtis, R-Kotzebue; Robert R. Blodgett, D-Nome; Charles E. Fagerstrom, D-Nome; and Axel C. Johnson, D-Kwiguk.

Prior to statehood, virtually every cabinet-level department of the federal government had some sort of interest in Alaska, and in every case that interest was pursued by an agency and several agents working in the territory, according to Territorial Gov. Scott Bone in a *Saturday Evening Post* article in the 1920s. And they usually were working at cross-purposes.

The Treasury Department was in charge of the customs service and the fur seal business; the Commerce Department monitored investments and controlled freight rates; the Agriculture Department ran experimental farms, grazing reserves, the national forests and the Bureau of Public Roads; the Labor Department monitored conditions in the mines and on the railroads; and the Interior Department ran the Bureau of Education, which ran the Alaska Native Service, which operated schools and hospitals, the latter for the Public Health Service. The Interior Department also ran the Fish and Wildlife Service, as well as the General Land Office and the national parks and monuments. The U.S. Navy and Army ran the telegraph line.

"It was a bewildering mess," said Alaska historian Stephen Haycox in an *Anchorage Times* article, titled "Disjointed government perplexed early governor," published on Feb. 12, 1984.

But the first state legislators worked diligently to untangle the web woven by the feds while also tackling issues like the amount for their own paychecks. Many Alaska residents raised eyebrows when the lawmakers initiated a bill to cover their pay at $35 per day (about $282 in 2015 dollars).

To put that pay into perspective, one could purchase a business lot in Homer for $1,150 or a parcel of land for $70 an acre; buy a pound of butter for 73 cents; and enjoy an Easter dinner at the new Westmark Hotel in Anchorage for $5 – dinner included crab cocktail, lobster tails, roast beef or ham with all the trimmings, according to an ad in the *Anchorage Daily Times*.

Lawmakers also introduced a bill providing for a $24,000 salary for the governor and $17,000 for the secretary of state. Setting the chief executives' yearly salaries became fodder for much debate as legislators also continued to wrangle over their own salaries while

One of the first actions of the 1959 Alaska Legislature was to establish Alaska's court system. The first state Supreme Court Justices were sworn in on Nov. 27, 1959. Seated from left to right are Walter Hodge of Nome, Chief Justice Buell A. Nesbett of Anchorage and John H. Dimond of Juneau. They all were to serve three-year terms.

Standing behind, from left, are Superior Court Justices Walter E. Walsh; Harry O. Arend; J. Earl Cooper; Everett W. Hepp; Hubert A. Gilbert; James A. von der Heydt; Edward V. Davis; and James M. Fitzgerald.

state bills waited their attention.

In March, the lawmakers passed the Statehood Organization Act that created 12 executive departments: administration, law, revenue, health and welfare, labor, commerce, military affairs, natural resources, public safety, public works, education and fish and game. They also passed a bill to set up Alaska's state court system, although there was a fight afoot over Superior Court judge salaries. The Senate had suggested a yearly salary of $21,500 and the House countered with $19,000, newspapers reported.

On March 13, legislators came to an agreement for the governor's salary and set it at $25,000 (more than $203,000 in 2015 dollars). They also passed the first state budget, which included $11.4 million for education – the largest item of the budget.

Acting Gov. Wade vetoed the budget soon after.

The *Anchorage Daily Times* reported on March 31 that Alaska's first duly elected lawmakers had voted $76,120 in additional funds to keep the Legislature in session so they could finish laws needed to get the new state on firm footing. The extension allowed them to finalize the framework for Alaska's first state government, which was signed into law on April 3. Department of Administration Commissioner Floyd Guertin became the first official to be sworn into office by Speaker of the House Warren A. Taylor. Guertin's salary was set at $17,000.

House leaders, however, criticized their Senate counterparts for "dragging their feet" on three "must-have" bills: revision of the employment security law, the blue skies securities act and a statute creating an Alaska Public Service Commission.

On April 13, the Legislature overturned Wade's veto and passed a state budget totaling $27.5 million. It also passed a bill to permit magistrates to levy fines in villages and give incorporated villages new powers and a bill that allowed dogs to be impounded if considered a menace to the community.

Two days later, the lawmakers adjourned their marathon session as they passed the employment security bill. Other accomplishments during this session included: establishing the Alaska Public Employees' Retirement System; prohibiting commercial fish traps; passing the Alaska Lands Act; creating the seal of the state; setting the drinking age at 21; permitting women serving as waitresses in restaurants to serve alcohol; establishing numerous professional licensing boards; and establishing a minimum wage of $1.50 per hour.

Alaska's first lawmakers were optimistic that federal transition grants, existing funds and the opportunity to select 103-plus million acres of land would be plenty to fund the transition to statehood. Later, of course, they learned that statehood would cost much more than anticipated. The next year, the Legislature faced a serious budget shortfall and enacted several tax measures to generate additional revenue that included increased personal income tax rates and increased taxes on cigarettes, liquor, wine and motor fuel.

Following his surgery and recovery, Gov. Egan returned to Juneau and was back to work on Monday, April 20. He thanked Wade and the Legislature for a job well done.

He then activated three new Alaska state agencies on May 1: law, labor and natural resources. He also vetoed a bill calling for 1 million acres of state lands for the University of Alaska, stating it was "inconsistent with constitutional concepts," according to newspaper reports.

He next appointed Buell A. Nesbett, a 49-year-old Anchorage lawyer, chief justice of the new state Supreme Court. Associate judges were Walter J. Hodge of Nome and John H. Dimond of Juneau. They all were to serve three-year terms.

The governor then went about the business of appointing his cabinet so that state government could move forward and propel Alaska well into the future. In July, however, he and the nation faced a new dilemma.

Where should the new 49-star flag first be raised on the Fourth of July?

President Eisenhower settled the controversy when, by special dispensation, he said the first flag-raising would take place at Fort McHenry in Baltimore, Maryland, the site of Francis Scott Key's creation of "The Star Spangled Banner."

Following that decision, Egan announced that any community in Alaska that unfurled the 49-star flag in its Independence Day ceremony would be regarded as the scene of the official flag raising, since Alaska had four different time zones. The governor spent the Fourth of July in Sitka, which observed Pacific Time, then flew back to Juneau to attend a ceremony there. At 3 p.m. he spoke to a crowd of 3,000 as the 49-star flag slowly rose up the flagpole at the Memorial Library, according to newspaper articles.

Many other communities across Alaska held flag-raising celebrations. In Anchorage, which was on Alaska Time, more than 8,000 people lined Fourth Avenue for the city's Fourth of July parade and to watch as Col. Cecil Bolton of the 23rd Battle Group raised the new 49-star flag at City Hall.

A few weeks later, Anchorage received a gift for its flag from Ketchikan. Many people thought the present was a joke.

Alaska State Library, Place File, ASL-Juneau-Parades-051

Juneau 1959 July 4
Raising of 49 Star Flag

Juneau residents gathered at the town library to celebrate raising the 49-star flag over the city on the Fourth of July 1959.

THE BIG YEAR

Hugh Wade

Alaska's first secretary of state had another first honor to his credit. Hugh J. Wade was among the first members of the first group of FBI agents recruited and trained by J. Edgar Hoover after Hoover became director of the agency in 1925. The nation's head lawman sent Wade to Seattle the next year to cover all of Washington state and the Territory of Alaska.

Wade, an attorney born in Dougherty, Iowa, traveled across Alaska and soon was tasked with heading the National Recovery Administration program in the Last Frontier. He settled in Juneau as its Alaska director.

After the recovery program ended in 1935, he turned his attention to serving as the area director for Alaska with the new Social Security Administration. Fifteen years later, the Bureau of Indian Affairs appointed him area director for the Alaska Native Service.

University of Alaska Fairbanks, Ernest H. Gruening Papers, UAF-1976-21-57312

Sen. William E. Beltz of Unalakleet, president of the Alaska Senate, discusses plans for establishing new state government with Acting Gov. Hugh J. Wade in the governor's office in 1959. Paul Solka and Burke Riley, assistants to the governor, look on.

He also won an election in the 1950s to become treasurer of Alaska – one of four elective offices in the territory, along with territorial attorney general, auditor and highway engineer. These officers, as well as Alaska's appointed governor, made up the territory's Board of Administration.

Wade was re-elected treasurer in 1958, but he never started that term because Congress passed the Alaska Statehood Act and Wade went on to win his bid for the first secretary of state to serve with the first elected governor of Alaska, William A. Egan.

Within hours of taking his oath of office on Jan. 3, 1959, Wade found himself acting governor for several months when Egan underwent abdominal surgery.

Wade rose to the challenge, according to his daughter, Suzanne McKeown. She remembered her father maintaining a normal routine at home, as well, such as taking family garbage to the dump.

"Evenin', Governor," the caretaker at the dump would call out when Wade arrived – sometimes at midnight during the 1959 legislative session.

"Evenin', yourself," Wade would reply as he ambled about to see what interesting items others may have dropped off at the capital's dump.

After Egan returned to full-time duties at the end of April that spring, Wade immersed himself in researching and writing Alaska's election code (Title 15), which the state Legislature approved in 1960.

When the Egan-Wade ticket lost to Walter J. Hickel and Keith Miller in 1966, Wade and wife Madge moved to Anchorage. He became regional solicitor for the Interior Department and then served as special counsel on Alaska Native claims settlement legislation.

After passage of the Alaska Native Claims Settlement Act in 1971, Wade retired. He and his wife returned to Juneau to live at their Tee Harbor cabin.

Madge died in 1977, and he died in 1995 at age 93.

4

FROM FOREST TO FLAGPOLE

A small spruce that peered skyward in a dense forest on Prince of Wales Island in the mid-1700s found its way to Anchorage when Alaska became America's 49th state. This Southeast sapling held no importance when Secretary of State William Seward finalized the purchase of Alaska from the Russians on March 30, 1867. And most Americans at the time thought Alaska unimportant, as well, and referred to it as "Seward's Ice Box."

But just as Alaska grew in importance for the nation, this little spruce tree grew in importance for the people of the Last Frontier. It became the tallest flagpole in the new state and displayed the new 49-star flag at Anchorage City Hall in 1959.

Newspaper accounts of how this tree became a giant flagpole in Anchorage vary. Some suggest it was a prank originated by people in Ketchikan.

One article appearing in the *Anchorage Daily News* on Sept. 10, 1959, reported that a man from Ketchikan claimed the huge pole, which measured 140 feet long, was selected because people in Ketchikan didn't think the folks in Anchorage would know what to do with it.

"The theory was that it was too big a project even for 'Big Anchorage' to complete," the article stated.

Indeed, many Anchorage residents thought it was a gag, too. The arrival of the long log in the summer of 1959 became the brunt

Ketchikan Pulp Co. felled a large Sitka spruce, like the one pictured here, on Prince of Wales Island to send to the people of Anchorage for a flagpole during the summer of 1959.

of many jokes. Some suggested their Southeast neighbors had sent Alaska's largest city a huge headache.

Another article appeared years later that again speculated the pole was sent to Anchorage in jest. "The Pole That A Gag Built," published in the *Anchorage Daily Times* in November 1970, said the Ketchikan Pulp Co. and Ketchikan Chamber of Commerce sent the giant spruce to Anchorage as a joke. The pole, 36 inches in diameter at its base and about 12 inches at its top, was selected because the "friendly Southeastern pranksters" thought it might cause a problem for the enthusiastic statehood supporters in Anchorage.

Following publication of that article, George H. Byer, who had been chairman of the Anchorage Parks and Recreation Commission at the time of the flagpole donation, wrote to the newspaper to set the record straight. The "gag" actually originated in Anchorage, he said in his letter dated Dec. 4, 1970.

" ... I thought it would be a nice gesture of one All-American City to another to do a real patriotic deed," he wrote. "And in view of statehood it would be great to have the tallest flagpole in the largest state in the biggest city to fly the newest 49th state flag."

He said some city councilmen were not crazy about the idea, however, and quoted one as saying: "I don't want any such sticks cluttering up our city hall lawn."

Undaunted, Byer wrote to Robert L. Jernberg, president of the Ketchikan Chamber of Commerce, to see if people in Ketchikan would consider sending Anchorage their tallest natural spruce log for a flagpole. After all, they had a "spirited background for sharing community interests."

Eventually, he received an enthusiastic response from Jernberg that the folks in Ketchikan thought it a terrific idea. They'd found a huge spruce and were preparing to ready it for transportation.

"A 140-foot log needs a straight shot roadway," Jernberg wrote Byer. "Besides, the whole project is one of magnitude with major engineering problems requiring a scheme of action."

It took 20 loggers to fall, trim, cut and bark the tree. They then had to bulldoze the log 40 miles to the loading wharf. From there, Foss Launch & Tug Co. hauled it 1,000 miles through the Gulf of Alaska and its treacherous storm-infested seas to the Port of Anchorage – free of charge.

"There were days of the barge creeping mileage against the galling waves and the big stick snapped and cracked with resisting sounds," wrote Byer, who became Anchorage's first full-time mayor and served from 1959 to 1961.

Once the giant log reached Anchorage, it was stored at the Delaney Park Strip until the city could figure out how to place such a large pole in downtown Anchorage.

"It'll take some study," city engineer Bob Smith said.

After coming up with a plan, city workers moved it by truck and dolly to City Hall on Aug. 17, 1959, where a 15-foot hole had been dug on the city hall lawn. Bad weather delayed its placement for a few days, however.

City workers brought the flagpole from the Park Strip to the city hall lawn on Aug. 19, 1959.

On Aug. 21, Municipal Light and Power employees hoisted the giant pole into the anchoring pit while cement men dumped tons of fast-hardening concrete into the hole to secure it.

"The once giant tree from Prince of Wales Island had reached its monumental destination," Byer wrote.

Townspeople attended a colorful ceremony on the city hall lawn to dedicate the flagpole on Labor Day, Sept. 8. More than 100 people gathered on Fourth Avenue to watch as Gov. William A. Egan unveiled a plaque on the pole that contained these words written by Daniel Webster, a prominent American politician who died in 1852:

"Let it be borne on the flag under which we rally in every exigency that we have one country, one constitution, one destiny."

Then a new American flag with 49 stars and an Alaska flag were raised with an American Legion color guard and veterans' organizations participating.

Other dignitaries at the grand event included Greater Anchorage Chamber of Commerce President Larry Landry, who presided as master of ceremonies; Anchorage Mayor Hewitt Lounsbury, who accepted the pole for the city; Ketchikan Chamber of Commerce representative Jernberg, who told the crowd that the tree that became Anchorage's flagpole had been a young spruce sapling growing in Southeast Alaska unseen by man while Russia controlled Alaska – before America became the United States.

"I can remember watching as they raised the flags for the first time," recalled Renee Boniface-Jones in a letter to the *Times* editor dated May 2, 1984. "Few had dry eyes that day."

Byer, also present at the ceremony, later wrote that the giant flagpole, standing 125 feet above ground, was the focal point of welcome in 1960 for Dwight D. Eisenhower, the first U.S. President to visit Alaska after it became a state.

"… on that day the huge 20-by-38-foot 49th state flag stretched by an accommodating breeze waved full length and was picture messaged around the world by the news media."

In keeping with the idea that the original purpose of the pole had been a gag contrived by pranksters in Ketchikan, an article appeared in the *Anchorage Daily Times* two days after the flagpole's dedication.

Anchorage townspeople gathered for a colorful ceremony on the city hall lawn to dedicate the flagpole on Labor Day, Sept. 8, 1959.

"With the gimmick gone, Ketchikan Mayor J. E. Winston made one final attempt to rub it in to Big Anchorage," the Sept. 10 article said. Winston sent a telegram to Anchorage Mayor Lounsbury that read:

"Congratulations on flagpole project. It is a pleasure for industrial and natural resource center of Alaska to participate in small way with state of Anchorage in this historic project."

The *Times* article concluded: "State of Anchorage, indeed."

Within a year of the dedication ceremony, construction began on a crown to top the tallest natural flagpole in the new state – a stainless steel globe.

Anchorage Daily Times photo

Chet Goodman Co. donated a crane to hoist the globe to the top of the pole on May 18, 1961.

Sheet metal worker John Elmer Gordon conceived the idea and organized union members to build the ball. Workers cut steel sections in orange-peel shapes to make a perfect sphere. They then welded continents made of copper to the globe. The equator, a ring of brass donated by sheet metal workers in Seattle, finished off the massive project that measured 46 inches in diameter.

Chet Goodman, of the Chet Goodman Co., donated a crane

to hoist the sphere to the top of the pole on May 18, 1961. They tilted the globe in recognition of the North Star, a directional symbol in the Alaska flag that faced northward. They then secured the ball to an automobile wheel in which pulleys for the halyards were placed. The wheel turned as wind direction changed, so the flags wouldn't wrap around the pole, according to a *Times* story.

Another project to enhance the flagpole soon was underway. Volunteers throughout Anchorage painted the pole and the Garden Club decorated the area for the globe's dedication. Members of the ironworkers union built the staging and Northern Roofing and Sheet Metal Co., Steel Fabricators, York Steel and Associated Contractors donated cables, copper and stainless steel to build the ball.

The city awoke on May 25, 1961, to find a painted and decorated pole with a sign hanging at its base that read: "Started by union help. Finished by management."

In his letter to the *Times* in 1970, Byer said that over the years that flagpole probably received more upward glances than any other Alaska site and "its high-flying American and Alaskan flags are

Anchorage Museum at Rasmuson Center, Ward Wells Collection, AMRC-wws-4262-1

The tallest flagpole in Alaska can be seen in the distance on Fourth Avenue and F Street with the globe on top in 1965. Businesses include Arctic Fur & Leather Co., The Uptown Beauty Salon, Alaska Treasure Shop, Dolly's Tailor Shop, Hub Clothing Co., National Bank of Alaska and Stolt Gift Center.

reminiscent of the statehood pledge that we have one country, one constitution and one destiny."

A mystery surrounded the flagpole and globe 15 years later when workers started repair on the pole's rotting base. While lowering the flagpole on Oct. 12, 1976, they noticed a message scratched on the globe: Jim Kinder, Feb. 20, 1962, 3:30 a.m., 36 degrees.

Someone had shimmied up the pole during the night in the middle of winter to make that inscription nine months after the globe was hoisted to the top – but no one knew anyone with that name.

A Matanuska Electric lineman solved the mystery a couple weeks later. Cy Mohr, of Eagle River, called *The Anchorage Times* to say that he and Kinder had worked together as linemen for General Telephone in Beaverton, Ore., during 1965.

Mohr said Kinder had told him that he climbed the flagpole on a dare while stationed at Elmendorf Air Force Base as a lineman. Kinder said he'd left his shirt on the flagpole, too!

Workers trimmed the deteriorating historic pole to 90 feet in 1987 and moved it from City Hall to the Delaney Park Strip to become the Veterans Memorial flagpole. Then it came down for good in 1999 when a 110-foot replacement pole was erected to "continue the tradition established in 1959 of displaying the flags of this great nation and the state in grandest honor."

A huge windstorm toppled that pole in September 2012. Onlookers later said they saw dry rot at its base. When the pole crashed to the ground, the beautiful globe that crowned its top split like a melon.

And that's when a battered Maxwell House coffee canister tumbled out. When pried open, its contents yielded a yellowed copy of the *Anchorage Daily News* from May 6, 1961, with headlines about Alan Shepard, the first American astronaut in space, and a story of the breakup on the Tanana River. The can also included a list of names, a 1960 penny and a Union 76 gas card bearing the name Charles Gillick.

Gillick, a 22-year-old volunteer firefighter in 1961, later said the globe had been stored at the downtown fire station before it had been hoisted atop the flagpole at City Hall. He and other firefighters decided to put a few items in a makeshift time capsule "for posterity."

Many other Alaskans were concerned with posterity during those first few years of statehood, too. And when a *Saturday Evening Post* article put Alaska in a less than favorable light in 1963, Alaskans loudly disputed the story's findings.

49-Star Flag Goes Down in History

June 14, 1960, unfurled the one and only Flag Day where Americans paid homage to a national flag that displayed 49 stars. Alaska's star was added on the Fourth of July the year before to represent Alaska's admittance into the Union as a full-fledged state. Hawaii's star would be added to the flag in July and make its debut in 1961, as the islands entered the Union in August 1959.

In days gone by, schoolchildren learned that Betsy Ross created the first American flag based on a pencil sketch given her by George Washington. Historians today dismiss that legend and say the similarity between Old Glory and Washington's coat of arms is coincidence. Sources say on only two or three occasions was a form of the Stars and Stripes carried into battle by Revolutionary troops.

Flag Day evolved from a resolution adopted on June 14, 1777, by the Second Continental Congress at Philadelphia. The resolution, offered by the Marine Committee, stated:

"Resolved that the flag of the United States be 13 stripes, alternate red and white, and the union be 13 stars, white in a blue field, representing a new constellation."

Historians say the white stands for purity and innocence; red for hardiness and valor; and blue for vigilance, perseverance and justice.

New stripes were added as the Union admitted new states. Soon the nation's flag became burdened with stripes. So Congress decreed that after July 4, 1818, the flag would have 13 stripes to symbolize the original states, 20 stars for all the states in the Union at that time, and then add a new star on the Independence Day following a new state's admission.

The stars grew from the original 13 to 50 over a period of 184 years and real estate played a part in the creation of each state.

Maryland set the stage when the Articles of Confederation, America's first Constitution, was written between 1776-1777. Maryland insisted that the larger states surrender claim to western lands. That stipulation allowed eight states to emerge from the territory from the Appalachians to the Mississippi under the Northwest Ordinance.

The land acquired through the 1803 Louisiana Purchase led to the creation of 14 more states. Negotiator Robert Livingston, in a Paris hotel room, penned his thoughts over the massive land deal:

"We have lived long, but this is the noblest work of our whole lives. It will transform vast solitudes into thriving districts. The United States takes rank this day among the first powers of the earth. The instrument we have just signed will cause no tears to be shed. They prepare ages of happiness for innumerable generations of human creatures."

America added more real estate as it acquired Florida from Spain, Texas by annexation, California, Arizona and southwestern New Mexico from Mexico, the Oregon Country from England, Hawaii by annexation and Alaska from Russia.

Alaska "joined the flag" on July 4, 1959. That 49-star flag only flew for a year, when Hawaii took over Alaska's place as the baby state of the federal family. The 50-star flag was hoisted on July 4, 1960.

University of Alaska Fairbanks, William A. Egan Papers, UAF-1985-120-128

The 49-star flag that graced the chambers of the U.S. Senate from Aug. 20, 1959, until the 50-star flag took its place on July 5, 1960, was given to Gov. William A. Egan for placement in the Alaska Historical Library and Museum.

FIRST FIVE YEARS OF STATEHOOD

5

POST ARTICLE CAUSES CONCERN

Alaska managed to take control of its destiny and develop its economy during its first five years of statehood. After jumping into the deep end of the pool, Alaskans came together to create new systems for government, courts and transportation. Most were proud of the achievements made by the fledgling state in such a short time.

So many were stunned when an article in *The Saturday Evening Post* titled "Alaska: Can it survive as a state?" hit national newsstands October 1963. It did not portray Alaska's economy in a positive light.

The article, written by former *Time Magazine* staff reporter Robert Schulman, began with a summary of what an airline pilot returning to the Lower 48 had to say about the 49th state: "Scenery magnificent. Hospitality tremendous. Politics puerile. Economy incredible."

That summed up what many visitors saw on the surface during Alaska's first five years of statehood, wrote Schulman, who only spent a few days in Alaska and did not interview the state's top leaders. The reporter said that the rosy picture painted by the pilot did not reflect what really was happening in the nation's newest state.

Schulman concluded that Alaska was suffering from a "severely sick economy" that was being supported by federal dollars. He ended the unflattering piece by saying that if the natural resources did not pan out, Alaska would "remain an invalid ward of the Federal Government."

That *Post* article unleashed a barrage of rebuttal articles and statements from Alaskans who thought Schulman had unfairly maligned the Last Frontier.

"A continually increasing number of new and old Alaskans could have provided Mr. Schulman with a ready answer to his question," Alaska Gov. William A. Egan wrote in a telegram to the *Post*. "Yes, Alaska not only will survive but will thrive as a state."

State Sen. Lester Bronson, D-Nome, said he thought Alaska was much better off as a state.

"I don't know what the man expects from a state just out of its diapers," Bronson said in an *Anchorage Daily News* rebuttal. "At last we're getting at our resources – the resources we've been robbed of for so many years, leaving Alaska a mere pittance."

Bronson added that Alaska had a worse economy before statehood.

"If he thinks Alaska's economy is sick, he should have seen it 35 years ago when I first came to Nome and everybody was fishing for

Prior to statehood, companies outside of Alaska controlled and profited from resource extraction out of the Last Frontier.

tomcods for a living," Bronson said. "Now at least they're living like human beings."

Anchorage Mayor George Sharrock addressed the reporter's article, too.

"Some of his comments about the economy might have applied to any part of the United States as the frontier moved west," Sharrock said.

While true that about 60 percent of the money flowing into the new state in its infancy came from federal transition grants to help Alaska move from federal control to independency, there were signs that Alaska was well on its way to becoming self-sufficient in 1963.

The gross volume of business had almost doubled. Per capita income was highest in the nation, increasing by 7.5 percent in 1963 alone. The state's first producing oil field on the Kenai Peninsula was developed. The Marine Highway System was becoming a reality. The tourist industry was booming. And fishing remained one of the mainstays of the state's economy.

But some people agreed with Schulman. Bob DeArmond, executive editor of the *Alaska Sportsman* and longtime statehood foe, claimed he had a hard time finding anyone who admitted that they voted for statehood – even though the 1958 vote had been 6 to 1 in favor. DeArmond said glowing figures about successful businesses and incomes were deceiving and that Alaska was indeed suffering from a sick economy.

To ease the transition from territory to state, the federal government had given Alaska $30 million in grants, but that was not enough to get state government projects going. Beginning in 1960, the state Legislature had to raise taxes to help offset the high cost of creating governing departments and programs. And with only about 60,000 taxpayers, the gap between available funds and expenditures grew, according to newspaper articles.

Many thought developing Alaska's natural resources was the only way to get Alaska on a sound fiscal footing. But prospects were uncertain, wrote Schulman, which was true at the time.

"Our annual take from bonus oil-land bids through 1968 could

An emerging oil resource, including this Union Oil Co. discovery near Soldotna on the Kenai Peninsula, was showing promise to build Alaska's economy.

be $750,000, or it could be ten times that," said Phil Holdsworth, commissioner of natural resources, in a newspaper interview in January 1963.

Several of the newly established state departments faced budget shortfalls in those early years. For instance, every new mile of road built in Alaska added $800 to $1,500 a year to maintenance costs. Since Alaska became a state, federal dollars could not be used for maintenance. Highway officials did not know where future funds would come from to cover the costs.

"There's a slight gaposis," new state Commissioner of Public Works Richard A. Downing told Ray J. Shrick, staff reporter for *The Wall Street Journal*, in March 1960.

Part of the "gaposis" may have been caused by language in the new state's constitution. It mandated the governor establish a highway department with more than 1,000 employees and also create or expand most other state services. Fulfilling that obligation increased the governance of Alaska from a staff of about 800 people during territorial days to 3,000 after statehood.

"You can't have New York City services on a clam-digging economy," said Bud Charles of the *Ketchikan News*.

Alaska aviator Robert "Bob" Reeve, owner/operator of Reeve Aleutian Airways, also voiced concern for Alaska's fiscal future in Schulman's *Post* article.

"We'd be in a helluva fix if it wasn't for the oil excitement," Reeve said, referring to $21 million in exploration fees for the Kenai Peninsula that kept the state from going into the red the year before. "How long can we count on it bailing us out?"

But most Alaskans believed that statehood had brought distinct advantages. Instead of 54 separate federal agencies and commissions running the government, Alaska now controlled its own destiny. Alaskans no longer had "pinstriped bureaucrats" in Washington, D.C., making decisions on their behalf. They had two elected senators and a representative in Congress who had their best interests at heart.

They also could boast that in the first five years of statehood, many new highways had been bulldozed across the state; a $10 million Standard of California oil refinery built near Anchorage handled a million tons of crude oil a year pumping from the Kenai Peninsula; the University of Alaska was on its way to becoming a first-rate space-communications and northern-latitudes research center; and big stores like J.C. Penney, Woolworth's and Safeway had come to Alaska, which showed that they had confidence in Alaska's future.

Millions more dollars poured into Anchorage during those first years from investors in California, Texas, New York and other East Coast entities for various public and quasi-public ventures, including the municipal dock, a natural gas pipeline from Kenai to Anchorage, the Anchorage Westward Hotel, the Alaska Methodist University, Providence Hospital and more.

Alaska's future also shined bright when a huge oil field was found in Cook Inlet, the first auction of coal leases was held and timber sawn and pulped in Southeast found a market with the Japanese for their rayon industry.

Alaska's Democratic U.S. Sen. E.L. "Bob" Bartlett may have best summed up the feelings of many Alaskans that statehood was the

Timber cut from forests in Southeast Alaska and processed by workers at the Ketchikan Pulp Mill found a market with the Japanese soon after statehood.

right decision and Schulman's article had not accurately portrayed what the new state had accomplished in a short amount of time.

"The amazing thing is that a stable foundation has been laid in only five years," Bartlett said. "Five years from now you won't find any doubters."

Sen. John Butrovich, R-Fairbanks, shared that sentiment and told Schulman that he saw bright skies ahead for the nation's 49th state.

"Our problems haven't made me change my mind. The people who are really going to make statehood go are young people with itchy feet, enthusiasm and a yen for the unknown," Butrovich said. "Youth is our passport, change is our course and development is our destiny."

One of the main contributors that advanced that change and development in Southeast Alaska was the new Alaska Marine Highway System, which had gone into service the same year as the *Post* article appeared.

6

BLUE CANOES MAKE DEBUT

Southeast Alaskans dreamt for years of a highway that could connect their island-bound towns with the outside world. Statehood became the catalyst to make it happen. Gov. William A. Egan appointed Richard A. Downing as the state's first commissioner of Public Works, and Downing made creating a passenger-car ferry system a priority.

In January 1963, Southeasterners saw their dream become a reality with the maiden voyage of the *M/V Malaspina*. When the first

Carl Cordell's decorated truck in the Fourth of July parade shows the serious side of Ketchikan's wish for a ferry system in 1917.

FIRST FIVE YEARS OF STATEHOOD

The *M/V Chilkoot* cruised by Columbia Glacier in the 1950s.

of three planned ferries sailed into Ketchikan, now the home base for the Alaska Marine Highway System, the 3,000 townspeople rejoiced as they watched the sleek blue and white vessel with eight-stars-of gold painted on its smokestack ease into the terminal for her first tie-up at the dock, according to the *Ketchikan Daily News*. They now could travel along the 450-mile length of Southeastern Alaska's panhandle from Ketchikan to Haines, at the head of Lynn Canal.

The genesis of the modern ferry system began in 1949 when Haines residents Steve Homer and Ray Gelotte founded the Chilkoot Motorship Lines. The men purchased and converted a surplus World War II LCT-Mark VI landing craft from the U.S. Navy and christened it the *M/V Chilkoot*. The vessel had a day lounge, bathrooms, a galley and crew quarters.

The 100-foot-long ship with a crew of seven could carry 20 passengers, 13 cars and travel at about 9 knots – a little more than 10 mph. It made weekly trips between its home base at Tee Harbor, 18 miles north of Juneau, to Haines-Port Chilkoot and Skagway, according to Stan Cohen, author of a book featuring the history of the

Alaska Marine Highway System titled *Highway on the Sea*. This service connected Alaska's capital with the Alaska-Canada Highway, built in 1942, at Haines Junction, 150 miles north of Haines.

The territorial government bought the company in 1951 and placed it under the Territorial Board of Road Commissioners. Six years later, the board replaced it with the *M/V Chilkat*, which stayed in service until 1988.

The *Chilkat* was a tad bit smaller, at 99 feet long, but could carry 59 passengers and 15 vehicles. Built by J.M. Martinac Shipbuilding Co. of Tacoma, Wash., it had a distinct bow ramp that allowed it to load from a beach as well as a dock. The new ship was painted with the blue and gold that now is synonymous with the ferries in the fleet and soon was dubbed the "Blue Canoe."

Alaskans could not add any more ships to help move passengers, however, as they were not allowed to float bonds for a ferry system or any other economic project under territorial government. And the federal government was hard pressed to spend unnecessary funds on "Seward's Icebox."

Printed with permission Ketchikan Daily News, Ketchikan Museums 93.2.15.214

The *M/V Chilkat*, which began serving Southeast Alaska with ferry service in 1957, is seen in this photo getting work done at Seward Marine Ways dry dock in Ketchikan.

The Alaska Steamship Co. had filled the void for more than 50 years as it carried freight and passengers between Seattle and Southeast. But it then dropped its passenger schedule in 1952. The new Alaska-Canada Highway and the proliferation of airliners cut into the steamship company's business so much that regularly scheduled sailings no longer proved profitable. The last steamer sailed away from Southeast Alaska in 1954.

Five years later, statehood brought renewed vigor for a ferry system. The first state Legislature set the stage for creating a department of public works. The second session in 1960 brought a proposal to provide funding to build a marine highway. Voters approved Bond Proposition No. 2 for $23 million – $182.5 million in 2015 dollars – to create a ferry system throughout Southeast and Southcentral Alaska.

Public Works Commissioner Downing consulted with experts in both Canada and the United States, which resulted in the "Study and Report on the Alaska Ferry System of February 1961," according to a newspaper article in the *Juneau Empire*. Downing acquired as much information as possible to make sure the ferry system would be practical, economical and of the most benefit to the people it would serve.

Controversy surrounded the idea of the ferry system from the beginning. Perhaps because much of Alaska's population did not live in Southeast and they didn't understand the importance of connecting the communities on the Panhandle. Some may have thought the price too high to pay.

Others saw it as a crazy idea that never would pay for itself. The author of this Alaska history series, Laurel Downing Bill, remembers some people calling the proposed ferry system "Downing's Folly" at the time – commissioner Downing was her father.

But after Downing analyzed all the information needed to proceed, he and his team drew up plans for four new vessels – each to carry 500 passengers, 105 vehicles, 44 staterooms and many reclining chairs in the fore and aft lounges for napping – along with new docks throughout the proposed system.

Alaska state ferry *M/V Malaspina* first arrived in Ketchikan on Jan. 23, 1963.

Building began immediately on terminal facilities at the mainline ports of Haines, Skagway, Juneau, Sitka, Petersburg, Wrangell, Ketchikan and Prince Rupert, British Columbia, which became known as "the little Canadian town that the Alaska ferries turned into a city," according to newspaper reports. Canadian officials improved and straightened the road from Prince Rupert to Canada Highway 16 to accommodate increased traffic expected as a result of the new ferry system.

Gov. Egan's wife, Neva, christened the 352-foot-long *M/V Malaspina* on June 8, 1962. Designed by Philip Spaulding, it was built for $4 million at Puget Sound Bridge and Dry Dock in Seattle. When the ship slid down rails into the water, Gov. Egan said it was "perhaps the most important and permanent achievement for Alaska since statehood."

The vessel, which cruised at 18 knots, arrived in Ketchikan on Jan. 23, 1963. Three days later, it docked in Wrangell for the first time. The *Wrangell Sentinel* covered the fanfare with a flourish.

"Three long blasts from the Wrangell Lumber Co.'s whistle at 6:45 yesterday morning welcomed the *M/V Malaspina* to this lumber capital of Alaska," the *Sentinel* reported.

Admiral B.E. Lewellen, head of the Marine Transportation Division, was aboard for the maiden voyage.

"She's running nicely," Lewellen told a reporter. "We're taking it easy, ironing out the kinks, and everything seems to be highly successful."

Gov. Egan also was aboard and greeted the official boarding delegation, as did Downing and his wife, Hazel, who were enjoying the inaugural run.

"The Commissioner was duly proud of the new vessel," a reporter noted.

Downing's wife, Hazel, christened the second ship – *M/V Taku* – that went into service in April that year. Admiral Lewellen's wife christened the third ship, *M/V Matanuska*, which followed in June. The ships, all named after glaciers, became known as the Alaska Marine Highway System.

"These vessels follow the same sea route traveled by thousands of sourdough gold seekers through the heavily forested islands of Alaska's mountainous Panhandle," a travel brochure proclaimed. "Visitors pass scores of dazzling glaciers flanked by magnificent fjords. Busy fishing ships of every size and description share this tireless view."

During its first year of service, the marine highway extended its reach from Ketchikan to Petersburg, Sitka, Skagway, Wrangell and Prince Rupert, B.C. The fleet moved more than 15,000 vehicles and 80,000 passengers.

The ocean-certified *M/V Tustumena* followed in 1964. The 240-foot-long ship, which became known as the "Trusty Tusty," brought the marine highway to Kodiak. The ship could carry 200 passengers and 40 vehicles along its route, which included stops at Anchorage, Seward and Homer, with occasional "flag stops" at Seldovia.

Tusty's design included a loading elevator on the stern so vehicles and cargo could be offloaded at any dock without a loading ramp, according to a *SitNews* article by Dave Kiffer titled "The Grand Ships of the Alaska Marine Highway System," dated July 8, 2006. Unfortunately, the ship suffered significant rolling when traveling the Gulf of Alaska, so it had to be modified five years later. It was lengthened by 56 feet, which alleviated the rolling problem.

The *Chilkat* moved to Prince William Sound, where it began service between Valdez and Cordova – then Valdez to Whittier. In 1969, *M/V E.L. Bartlett* joined the *Chilkat* in Southcentral Alaska and soon established a marine highway between the Kenai Peninsula and the Kodiak area. The 193-foot ferry, which traveled at 12 knots, could carry 190 passengers and 41 vehicles. Named for much-loved politician Edward Lewis "Bob" Bartlett, who died in December 1968, this was the first Alaska ferry specifically built for the marine highway that was not named for a glacier.

"… families with their cars can travel the fabled Inside Passage all the way from Vancouver Island through the scenic Alaska Panhandle to Haines, where a 158-mile highway will take them to the Alaska Highway and into the great heartland of the 49th state," reported the *Fairbanks Daily News-Miner* on March 17, 1966, as it announced the link up of Canada's *M/V Queen of Prince Rupert* in British Columbia with the Alaska ferries.

When a rockslide took out a section of the Alaska Highway in 1967, and the *Queen of Prince Rupert* ran aground, the transfer ability of passengers using the ferry service between Alaska, Canada and Washington became restricted.

Then-Gov. Walter J. Hickel ordered the Alaska Marine Highway System to send a ship south to Seattle as he worked with the federal government to reclassify the route from "outside waters" to "inside waters," as none of the state ferries had the necessary ocean-going certifications to travel on outside waters. The feds agreed to do so, which left the system with a significantly longer route and no new ships to serve it.

In an effort to get a new ship into service quickly, marine highway officials purchased a 1-year-old vessel named the *Stena Britannica* and rechristened it the *M/V Wickersham*, after a much-respected early

Alaska State Library, Alaska Division of Tourism Collection, ASL-P22-07-024

The sturdy little auto and passenger ship *M/V Chilkat* was sent to the historic ports of Valdez and Cordova after larger ferries went into service in Southeast Alaska during 1963.

Author Laurel Downing Bill remembers her mother, Hazel Downing, telling her stories of how she and Gov. William Egan's wife, Neva, spent several days painting the inside of the ship as it made is way from Southeast to its new home in Prince William Sound. The women wanted to spruce it up and make it shine for the people of Southcentral Alaska.

The *Chilkat* provided water-and-mountain-locked Cordova with the city's only surface link to Valdez and the Richardson Highway. It began with three weekly trips during the summer months and two trips monthly during the winter. The 87-mile ferry trip between the two ports took 7-1/2 hours.

After the Good Friday 1964 earthquake, the ferry was shifted to the Valdez-Whittier run. And then, in 1969, it returned to Southeast for the Juneau to Hoonah run. In 1977, it was put on the Ketchikan-Hollis-Metlakatla route.

In 1988, Alaska's oldest ferry was sold and - up into the early 2000s – it was still part of the regional fishing industry.

Alaska State Library, Herbert J. "Red" Lockert Collection, ASL-P452-169

From 1968 to 1972, the *M/V Wickersham* could only operate between U.S. ports if it stopped in Prince Rupert, B.C. Its bow loading system limited its Alaska service to Ketchikan, Juneau, Sitka and Haines, too.

The deep draft of the *Wickersham* also made it impossible to traverse narrow, shallow areas like Peril Strait near Sitka, which led to some adventurous stormy trips in the open ocean on the outside of Baranof Island and elsewhere during the winters.

While the *Wickersham* was not a luxurious ship, it was definitely fancier than the other, more utilitarian members of the fleet.

judge, political leader and advocate for Alaska statehood. The 363-foot ocean-going ship, which carried 1,300 passengers, was never reflagged as an American ship, however.

The *Wickersham's* commercial operation between two American ports of call was in violation of the Jones Act. Enacted in the 1920s to protect U.S. shipbuilders, the act prohibits foreign vessels from traveling between American ports unless there is an intermediate stop in a foreign country. The state attempted to get a waiver, but federal officials would not agree.

So while the *Wickersham* could pick up passengers in Seattle, and deliver them to Alaska by stopping in Canada on the way, it could not move passengers within Alaska. The ship also had not been built with Alaska ports in mind, so she could not physically dock at several places.

The 1,000-passenger *M/V Columbia*, specifically built for the marine highway system, replaced the *Wickersham* in 1974. The 418-foot ship cost $22 million and became the largest ferry in the fleet.

Alaska's marine highway proved so successful, that both the *Matanuska* and *Malaspina* had to be stretched by 56 feet at their midsections to accommodate more passengers and vehicles, which left the *Taku* as the only ship in Southeast that could serve the smaller communities.

The fleet also added the *M/V LeConte* in 1974, and her sister ship, *M/V Aurora*, in 1978. These 235-foot Wisconsin-built vessels each carried 250 passengers and 34 vehicles and were the last new ships of the feet for the next 20 years. They completed the initial construction phase of the marine highway.

A few more ferries were added in later years, and the Alaska Marine Highway System now extends 3,500 miles. It has a network of ferries that stop at 35 ports from Bellingham, Wash., to Southeast to Prince William Sound to Kodiak to the Aleutians.

The system also proved economical for the state, according to a report written by Dr. George W. Rogers for the University of Alaska in 1970.

"The annual net public cost of operating the Alaska Marine Highway System for the five-year period (1965 to 1969) was $2.9 million, as compared with $58.3 million for all roads in the state," Rogers reported. "… This resulted in per capita annual cost of providing highway systems to the public (directly served) of $31.76 for the Marine Highway against $260.94 for the Land Highway."

Commissioner Downing, who died in 1988, would be pleased to know that the Blue Canoes sailing Alaska's saltwater highways not only fulfilled his desire for economy and efficiency, but also have led to economic and travel opportunities that continue to expand the horizons of once-isolated Alaska communities.

Alaska Marine Highway System 1963

When the Alaska Marine Highway System debuted in 1963, its three ferries – *M/V Matanuska, M/V Taku and M/V Malaspina* – opened a new world of exploration to the American driving public. Prior to ferry service Alaska's panhandle region, which features countless islands, massive glaciers and deep-forested fjords, only could be viewed by air or steamship.

The south terminal of the 450-mile route was Prince Rupert, British Columbia. From there, it connected to the seven Alaska towns of Ketchikan, Wrangell, Petersburg, Sitka, Juneau, Haines and Skagway. Passengers could connect to Alaska's road system once they reached Haines.

The Marine Highway not only brought tourists to this once-isolated section of Alaska, but it brought many opportunities, as well.

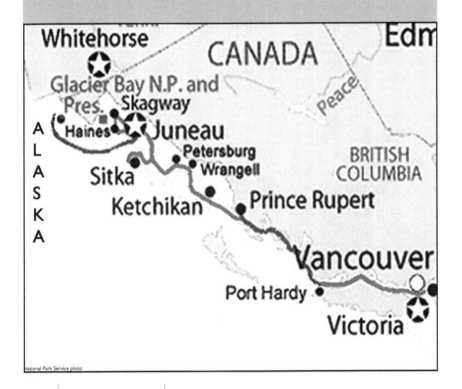

National Park Service photo

FIRST FIVE YEARS OF STATEHOOD

Ketchikan

The Alaska Marine Highway System's first northbound stop was Ketchikan, known as "Salmon Capital of the World." It also was home for the world's largest collection of totem poles and the site of Alaska's first pulp mill.

Anchorage Museum at Rasmuson Center, Steve McCutcheon Collection, AMRC-B1990-014-5-AKNative-44-139

Wrangell

Wrangell, the third-oldest town in Alaska, boasted salmon, crab and shrimp canneries during the 1960s. It featured the busiest sawmills in the state, too.

University of Alaska Fairbanks, George King Collection, UAF-1988-131-12

Petersburg

One of the most picturesque places in Southeast Alaska, Petersburg was known for its white halibut fishing fleet, manned by the descendants of Scandinavian fishermen who first settled the city. It showcased the world-record 126-pound king salmon in the 1960s.

Sitka

The influence of old Czarist Russia permeates Sitka, Alaska's first capital after it became part of the United States in 1867. Old St. Michael's Russian Orthodox Cathedral, built in the 1840s, housed religious treasures. It burned down in 1966 and later was rebuilt.

Juneau

Proclaimed by many as "The Nation's Most Scenic Capital," Juneau, shown above, sits near Mendenhall Glacier – the most photographed glacier in the world. It is home to the first major gold rush north after rich deposits were found in Silver Bow Basin in 1880.

Haines

Haines and Port Chilkoot, twin cities of the ferry route, sit on the coastal end of the Haines Highway that connects to the Alaska Highway near Whitehorse, B.C. Visitors during the 1960s enjoyed "Totem Village," where they watched authentic Chilkat Indian dancers, observed totem pole carvers and wandered through a recreated tribal house.

Skagway

The farthest north stop on the Alaska Marine Highway System was Skagway, gateway to the Klondike gold fields of 1898. A narrow-gauge railway connects to Whitehorse, B.C., and the Yukon Territory. Skagway embraces the gold-rush era with its amazing museum and "Days of '98" shows.

7

THE LOST ALASKANS

The opening of the Alaska Psychiatric Institute in 1962 marked a dramatic change in the way Alaska handled those who suffered from mental illness. Construction of the facility, made possible by $6.5 million allocated from the 1956 Alaska Mental Health Enabling Act, meant Alaskans might find treatment for their mental illnesses without traveling outside the state. Prior to that, those with mental illness were shipped off to Morningside Hospital in Portland, Ore. – and most families never heard from their loved ones again. They became known as "The Lost Alaskans."

The hospital, founded in 1899 by Dr. Henry Waldo Coe, was awarded a contract from the U.S. Department of Interior to care for mentally ill and mentally handicapped patients from the Territory of Alaska. Coe started the hospital out of his home and then purchased the Massachusetts Building from the Lewis and Clark Exposition in 1905. He moved it from the exposition site to Mount Tabor, where he converted it into a psychiatric hospital. Five years later, he moved his operation to a 47-acre site in east Portland, according to the Morningside Website.

At the time, mental illness was considered a crime and Alaskan adults and children were arrested, convicted of insanity and sent by the federal government via dog teams, trains and ships to live at Morningside. Between 1905 and 1962, the hospital admitted about 3,500 Alaskans.

Marshals and volunteer deputies accompanied those convicted of insanity from Fairbanks to Valdez in horse-drawn stagecoaches during winter. Stagecoaches often stopped at Salchaket, seen here, to rest along the way.

The procedure for determining mental illness was rather simple. A person said to be mentally ill was brought before a jury of six people who would rule him sane or insane. If he was found insane, he then was sent to jail until his release or transfer to Morningside. Nowhere in this process was a medical or psychiatric examination required.

Oftentimes jails housed both criminals and the insane until their court hearings were held, which could take up to a year at times due to the early practice of traveling courts. Once convicted, marshals would advertise for honest civilians looking for a paid trip to Seattle who then would be hired as temporary deputies to help take the "prisoners" south.

A *Fairbanks Daily News* article titled "Insane Patients Soon to Go Outside," published on Dec. 17, 1908, was typical of the announcements placed in the newspaper when the marshals needed to find volunteers to help escort the insane out of the territory.

"Marshal Love stated today that he was now perfecting plans for sending the patients outside and that they will go over the trail shortly after the first of year, if no hitch occurs in court proceedings."

Once arrangements were made, the marshal would deputize guards who wanted to go "outside" and were willing to undertake the delicate task of handling the patients.

"These men, will, of course, be paid their expenses and a per diem for the trip, and it affords an opportunity for those who are desirous of getting out, if they are of sufficient responsibility to meet the marshal's requirements," the article stated.

The deputies often transported actual criminals and the insane together. They traveled by horse-drawn stagecoach from Fairbanks, where winter temperatures routinely dipped to 50-below, along a 400-mile-long trail to Valdez. There they boarded ships to Seattle, and then continued on by train to Oregon. Sometimes the volunteers kept all the "prisoners" in restraints – and once in a while one had to be strapped to a cot for the entire trip due to his insanity and violence.

Some of those sent to Morningside Hospital did not suffer from mental illness, records show. A few who went south had contracted tuberculosis and one, James Ebana, appears to have had epilepsy.

Apparently, missionaries at the Church Christ Mission in Anvik arranged to have Ebana, then 17, sent to Morningside after he had a seizure in 1932. Like many people sent to the facility, Ebana's family

Missionaries at the Christ Church Mission in Anvik, seen here in 1921, sent a young man to the Morningside Hospital in Oregon because he suffered from epilepsy.

Thursday, October 25, 1906

Fairbanks Evening News

Insanity Raging

Man Being Brought from Richardson Is The Third Case
Which Has Developed Within Past Three Weeks

Marshal Perry is in receipt of a telegram from Richardson, stating that two men, Maher and Espy by name, left the Tenderfoot town yesterday with an Insane person in charge, who will be kept here until there is some improvement in his condition or otherwise, until he can be sent outside to Mount Tabor (the early name for Morningside Hospital).

This is the third case of insanity that has developed in the Tanana during the past three weeks. Jack Spencer was brought up from Gibbon and tried before Commissioner Erwin, and, although he was discharged, the general opinion appeared to be that he was a fit subject for the wheelhouse, unless he could be kept away from the influence of hootch (whiskey). Jack was indicted by the jury, which tried his case, or a recommendation was made to that effect.

The case of Mrs. Black is hardly a week old. Mrs. Black, the mother of a family at Gibbon, went violently insane at that place, and the commissioner there having no jurisdiction to try the case, the afflicted woman is now on her way to Rampart, where she will be held awaiting some improvement in her condition or until her case is dispensed of by Commissioner Green.

Commissioner Hedger has already dispensed of the case of the patient at Richardson, but there being no place at that point where such cases can be properly handled, it was thought best to send the insane person to Fairbanks. The name of the man is not known here, the Richardson commissioner having failed to mention it in his various dispatches.

never knew what happened to him after he left Anvik. The young man's death certificate stated he died of "Tuberculosis of the Lungs" in 1942, according to records at Morningside.

Some sent to the hospital responded to treatment and returned home. But many died without ever seeing their loved ones again.

The American Medical Association and the Department of the Interior revisited the practice of sending these patients to Oregon in the late 1940s and early 1950s. Soon after, the U.S. House of Representatives launched a series of investigations into the care provided when Congress debated the fate of those with mental illness in Alaska.

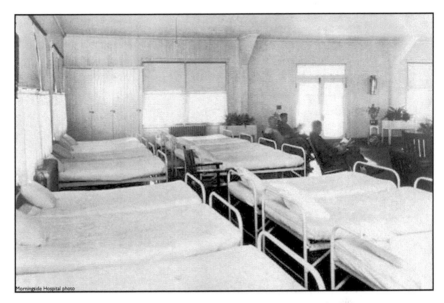

Authorities sent Alaskans with mental health issues to Morningside Hospital in Portland, Ore. This is a photo of the men's ward.

The investigations found widespread deficiencies in the program, including financial abuse by the Coe family. Investigators learned the family was subverting money intended for patient care to personal gain, including trips to South Africa and Mexico. They also found the Coes had used patient labor for building and maintenance of the facility under the guise of occupational therapy, according to Morningside's Website.

No criminal charges came out of the investigations, and the *Oregonian* later featured Morningside in an article about its success as an "open hospital," where patients were controlled through drugs rather than by lock and key.

The cumulative findings from the House investigations, which also revealed that the long trip from Alaska to Portland had negative effects on the patients, as well as their families, laid the groundwork for a new era in the way mental health was provided. Authorities recommended a total overhaul of the system and development of a mental health program in Alaska.

Morningside Hospital officials grew vegetables outside the mental health facility.

Alaska only had one nonvoting delegate in Congress at that time – E.L. "Bob" Bartlett. Bartlett wrote H.R. 6376, the Alaska Mental Health Bill, and Oregon's Rep. Edith Green introduced it in the House on Jan. 16, 1956. It received bipartisan support and passed unanimously two days later.

Oregon Sen. Richard L. Neuberger sponsored its equivalent, S. 2518, in the Senate. That's when all hell broke loose. The bill became the focus of major political controversy after opponents nicknamed it the "Siberia Bill" and claimed it was part of a Communist plot to institutionalize and brainwash Americans.

Anticommunist groups said that the commitment language in the bill "takes away all of the rights of the American citizen to ask for a jury trial and protect him[self] from being railroaded to an asylum by a greedy relative or 'friend' or, as the Alaska bill states, 'an interested party.'"

Another California "super patriot" group, called the Keep America Committee, said mental hygiene was part of the "unholy three" of the "Communistic World Government" and claimed "mental hygiene is a subtle and diabolical plan of the enemy to transform a free and intelligent people into a cringing horde of zombies."

And yet others thought the bill was a product of a conspiracy by the American Psychiatric Association to ram home the "Siberia Bill," which called for "a secret concentration camp in the wastes of Alaska."

The Church of Scientology opposed the bill, as well, and asserted the bill was "psychiatry's attempt to establish a million-acre Siberia-type camp for mental health patients in Alaska, far from the prying eyes of civil libertarians," which "presumably ... was far enough away from the well-traveled roads of the world to allow psychiatrists to conduct their mind control and other experiments on a captive population, unhindered by the glare of publicity," according to the church's official Website.

In an effort to bring rational debate to the issue, the late U.S. Sen. Ted Stevens explained the federal commitment process for

Some Alaska orphans also found a home at Morningside Hospital in Oregon.

the mentally ill to members of Congress. Stevens, then a young lawyer working for the U.S. Department of Justice, told them of his experience with the criminal proceedings used to commit adults and children to Morningside. He said the insanity jury system was archaic and that he had "a very great respect for juries, but not insanity," according to Terrence Cole in his book, "Fighting for the Forty-Ninth Star: C.W. Snedden and the Crusade for Alaska Statehood."

Republican Sen. Barry Goldwater helped craft a new version of the bill without the commitment provisions that had been the target of such intense opposition. His and Stevens' efforts helped lead to passage of the Alaska Mental Health Enabling Act.

Language in the act provided funding for Alaska's mental health care system through lands allocated to a mental health trust. Although politicians later transferred most of the valuable land to state agencies and private individuals, the legal system ruled their actions illegal and a reconstituted mental health trust was established in the mid-1980s.

After the Alaska psychiatric facility opened in the early 1960s, many patients left Morningside and returned to their homeland. Their departure left openings at the Oregon hospital.

"Hospital officials feel that Morningside's present facilities and rehabilitation programs geared to both mentally ill and mentally retarded can be adapted to private patients with a few changes," an article in the *Oregonian* newspaper reported.

Morningside never recovered from the loss of those Alaskan patients, however. After the psychiatric hospital discharged its last three patients in the summer of 1968, the hospital closed its doors forever.

Many businesses in Southcentral Alaska had to close their doors, too, after the largest earthquake in North America's recorded history hit in 1964 to start off the second five years of Alaska statehood with a jolt.

EARTHQUAKE!

8

GOOD FRIDAY 1964

Two hundred cattle moved away from their low-lying grazing land around 3 p.m. and climbed to higher ground on Louis Beaty's ranch on Narrow Cape, about 50 miles southeast of Kodiak. The rancher looked around and saw nothing but blue skies, sunshine and calm seas that crisp Good Friday, March 27, 1964. He vaguely wondered why the cows were heading upland, as they had never before gone to higher ground so early in the day.

Two-and-a-half hours later, Beaty learned what his clairvoyant cattle may have sensed when the frozen ground and thick ice started to shake and crack. The second-largest earthquake in recorded history struck at 5:36 p.m. Anchorage time. It measured 8.4 on the Richter Scale – experts later upgraded it to 9.2 on the Moment Magnitude Scale as the Richter Scale was determined to be inaccurate at measuring earthquakes above 8.0.

The temblor's epicenter was about 75 miles southeast of Anchorage, 54 miles west of Valdez and 15 miles beneath the tranquil waters of Prince William Sound. Centuries of pressure and strain finally broke loose when the crust of the Pacific Plate moved an estimated 25 to 30 feet northward, driving beneath the North American Plate with such force it released 200,000 megatons of energy in an instant – more energy than 10 million Hiroshima-vintage atomic bombs.

The effects were felt around the world – even in Chile, where the largest quake ever recorded at 9.5 hit on May 22, 1960. While 114 people died in Alaska, another 12 were killed in Crescent City, Calif., and four children camping on Beverly Beach State Park in Oregon lost their lives when tsunamis hit the Pacific Coast. Tsunami, an adapted Japanese word meaning "port wave," refers to the fact that the wave's danger and destructive power only becomes evident as it approaches the shore.

The tsunamis also damaged boats in Los Angeles and Hawaii. Tide gauges in Freeport, Texas, recorded waves similar to seismic waves. And surfers at Collaroy Beach in Sydney, Australia, reported their usually gentle and small waves peaked violently at more than 20 feet on Easter Sunday.

Entire towns across Southcentral Alaska crumbled, streets buckled and cars, stores and homes dropped into wide crevices that split across the ground. This earthquake altered more of the Earth's crust than any other earthquake on record, according to U.S. Geological Survey reports. On uninhabited Montague Island, near the quake's epicenter, the quake raised the land as much as 33 feet. It lowered the ocean floor up to 150 feet under the devastated harbors of Seward and Valdez. The shoreline in parts of the Kenai Peninsula lifted 8 feet. Kodiak Island dropped 5.5 feet. And Anchorage shifted laterally 6 feet.

The Good Friday earthquake, which disrupted 185,000 square miles – larger than California – was the first "properly interpreted" megathrust quake, according to the U.S. Geological Survey. Megathrust quakes occur in subduction zones, where tectonic plates converge. When forces build up and those plates slip, the results can be catastrophic, as in Alaska.

Some said the quake that shook, cut, dropped, heaved and twisted Southcentral Alaska started with a gentle roll. Others said they heard a thunder-like roar. Still others said it began with a single, sharp crack. But all who experienced the almost five minutes of terror will never forget the day when needles on seismographs thousands of miles away went clear off their machines and tsunamis swept across the Pacific Ocean at more than 400 mph and flooded towns in Alaska and the West Coast.

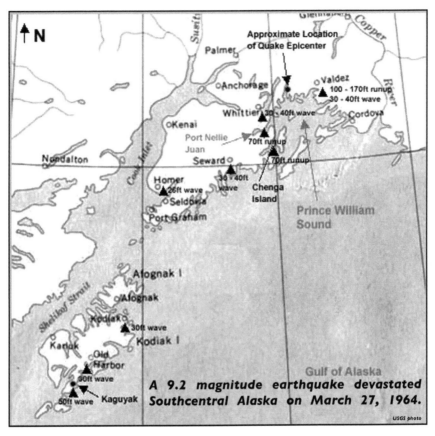

A 9.2 magnitude earthquake devastated Southcentral Alaska on March 27, 1964.

USGS photo

Many people struggled to stand as the ground rolled like waves. They saw treetops slap the ground and fissures up to 30 feet wide split the earth, then snap shut. Depending on where they were when the quake hit, people climbed trees, clutched power poles or tried to run to keep from being hurled into massive cracks or carried out to sea by giant waves.

The immense quake and resulting tsunamis caused massive property damage, but the death toll was remarkably low. Experts say the low death toll can be attributed to a few things: the low population density of the state; few tall buildings in the towns; the time of day the quake occurred; and it hit on a holiday when most Alaskans were home.

While the devastation to property was enormous, of more concern to most Alaskans was whether loved ones had survived the horrific event. Communication systems were severely damaged, or nonexistent in some cases. Relatives and friends, both inside and outside Alaska, had no way to help and no way to communicate.

Aftershocks as large at 6.5 rattled the land and the nerves just about every hour for a few days, and anxiety and concern reigned as Alaskans gathered together without heat, power or information in subfreezing temperatures. For the first few hours, only those lucky enough to have ham radios heard bits and pieces of news – and rumors – as voices crackled through the airwaves that long, dark night.

"Just heard Valdez is gone," wrote Phyllis Downing Carlson in her diary after hearing a ham radio operator sharing the news. Ever

Phyllis Downing Carlson, paternal aunt of author Laurel Downing Bill, lived near Kodiak when the 1964 earthquake hit. She wrote in her diary that a ham operator relayed a message saying the massive quake and tsunamis that followed had devastated Valdez.

U.S. military troops soon were delivering C rations to communities affected by the 1964 earthquake, as seen in this photo taken in Valdez.

the journalist and historian, Aunt Phil – who was living 2.6 miles east of Kodiak on Woody Island and working for the Federal Aviation Administration at the time – recorded this major event as it unfolded and her own home shook to its core.

She learned that tidal waves had inundated Kodiak, fissures and landslides covered Anchorage and no one had yet heard from other communities along Alaska's coast. She also heard several operators saying prayers for the missing and their families.

The military and Alaska Communication System labored all night to restore phone lines to the Lower 48, and local radio stations moved swiftly to get back on the air so people with transistor radios could keep abreast of vital news. The American Red Cross and The Salvation Army jumped into high gear, as well.

Soon more than 800 U.S. Army troops were guarding devastated areas, providing medical support and assisting U.S. Army Corps of

Engineers crews clear slides and open roads and railroad tracks. The U.S. Air Force immediately donated food, medical and other supplies for Alaska residents. And the Alaskan Air Command quickly moved hundreds of thousands of pounds of cargo throughout stricken areas.

The grim news reached the LBJ Ranch in Texas, where President Lyndon B. Johnson was spending the Easter weekend. Advisors woke the president twice during the night to give him updates on the devastation, according to newspaper articles. In the morning, Johnson officially declared the 49th state a disaster area.

One Anchorage policeman said it was worse than a disaster. After assisting with emergency services for 24 hours, he told a *Newsweek* reporter "it was hell."

Bustling Anchorage, Alaska's largest city with a population close to 50,000 at the time, suffered the most property damage. Three giant waves washed into Whittier within three minutes. Ruptured oil tanks ignited and set the town of Seward ablaze. Tsunami waves swept away Valdez. Tidal waves devastated Kodiak's downtown district. And several villages were obliterated.

Anchorage suffered heavy damage from the 1964 earthquake.

USGS photo

Broken cars and buildings lie in heaps in Crescent City, Calif. – 2,000-plus miles from Anchorage – after 12-foot tidal waves roared ashore. The tsunami devastated the city's business district and started a big oil-tank fire.

The tsunami waves continued south at more than 400 mph, damaging a logging camp and several houses in British Columbia, and on to Washington, California and Oregon.

By the time it reached Hawaii, it damaged a few yachts and then was barely visible when it hit the coast of Japan.

The following chapters share the stories of people who lived through the disaster, some of whom shared their experiences with radio and television newscaster Genie Chance. Chance spent the first 59 hours in the wake of the disaster serving as public information officer for Anchorage's local disaster organization. She broadcast messages for individuals and officials from her post at the Anchorage Public Safety Building in downtown Anchorage, only a few blocks away from Fourth Avenue, which had dropped 10 to 20 feet during the first few minutes of the earthquake.

Following that marathon broadcast, Chance spent the next few weeks interviewing and tape-recording eyewitnesses to find out what happened in Alaska's communities as the massive quake and tsunamis hit. She published these firsthand accounts in a document titled "Chronology of Physical Events of the Alaskan Earthquake," prepared under a National Science Foundation grant to the University of Alaska in 1966.

Alaska State Library Portrait File, ASL-Chance-Genie-1

Radio and television newscaster Genie Chance interviewed dozens of people across Alaska who survived the Good Friday Earthquake on March 27, 1964. She then compiled the interviews and published a document in 1966 titled "Chronology of Physical Events of the Alaskan Earthquake," funded through a grant from the National Science Foundation to the University of Alaska. Chance manned a mobile radio from her car to broadcast public safety messages in Anchorage following the terrifying earthquake. She later served in the state House (1969-1975) and state Senate (1975-1979).

EARTHQUAKE!

9

ANCHORAGE HIT HARD

T he massive shockwave at 5:36 p.m. on Good Friday, March 27, 1964, sent Anchorage suburb Turnagain-By-The-Sea into terrifying motion. The earth slumped, slid and dropped toward the shores of Cook Inlet. Alaska's most beautiful homes twisted and split as a bluff 8,450 feet long and 895 feet wide broke into pieces and fell into a pit 50 to 100 feet deep. Other homes moved hundreds of yards from their foundations. Within minutes, 75 houses were lost and three residents of the subdivision were dead.

Robert Atwood, editor and publisher of the *Anchorage Daily Times*, was one of those who escaped as his home on Marston Drive was torn apart. He told his story to radio interviewer Genie Chance, who later recorded firsthand accounts of people who experienced the world's second-largest recorded earthquake.

While some subdivision residents rode tabletop size pieces of land down the bluff and others clung to each other in an effort to stay put, Atwood's story of watching his house fall apart and his determination to survive the quake is similar to others who were home in the subdivision at dusk that slightly overcast Good Friday afternoon.

The veteran newspaperman had just picked up his new trumpet to begin practicing in the living room of his spacious log home when the house began to rock. He saw the chandelier hanging from the open-beam ceiling start to swing.

The earthquake of March 1964 destroyed homes in the Turnagain area of Anchorage.

"When I noticed things falling that don't usually fall in an earthquake, it was very easy to see that this was more than an ordinary one," Atwood told Chance.

He quickly realized the house would not stand long with the quake shaking it violently at different angles, so he stumbled out the front door. When he reached his driveway, he turned just in time to see his house destroyed.

Atwood said the earth beneath the home twisted the two ends of his house in opposite directions, which seemed to lengthen and then shrink it.

"The noise was terrific," he said. "Just the noise of a dying house … the glass breaking, the timbers giving, snapping, cracking, splitting – everything tearing apart. …"

Then trees began falling around him and the earth started opening up and taking on odd, angular forms. Some pieces dashed upward, others tilted down. Chasms opened all around him in crazy patterns. He wondered where he should stand to be safe. Then he began to fall.

EARTHQUAKE!

"The earth just opened up, and I was going down," he said. "It seemed an awful long distance."

Atwood landed in soft, dry sand at the bottom of a darkened V-shape crevice that kept getting wider. Tree stumps, fence posts, frozen boulder-size chunks of soil and other debris fell on top of him.

"Then I saw this chasm elongate, and it went over to my neighbor's house," he said. Atwood told Chance that up to that point he had thought his house was the only one affected by the quake. But when he heard his neighbor's house begin to fall apart, the enormity of the situation began to register.

He remained at the bottom of the chasm and struggled to free his right arm, buried up to the shoulder in sand. When he unclenched his grip on his trumpet, his arm came out easily. He then scrambled to keep above the debris that kept falling in on top of him.

University of Alaska Fairbanks, Alaska Earthquake Archives Committee Records, UAF-1972-152-4

People could not believe the devastion in their neighborhood at Turnagain-By-The-Sea subdivision. The earth split and huge crevices opened during the Good Friday earthquake on March 27, 1964.

"The roar of an earthquake is a sound in itself," he said. "I don't know how you'd describe it. It's a rumble and a slithery sound all mixed up. And it's got some crackle to it, too. That's when the frozen earth breaks and slides around, I guess."

When things quieted down, he clamored up the side of the chasm to the surface.

"I looked around, and as far as I could see, I saw nothing but desolation in what used to be our neighborhood," he said. "Houses galore at all angles – and topsy-turvy. And everything silent, except for the last snapping and cracking of the house as the earth still moved a bit and things still gave."

His house, which had stood about 100 feet above the water overlooking the Knik Arm, now was nothing but kindling wood down on the beach. Helicopter pilots used his roof, which had remained intact, as a heliport the next day.

This aerial photograph shows the devastation of the landslides in Turnagain-By-The-Sea subdivision in Anchorage on March 27, 1964.

EARTHQUAKE!

Still dressed in his suit coat, slacks and oxford shoes, Atwood wondered if anyone else in the subdivision had survived the giant quake. Then he heard the voice of his 15-year-old neighbor, Warren Hines, who was holding his 4-year-old sister, Mitzi.

Atwood carefully made his way toward the youngsters. He had to navigate frozen ground covered with a foot of snow and frozen brush, which was slippery. He had a tough time maintaining his footing. Then he got into soft sand, where he slid, and then found himself dropping into blue clay and sinking up to his knees.

When he finally got to the Hines' children, he found Warren barefoot and wearing a silk shirt and Mitzi dressed in pajamas.

"It's interesting how values change when an earthquake hits," Atwood later recalled, adding that at that moment he would have given anything for a piece of wool to warm the little girl.

The trio made their way up and down chasm walls and under dangerous overhanging pieces of frozen ground until they reached safety and the children's mother. Soon rescuers made their way to the group and helped them out of the disaster area.

Less than a mile away from the subdivision, Alaska manager for Scandinavian Airways Chris von Imhof was sitting in his second-floor office in the Anchorage International Airport terminal building when the earth began to move.

"As it got stronger, I tried to go out to the ramp," von Imhof told Chance a few days after the quake. But he found the doors locked because workers were rebuilding the airport. "So as it got stronger, I had no choice but to jump out the window."

He first slammed his foot through the glass and then leapt out onto the pavement below. That's when he saw the seven-story Federal Aviation Administration flight tower fall.

"It just cracked together like a piece of match," he said. "It more or less just fell onto itself – just collapsed."

Although suffering cuts on his chest and arms, von Imhof joined others in the area and raced toward the wreckage.

With help from a 20-ton mobile crane supplied by Elmendorf's 5040th Civil Engineer Group, they dug through 30 feet of debris

The great earthquake of March 27, 1964, destroyed the air traffic control tower at Anchorage International Airport, killing one traffic controller on duty that day.

to rescue a cook and a waitress who had been in the flight kitchen beneath the tower when the quake hit. They also removed the body of William Taylor, control specialist for the FAA who had been on duty when the tower collapsed.

Von Imhof had a unique perspective on the massive quake, which ripped cracks in the runway near the airport and also damaged the terminal. He compared it to warfare, as he had lived in Europe during World War II.

"The effects are the same, whether it's a bomb blast or an earthquake," he told Chance. "Except the bomb blast sometimes takes longer and this just took a few seconds and the whole tower collapsed. It's the worst thing I've ever seen."

Luckily, not many people had been in the building at the time of the earthquake, because the scheduled Alaska Airlines jet had departed on time 15 minutes earlier.

Closer to downtown Anchorage, radio announcer Bob Fleming was in the basement cafeteria of the Presbyterian Community Hospital at Ninth Avenue and L Street when the earthquake struck. He told interviewer Chance that the quake began as a tremble in the basement. He then felt the building buck and sway. Then a rolling motion hit that almost made him dizzy.

While he and a couple nurses braced themselves inside a doorway, he glanced south and noticed the entire building looked like it was on a swing – swinging back and forth.

Dishes, equipment and food smashed to the floor. Fleming then heard a huge crash as the big soft-drink machine overturned down the hall.

After the shaking subsided, he made his way to the first floor where he found his wife. They hurried up to the hospital on the fourth floor and found tremendous damage to the facility.

"Everything had come down," Fleming said. "And these big containers of ether had opened up and the place was full of the fumes of ether. And we began to smell gas."

He said he then looked out the window.

The ground dropped several feet around Ninth Avenue and L Street, as seen in this photograph. Wreckage of the Four Seasons apartment house at Ninth Avenue and M Street fills the background.

"L Street had sunk about 15 or 20 feet," he said. "And another street had sunk and the houses had just dropped into chasms and cars were in holes down the street."

He helped the staff evacuate all the patients to Providence Hospital, a short distance away. The evacuation took quite a while, however, as the traffic was heavy and the signal lights were all out. Once they reached Providence, they found it overflowing with people.

"Everybody they could find was working," Fleming said.

Just down the street from the Presbyterian Community Hospital, the quake proved too much for an almost completed six-story concrete apartment house at Ninth Avenue and M Street. The violent shaking took its toll on the Four Seasons, and the structure – slated to be the first "luxury" apartments in Alaska – collapsed into a heap.

The owner of an apartment house on K Street near Seventh Avenue rode out the quake by sitting on the floor inside the building where he was painting walls. When the shaking stopped, he found the building had sunk about 9 feet as a graben, or trench, formed in the earth beneath it and the land to the west had moved westward.

More buildings and streets collapsed in downtown Anchorage, as well, catching many people off guard.

Blanche Clark had just walked out of the new J.C. Penney building on Fifth Avenue and climbed into her car when the first tremor hit. She sat waiting for the light to turn green so she could pull away from the curb next to the building.

"The car started acting up, just pitching back and forth," she later told Chance. "I figured something had gone wrong with the mechanism of the car."

She then looked up and saw a woman attempting to get up on the street ahead of her. That's when she realized it was an earthquake. Clark then saw the pavement rolling in huge waves.

"I knew that the building next to me would probably fall," Clark said. "But I couldn't get the car in motion to get away from it."

As she debated whether to get out of the car and make a run for it, she noticed the woman in the street wasn't having much luck walking so she decided to stay put.

The violent earthquake ripped two concrete panels off the front of the J.C. Penny building in downtown Anchorage. Two people died as a result.

U.S. Army Pfc. Clarence Myers Jr., who was in front of Penney's when the quake began, saw Clark sitting in her parked car and witnessed the concrete walls of the store begin to separate from the building.

Meyers said he saw "… the walls on Penney's swaying back and forth and one panel slid down." He told Chance that the east panel on the north wall was the first to go and tons of concrete came crashing down on Clark's 1963 Chevrolet station wagon.

Meyers then watched in horror as another slab of the concrete paneling fell from the north wall and struck a woman running from the building. It cut her in two, burying one half under the debris and hurling the other into the middle of the street.

He then rushed to join a group of men attempting to rescue Clark, whose car was crushed to a height of about three feet.

Clark told Chance that she was not in much pain, even though the weight of the debris had pinned her shoulder and chest.

"I thought if I could get the door open, I could get out and walk away," she later said. "But the door wouldn't open."

Meyers and other rescuers talked to her while they attempted to get her out of the vehicle.

The men tried to lift the slabs of concrete off the car with a winch-truck, then two winch-trucks and then three. They attached a winch and cable to her steering wheel, and then using a winch on either end, they slid the slabs apart a bit. The rescuers finally brought in jacks to raise the slabs in the center and used a cutting torch to open the car and remove her.

Clark, who remained conscious throughout the entire ordeal, was on her way to Providence Hospital 30 minutes after the onset of the quake. Doctors found she had a broken neck, broken right arm, fractured ribs and a punctured lung.

Several other Anchorage residents shared their stories of almost five minutes of terror with Chance, too. Parents and children, out of school that day, stumbled and fell on shifting floors as they tried to escape outdoors. Windows broke out of stores all around them.

Drivers hung on to their steering wheels as their cars bounced along streets that wrinkled and split. They watched huge cracks open roadways and numerous chimneys fall apart and drop near their cars.

"Everybody was all shook up," said U.S. Army Specialist-4 Martin R. Paulhemus, who tried to navigate the waving sidewalk at the intersection of Fourth Avenue and C Street. "Nobody knew what to do – trying to get away from falling power lines and flying glass."

Danny Plotnik was in his clothing store on Fourth Avenue when the earthquake struck. He stayed in the building as it began sinking about two minutes into the quake.

"It felt like to me I was going down in an elevator," he said of the experience as the building dropped about 10 feet. "It was a slow, gradual movement."

Plotnik said he thought he was being swallowed up alive by the earth.

After the building stopped moving, he made his way to the front door and climbed up the steep walls of the graben to street level. Once there, he noticed that the second floor of the Denali Theater was at street level and its marquee was resting on the pavement. Luckily, the theater was empty because the first showing of an adult-only movie titled "Irma La Douce" was not scheduled to begin until 6 p.m.

Fourth Avenue in downtown Anchorage was heavily damaged, as seen in these photographs. Notice Denali Theater dropped one story.

Anchorage's Government Hill Elementary School lies split in half in the wake of the Good Friday earthquake, which rocked the southern coastal region of Alaska. Many schools in the area sustained heavy damage, necessitating double-shifting of students in those facilities still open.

The earthquake caused massive damage to downtown Anchorage, including leveling an apartment building and two parking garages; causing an elementary school and several homes to slide into Ship Creek Valley and settle on top of an Alaska Railroad warehouse; and dropping businesses on three blocks of Fourth Avenue 10 to 20 feet into the ground, according to a U.S. Army Corps of Engineers report.

Nine people died in Anchorage that afternoon: three in the Turnagain-By-The-Sea subdivision, five crushed in the downtown area, and one as the control tower at the airport collapsed.

Shell-shocked survivors huddled in neighbors' homes, community centers like the YMCA, churches and makeshift shelters. They settled in for a night without power, heat or communications.

It may have seemed like a city of silence that night, but many people were working through the darkness to find the missing and sift through debris.

Utility workers showed up in droves. Policemen, firemen and

other first responders gathered. The Salvation Army and American Red Cross sprang into action. Doctors and nurses mustered at the Providence and Alaska Native hospitals.

Alaska Gov. William A. Egan sent word from Juneau via an amateur radio operator to utilize the Alaska National Guard troops, who had just completed a two-week training encampment at Fort Richardson, to patrol and guard the damaged areas against looters.

And under direction from the Alaskan Command, all branches of the military based in Anchorage teamed up to assist during this emergency.

One of the first critical issues they faced was repairing communications. Initially, taxis with their mobile power units were strategically placed throughout the area and became major communication points between Elmendorf Air Force base and the

Alaska National Guard photo

Eskimo Scouts helped guard businesses in downtown Anchorage and directed traffic the day after the massive earthquake.

U.S. Army at Fort Richardson. Then the military sent a squad car into Anchorage, which provided the first communication with the city. It stood by at the Public Safety Building to relay damage reports and requests for assistance until wire communications could be restored.

Within 90 minutes of the first tremor, both Anchorage bases had restored 95 percent of their communications in a limited capacity. Telephone communication into the city was back in service in two hours, and calls for assistance poured into the command center.

Telegraph circuits for the American Red Cross were provided between Anchorage and Seattle, and two-and-a-half hours after the quake, two teletypes and three phones were set up in the lobby of the Alaska Communications System building on Government Hill for public use.

University of Alaska Fairbanks, Alaska Earthquake Archives Committee Records, UAF-1972-152-131

Anchorage residents began cleaning up their city as soon as they were able. This photo shows trucks, workers and others on Fourth Avenue on March 31, 1964.

Some businesses, like the Matanuska Valley Bank, set up temporary offices in trailers in Anchorage after the earthquake.

Military personnel also addressed the need for potable water. Right after the quake, people had to melt snow for drinking water, washing and flushing toilets.

Three hours after the earthquake, troops hauled five water trailers to the Anchorage Public Safety Building. More showed up a while later.

"From Friday night until Monday morning, six trucks shuttled water trailers back and forth from Fort Richardson," according to a military document titled "Operation Helping Hand."

"They were placed at hospitals, in school yards, at major public buildings and in the park strip. At the peak of the effort, 33 water trailers were in use," according to the military's account.

The report stated the water hydrant at Orah Dee Clark Junior High School in Mountain View became usable on Monday, and turned into the primary water point where water trailers filled up.

The earth cracked in several places on this section between Third and Fourth avenues in downtown Anchorage.

Below-freezing temperatures kept blowtorch-armed patrols busy all night to protect the water trailers from freezing.

By Tuesday, water service had been restored to most of Anchorage after four water purification units were flown into town from Fort Lewis, Wash. The units were put at four key points in the city. The military provided Anchorage's water supply until Sunday, April 5, when the city system could begin providing potable water to most of the citizens.

The military helped feed the masses, as well, since homes had been destroyed and utilities disrupted. While many Alaskans had a supply of canned moose, salmon and vegetables to tide them over the first few days, others – including those left homeless who were sleeping in base barracks, volunteer workers and the troops themselves – needed to be fed. The Army set up field mess halls around town, although the first meals consisted of C-rations.

The 5040th Food Service Squadron at Elmendorf served 44,487

regular meals and 11,820 C-ration meals in four days, according to military records. With all civilian bakeries down, too, the Elmendorf bakery shifted into high gear and worked around the clock to make 14,000 pounds of bread every day for four days.

Disease was another immediate concern since sewer lines had broken and standing water was common. Two Army ambulances and eight medics made themselves available to the Anchorage Police Department. The military also provided a multitude of beds, mattresses and blankets to Anchorage hospitals, distributed typhoid vaccines and assisted medical professionals with many other services.

They also helped search all the damaged buildings downtown, and when rehabilitation of the Turnagain residential area slowed because equipment was scarce, Elmendorf's motor pool supplied 20 trucks, a huge wrecker and two radio units plus personnel. The bases provided many more vehicles and pieces of heavy equipment to help with the cleanup effort, too.

Army Corp of Engineers 1964 Earthquake Photographs Collection: Anchorage Museum, B1977.118.54

Anchorage residents immediately went to work clearing away debris and rebuilding their city. This photo shows destroyed buildings downtown being hauled away along Fourth Avenue, in center running left to right, with damaged J.C. Penney building at middle right.

Thanks to the assistance offered by the military, Anchorage residents soon were able to turn their attention to rebuilding their community. Public schools opened in a week, although many were double-shifted as several schools underwent repairs.

While Anchorage sustained losses of more than $200 million to its public and private facilities, most facilities and services were federally owned and controlled so federal dollars flowed for reconstruction.

The Office of Emergency Planning moved quickly to provide financial assistance. Congress extended the Alaska Omnibus Act, which had provided Alaska transitional funds from territorial to state status during the first five years of statehood, and amendments to the act boosted the federal share of funding several projects to more than 90 percent.

The city rebuilt rapidly, as the construction industry had been in decline before the quake and a supply of labor and resources were readily available. The Port of Anchorage, which sustained little damage, was the only operational port for oil companies and shipping giants. It benefited in the long term as businesses began building warehouses, storage tanks and other new installations in the Anchorage industrial park. Anchorage soon became the main port for the state.

In 1965, the National Civic League awarded Anchorage with the coveted All-America City award – along with Seward and Valdez – for how it recovered and rebuilt following the Good Friday earthquake. Annually, since 1949, the league has given this award to 10 communities in the United States to recognize those whose citizens work together to identify and tackle communitywide challenges and receive uncommon results.

10

WILD WAVES BASH WHITTIER

The ice-free, deep-water port of Whittier, which lies at the western end of Passage Canal, was devastated at lightening speed by giant waves that crashed ashore before the earth stopped shaking on March 27, 1964. Underwater landslides that Good Friday caused three 30- to 40-foot localized tsunamis to come ashore 90 seconds apart. They killed 13 people.

Alaska Railroad employee Jerry Wade told interviewer Genie Chance that he was standing near his trailer home on a bluff 15 feet above the beach. When the violent shaking stopped, he watched as water "rushed out of the inlet as through a mighty funnel." He then saw the gravel bottom exposed where water is usually 30 to 35 feet deep.

Then a wave, which he estimated to be about 20 feet high, rushed onto the beach and swept him, his wife and baby daughter, their trailer home and a railroad flatcar about 400 feet up the beach. His daughter died.

That same wave tipped over the Union Oil Co. tank farm. The fuel storage tanks at the waterfront then exploded and sent burning oil miles out into the bay.

Several witnesses told Chance that the waves did not appear to come across the inlet, but rather appeared to form in the center of the inlet before sweeping toward Whittier. And a "black cloud boiled" in the water after the first failure of an oil storage tank occurred.

Tidal waves hit Whittier with such force that the water drove a thick plank of wood through a tractor tire.

EARTHQUAKE!

Others said the next huge wave floated a solid concrete pump house several inches above its foundation, drove a 2x4 plank of wood through a 10-ply tire on a forklift at the sawmill, and moved an oil storage tank 48 feet off its pad.

Douglas Keating said the waves struck Whittier from the northwest and northeast simultaneously. One seismic wave took out the Columbia Lumber Mill, along with 12 people who never were found. The waves destroyed the Alaska Railroad depot, the stub pier and small boat harbor, the car-barge slip dock and several homes. They also deposited two-ton boulders on shore.

There were no eyewitnesses to other parts of Passage Canal, but evidence showed waves along the shore northwest of Whittier reached as high as 104 feet.

The earthquake and giant waves destroyed all communications out of Whittier and cut the spur connecting the town to the Alaska Railroad line out to Portage.

A U.S. Coast Guard plane flew over Whittier the next morning and those on board saw oil tanks burning. Just after noon, a Pacific Northern Airlines pilot reported Whittier was "all aflame" as he passed overhead.

Then an Alaska State Trooper reported to the Civil Defense headquarters around 2:30 p.m. what he had found in Whittier. The tunnel to the town was open, one person had died and 12 people were missing. The remaining 52 residents were all right.

An Army helicopter finally made it into the isolated community late Saturday and evacuated Alaska Railroad employee Jerry Wade, his wife and their deceased child, the only recovered fatality at Whittier. The Army pilot then picked up 16 more women and children along the highway between Portage and Anchorage.

The port was not as badly damaged as initially thought. The power plant remained in operation and major port buildings suffered little damage.

Townspeople restored Whittier's electricity in six hours and the running water in 10. As aftershocks continued, the small community moved into the school gymnasium and set up a community kitchen in

The tidal waves that hit Whittier following the earthquake on March 27, 1964, caused much damage to the dock area.

the cafeteria. After three days, they began to return to a more normal life, except they continued to use the community dining room.

On April 6, Fort Richardson flew in troops and three jeeps via helicopter to help with heavy cleanup work. They tore down unstable structures, cleared debris and salvaged supplies.

"A boon to the ladies of the port was the kitchen crew that accompanied the detachment," read a military report featured in a document titled "Operation Helping Hand."

They were able to close the community kitchen when Army cooks took over. They then fed the residents of Whittier, along with the troops, railroad employees and others working the docks until May 1.

The tunnels and tracks of the Alaska Railroad had to be cleared and repaired before cargo from the Whittier dock could be moved to Anchorage, and railroad employees proved up to the challenge. They worked 70 to 80 hours a week making stopgap repairs to get cars moving on the tracks in less than three weeks from the first tremor.

"In the weeks after the quake, ARR personnel – supervisory and union – were out working 16 hour days, seven days a week, daylight and dark," according to an article titled "Alaska RR Comeback From Disaster," which appeared in *Railway Age Weekly* in January 1965.

The City of Whittier, incorporated in 1969, grew to around 300 people who now call it home. The town became known for commercial fishing, recreation and tourism.

11

SEAWATER SEEPS INTO PORTAGE

"It was impossible to stand," Portage Postmaster N. Upchurch told interviewer Genie Chance a few weeks after the Great Earthquake. "It pounded me against the earth like a rubber ball."

Trees swayed to a 45-degree angle, their tops smacking the snow-covered tundra. Many cracks appeared in the ground within 30 seconds of the quake's onset, with an average length one-quarter mile, average width 6 feet and average depth 10 feet. And some sections of earth rose 8 feet.

Upchurch said she heard water running in the ground cracks immediately after the quake. Some water and mud spouted as high as 50 feet from the cracks. Upchurch noted that the largest piece of earth not cracked was only about 50 square feet and "not one highway-bridge was left standing."

The earthquake lasted 18 minutes in Portage due to the area's thick underlying beds of clay, according to Alaska Railroad records. Rivers and streams in the area immediately went dry following the quake. They did not start running again for three days.

George Larson and his wife, owners of Portage House, were in their restaurant at the time of the quake. The large building, located on the east side of the highway, also housed the Alaska Railroad station. Larson said the entire building rose up and down in a series of waves, and he feared it would collapse on top of them. About two minutes into the violent shaking, the stone fireplace in the north end "exploded," sending stones away from the building.

The Larsons, in an effort to not be buried under their building in case it collapsed, ran out the door and jumped into their car, which was "rocking and rolling." Just then, the earth cracked between the car and the building. They then watched as many cracks developed, running in all directions, and the earth broke into pieces. Mud and water shot into the air about 25 to 35 feet high as the cracks opened and closed.

The couple heaved a sigh of relief when the earthquake ended and saw, that although severely damaged, their building had not collapsed.

Two men on the west side of the highway ran out of a service station as its concrete floor began to crack. They made it a few feet away from the building before a 3-foot-wide crack opened between them. Then cracks formed around them, which left each man on a small island that moved up and down.

Kenneth J. Huseby photographs, Archives and Special Collections, Consortium Library, University of Alaska Anchorage

Witnesses who rode out the earthquake in Portage reported the earth splitting in chunks all around them, as seen in this photo at the Portage Inn. Helicopters rescued those stranded in the area.

Alaska Railroad Collection; Anchorage Museum, B1979.002.791

Above: The land near Portage dropped several feet during the 1964 earthquake, which made the area flood at high tide.

Below: U.S. Army Corps of Engineers workers stacked sandbags to prevent more flooding near Girdwood.

Woodman Photograph Collection; Anchorage Museum, B1980.027.12

The earthquake destroyed the bridge connecting Portage to the outside world. The military sent in helicopters to rescue the residents in that area.

"It was like riding an open elevator," one man said, adding that as he went up, the other man went down. Then they'd pass each other going in opposite directions.

All the earth around them broke into similar pieces, and as the blocks of frozen earth moved up and down, the cracks opened and closed causing muddy water to spout as high as 50 feet in the air. When the shaking stopped, water filled the open cracks.

A vast area along the Seward Highway near Girdwood dropped several feet, sinking into Cook Inlet. The trees, which suddenly absorbed seawater, died.

The residents of Portage had not been able to evacuate due to the destruction of highway bridges and landslides on both sides of town. They spent a fearful night with mighty aftershocks hitting often, and they worried about tidal waves.

EARTHQUAKE!

The earthquake split the New Seward Highway in several places, breaking the pavement into chunks.

The American Red Cross used dog teams and military aircraft to shuttle emergency and relief supplies to communities like Hope following the earthquake on March 27, 1964.

This photo captured Carolyn S. Murray, a Red Cross disaster worker from Los Angeles, helping to unload a sled of supplies for Helen DeFrance, a widow whose home was destroyed.

Reports coming into Anchorage about the devastation in Seward mobilized the military within hours of the earthquake. By 10:30 p.m., an Army platoon had left Fort Richardson and was heading down the Seward Highway. A few minutes later, a battalion and two more platoons followed with two bulldozers.

While these troops had been ordered to get to Seward, it soon became clear that the task could take several days due to the damage and debris along the highway. The force first found a large fissure at Rabbit Creek, which the bulldozers filled with earth and snow.

The group cautiously continued on to Bird Creek, where they saw the bridge was cracked but useable. The convoy filled in cracks along the way with dirt, gravel, timber, ice and snow.

They hit their first major obstacle about 10 miles short of Girdwood, where a massive slide had covered the road with a mix of dirt, rocks and trees.

Along with three bulldozers from the state highway department, the Army troops and their dozers pushed through the slide. Engineers and infantrymen then worked side-by-side to clear the bulldozer trail by hand.

Military rescue workers had to bulldoze their way through several avalanches and landslides along the Seward Highway.

Mid-Saturday they found a bridge collapsed just before Girdwood at Glacier Creek. That's when the mission changed. Many of the troops were recalled to Fort Richardson, and one platoon stayed with 50 men of the U.S. Army Corps of Engineers to put in a 150-foot pre-fabricated, portable truss bridge called a Bailey bridge across the creek. The new orders for these troops were to clear the road enough to evacuate 140 people stranded at Girdwood, Alyeska and Portage.

The engineers continued on to Virgin Creek, where they found its bridge torn out. There they installed an 80-foot Bailey bridge.

On the 12-mile stretch between Girdwood and Portage, the troops came across 15 slides that cut the road. Some measured up to 300 feet long and 30 to 40 feet deep.

"The bulldozers worked up to 10 hours clearing a single slide," stated a military report titled "Operation Helping Hand." "Even after such labor, the paths they sliced through some of the slides were so narrow the mirrors on the cabs of big trucks dragged along the snowbank on either side of the cut."

They also came across huge fissures where cracks in the ground reached two and three feet wide. The men only filled in those that they could not go around.

"Every bridge and major culvert on the road was damaged or destroyed," according to military records. "Hasty repairs were made, or the dozers bucked rough roadways around them."

They found the highway bridge at Twentymile Creek gone and the concrete decking lying in the creek bed.

"The incredible force of the earthquake had driven wooden pilings through the concrete like a steel awl through cheese," the report said.

The railroad bridge still stood, however. So the bulldozers cut new approaches across the tide flats and troops decked the trestle to allow wheeled vehicles to cross.

The Army finally reached Portage on Tuesday afternoon, four days after the earthquake, and they had fought the highway around the clock to get there. Once at Portage, the troops learned Army and Air Force helicopters already had evacuated many residents. The 35

The earthquake destroyed the Twentymile Bridge along the Seward Highway.

who chose to remain were living in Diamond Jim's, an old log lodge that was the only building left intact.

The remaining few welcomed the 40 gallons of potable water brought by the troops, the first drinking water they'd seen since the quake. A few days later, a water trailer and purification unit came over the road from Fort Richardson.

The military began reconnaissance and rescue missions the day after the earthquake. They had transported survivors from not only Portage but all populated areas along the Seward Highway between Anchorage and Seward, including three people at Hope and some at Silver Tip. They also flew over Cook Inlet to Tyonek.

The Civil Air Patrol flew 50 pounds of medical supplies to Portage, along with 200 pounds of meat and 50 pounds of typhoid serum to Hope on April 4. Another mission to Hope brought baled hay for starving livestock.

By the weekend of April 11-12, only a handful of Portage residents remained as the majority had decided to leave. However, when high spring tides flooded their village and carried giant chunks of ice through their already battered community, they sent out an urgent call for rescue. Two military helicopters responded to evacuate 12 people – 10 went to Girdwood and two to Elmendorf Air Force Base in Anchorage. An Army chopper carried another eight people to the high school at Girdwood. The tides that evening sent 43 inches of water into Diamond Jim's lodge.

Army engineers then put 27,000 sandbags along the approaches to Girdwood. While the bags did not keep the water from flooding the community, they did keep the ice chunks from destroying the buildings, military records show.

The high tides wiped out the approaches to the 80-foot Bailey bridge at Virgin Creek, so Army Engineers dismantled it and placed a 130-foot replacement bridge that would suffice until the state could build a new bridge across that creek.

Following the earthquake, Girdwood ended up below sea level after the earth shifted. That meant the residents suffered through muddy feet and flooded homes and businesses when Turnagain Arm flooded at high tide. After careful consideration, the community of Girdwood later decided to move its settlement at least 300 yards north where the average land height stood 15 to 20 feet above the old site. It also was closer to the proposed route of the New Seward Highway relocation.

Once the property owners' land was declared to be below mean high tide, it reverted to the state and the displaced property owners received parcels of land in the new townsite.

At the time of the earthquake, the community of Girdwood was comprised of three men working for the railroad and three men with the state highway department. The remaining 76 people worked in or were associated with recreation work, according to a newspaper article at the time.

12

ALASKA RAILROAD DAMAGED

D amage to the Alaska Railroad from the Good Friday earthquake was close to $30 million. After the shaking and tidal waves ceased, much of the railroad south of Anchorage lay in ruins. The section north from Anchorage across the Knik and Matanuska river flats and up the Palmer branch also sustained heavy damage. Bridges up to 170 miles north of Anchorage suffered light damage, according to Alaska Railroad reports.

Underwater slides and tidal waves devastated the deep-water docks and transit sheds at Seward, along with six miles of yard and dock tracks and the new engine house. Two giant gantry cranes and six large straddle buggies, worth $300,000, toppled into Resurrection Bay.

A 30-foot tidal wave wiped away one wing of the railroad depot building at Whittier, but did not take the rest of the building. The railroad yard stayed pretty much in tact, too.

Railroad facilities in Anchorage, including the office annex building, wheel shop and an equipment storage building received severe damage and had to be torn down.

Railroad officials met early Saturday morning in the Anchorage dispatchers' office, with no heat or electricity, to figure out a plan of action. No one knew the extent of the damage to the line at that time.

Soon employees spread out via helicopter and car to check on the status of the destruction. Reports from Seward and Whittier finally

Above: The Good Friday earthquake destroyed the waiting room of the Alaska Railroad Depot at Whittier.

Below: The violent quake twisted and broke railroad tracks and bridges near Portage.

The earthquake and tidal waves that hit Seward destroyed Alaska Railroad cars and tracks.

came in when communications were restored, according to railroad documents.

Decision makers decided to make repairs to the northern section of the railroad first. That section was least damaged and they wanted to make sure that coal deliveries for the Elmendorf Air Force Base and the U.S. Army base at Fort Richardson could resume from the Matanuska coalfields.

Railroad employees worked day and night and got freight service from Anchorage to Fairbanks resumed on April 6. Passenger service went back on line April 11.

Other railroaders "ripped and dozed, hammered and shoveled" their way toward Portage, according to chief engineer Thomas "Cliff" Fuglestad, who later wrote about the repairs to the line. They thought they could have service to Whittier back on line around the same time as that northern section.

But workers discovered that towns, tracks and land along that section had dropped 5.5 feet from the great movement of the earth's crust. They would need to bring in massive amounts of fill to raise and move the tracks.

Army engineers, who had bulldozed their way to Portage in the days following the earthquake, assisted Alaska Railroad crews in raising the sunken roadbed and aided in getting emergency repairs completed to get the rail line open into Whittier. The military moved communications equipment to Portage to temporarily replace damaged railroad and Federal Aviation Administration systems, which finally allowed communications between Anchorage, Whittier and Seward.

High tides carrying ice floes threatened to take out the damaged, inverted trusses of the bridge at Twentymile, so before heading back to Anchorage on April 11, Fuglestad and his crew grabbed nine cars loaded with ties out of the Portage railroad yard and used a dozer to push them onto the long steel bridge. They hoped the added weight would save the bridge.

"I went down the next morning by helicopter to watch the high tide as it came flooding in like an evil and malevolent thing," Fuglestad wrote in his account. He then had the helicopter land, and he instructed a lineman to paddle to a pole and tie a ribbon on it, one foot above the still visible high-water mark.

"That would be our design grade for raising as much track as possible before the high tides of early May," he wrote when he recounted the event in 1979.

Thanks to the dedication and perseverance of Alaska Railroad engineers, union workers and gandy dancers, freight service from Whittier was restored on April 21 when the first train with 125 cars of freight crawled at 10 mph to Anchorage. The railroad schedule revolved around the high tides for the next several months.

Workers began rebuilding the section from Portage south to Seward in late June 1964. Due to the change in land elevation, the damage to the tracks and the destruction of dock facilities, that work was not fully completed until 1966.

13

SEWARD BURNS

"An isolated ghost town populated by the living" was the *Seattle Times'* view of Seward following the Good Friday earthquake of 1964. Just a day before it had shared the news that the town on Resurrection Bay had been named an All-America City by the National Civic League.

Standard Oil Co. seaman Ted Pederson was on the Seward dock checking and adjusting valves between his ship and the bulk storage tanks when he felt the second-largest earthquake in recorded human history hit at 5:36 p.m. on March 27.

"Earthquake!" he shouted as he ran toward his ship, *Alaska Standard*. Within 30 seconds of the first violent shake, he saw the oil tanker buck and then slam into the dock, he later told interviewer Genie Chance.

He continued up the dock toward the beach – then saw all the oil pipelines leading from the beach to the dock break in one place. Geysers of gasoline shot skyward. Pilings then flew upward, a 200-foot warehouse sank and the *Alaska Standard* pitched and dropped 30 feet to hit land.

Pedersen said he flew into the water when the dock collapsed. As he struggled to stay afloat in the turbulence, he saw a giant wave filled with debris heading toward him. He then fell unconscious when something hit him on the back of his head.

The Good Friday earthquake of 1964 and the tidal waves that followed destroyed most of the buildings and docks in Seward.

The massive wave tossed him onto the catwalk of his ship, eight feet above the deck. When he came to, he found his fellow crewmates fighting flames aboard the tanker and he had a broken leg.

Dean Smith was working in the cabin of a gantry crane about 50 feet above the Alaska Railroad dock when the quake struck. He later reported the top of the crane flipped back and forth "like a long whip," and when the wheels came off the tracks, his crane began "walking around like some stiff-legged spider." Smith quickly scrambled down and began leaping over cracks appearing in the pavement on the dock that were a foot wide and "getting bigger all the time."

As he and a fellow worker made their way to higher ground, they saw East Point Cannery float on top of a huge wave and then sink into Resurrection Bay. Smith told Chance they also saw the wave pick up many vehicles parked at the dock, and then a burst of flames shot 200 feet in the air from the Standard Oil storage tanks.

Moments before the explosion, Val Anderson had just walked into his house on Sixth Avenue after working a full day as a longshoreman on the Standard Oil dock. His wife, Jean, was in the bathroom and his three children – Susie, 9, Sharon, 6, and Eric, 4 – were sitting on the living room floor watching "Puppet Spaceship XL," their favorite television show.

"I'm so thankful for that," Anderson said in an interview for *Aunt Phil's Trunk* in 2013. On most days, his children would have been outdoors playing somewhere in the neighborhood. "Other parents didn't find their kids until the next day."

Within seconds he heard an overwhelming rumble. Then he felt the house shake so hard that the hanging light in the living room almost hit him in his head. The kitchen refrigerator lurched sideways.

About 20 seconds after the first jolt, Anderson heard a giant "whoosh!" and felt heat as a Standard Oil tank exploded and flames shot more than 100 feet straight up – higher than the tree tops out his living room window.

US Army Corps of Engineers 1964 Earthquake Photographs Collection, Anchorage Museum, B1979.038.32

Oil tanks near the docks in Seward exploded and burned during the 1964 Good Friday earthquake.

EARTHQUAKE!

He had one thought: Get the children and his wife out of the house immediately as it was only a few blocks from what he felt would become a massive fire. He knew there were more tanks and hundreds of 10-gallon cases of aviation gas in that warehouse on the dock.

"Get in the car!" he shouted to the children and then rushed to the bathroom to get his wife. He found her hanging onto the sink and grabbed her. The two managed to get back down the hall to the front door. But then Jean fell down the steps.

Anderson stumbled down to her and lifted her back onto her feet. She took a few steps, then fell again and slid under the car.

The longshoreman pulled her up once more, pushed her into their sedan and took off, leaving the front door of their home wide open.

"We just had to get away from the fire," he said.

As the family drove toward the first bridge out of town, Anderson glanced toward the boat harbor. He saw a large power barge heaved in the air on a 15- or 20-foot wave above the breakwater. His wife saw water splashing over the railroad tracks.

When they reached the first of the three bridges leading out of Seward, they found a crack had split the road about two feet before the deck of the bridge. Anderson then knew they would not be escaping out of town, as the other bridges probably had suffered similar damage.

So he doubled back and made his way to higher ground at Forest Acres, along with many other Seward residents, about two miles from his house.

Others fleeing the fire drove down Third Avenue only to find that a wave had deposited railroad cars, parts of houses and other debris on the road. Some came across Al Wisdom using a bulldozer to try and clear the road. About 20 minutes later another tidal wave swept over Seward and no one ever saw Wisdom again.

"It was quite a night," Anderson said. "We listened to the roar of Standard Oil tanks exploding, and at times tidal waves moving in, and watching the great, red glare of the fire lighting the sky and mountainsides."

Above: Tidal waves carried fires from ruptured fuel tanks across Seward.

Below: Fire and tidal waves devastated the little town of Seward on Resurrection Bay.

EARTHQUAKE!

The refuges also felt strong aftershocks about every hour, which kept nerves on edge.

"Around midnight, someone came along for a head count," Anderson said, adding that the final death count was 12 in Seward.

"Whenever someone saw a kid, they'd pick him up and take him to safety," he said. "So many parents didn't know for a long time if their kids were gone or safe."

Anderson never thought his house would survive the blazing inferno that appeared to be engulfing the town. The next morning, however, he found his home in tact when he drove into Seward. But he also found much of the town destroyed.

Waves from various sources had created havoc on the small town, including an underwater landslide beneath the waterfront; the sloshing effect in Resurrection Bay; and displacement water from the earthquake fracturing the floor beneath Prince William Sound.

Burning oil covered most of the water surface. Flames from that oil spread to many parts of Seward as the waves swept further inland to the Texaco Petroleum tank farm, starting another fire. Water and burning fuel surged across the railroad tracks and into the city's north end, crushing dozens of homes, house trailers, waterfront stores and the radio station. Flames set debris ablaze and swept up against the foot of the mountains behind the city. As it crossed the highway leading to higher ground, a giant wave overtook several people who were fleeing in their vehicles and moved a 60-ton locomotive six blocks.

But it could have been worse, according to Richard Lemke, who visited Seward shortly after the earthquake and wrote a report for the U.S. Geological Survey.

"Had not a gentle wind been blowing eastward across the bay, the entire town probably would have burned," he surmised.

The earthquake, tidal waves and fires left Seward helpless. The disaster wiped out the town's harbor, utilities, road and rail lines, and communications. The airport remained the only useable facility, and it would play a critical role linking the battered town to civilization for many days.

U.S. military troops helped Sewardites look for the missing and clear debris.

Twenty-one U.S. Army soldiers were in Seward the day the earthquake struck. They were preparing to open the Army Recreation Center during the All-America City celebration slated for the following weekend.

Most, in the dining hall at the time of the shaker, escaped to higher ground, grabbing children from nearby houses as they ran. Once they recovered from the shock of the event, several soldiers made their way to the Seward hospital to help out with casualties.

The three cooks in the group went to the Jesse Lee Home orphanage and got the kitchen working on Army field ranges. They manned the kitchen all night and into Saturday afternoon, feeding the residents of the home and any other hungry Seward residents, according to a military document titled "Operation Helping Hand."

The soldiers worked with the police and townspeople as they searched through the wreckage of the devastated city looking for the injured and bodies.

By 10 a.m. Saturday, the military was flying more than 150

military troops to Seward – including 36 Alaska Army National Guardsmen who had been in Anchorage for a two-week tour of active duty at Fort Richardson. They brought a radio-teletype with them, which finally gave Seward communications with the outside world. It remained the only link until late on March 31, when two telephone lines went into operation.

One of the first messages sent out let the state Civil Defense Headquarters in Anchorage know that Seward badly needed utility experts to help reestablish water, sewer and electricity.

A demolitions expert had been sent along to Seward, also. City leaders had hoped he would be able to blow the fire out of the burning oil tanks, but that proved impossible. However, he was able to knock down some dangerously damaged buildings, blast pits for latrines and did a few other jobs that needed explosives.

The military brought a water purification unit, too, which was set up at a small lake near the city. Six water trailers then were placed around town for public use. The unit produced 10,000 gallons of

Seward's water supply became polluted with garbage and sewage following the earthquake and tidal waves. The U.S. military brought a water purification unit into town and set up water trailers.

Alaska National Guard cooks made meals for the residents of Seward at the Jesse Lee Home orphanage, which sat on high ground and was safe from the tsunamis.

water that Saturday and continued at peak capacity until not needed on April 9.

Cooks from the Alaska National Guard took over cooking at the Jesse Lee Home, and the Army cooks then opened a mess hall at the high school to feed those left in Seward. Food was gathered from damaged stores and homes. This community kitchen prepared, on average, 800 meals a day for citizens and volunteers. Another military field kitchen fed the soldiers who were helping out.

The Alaskan Air Command delivered nearly 200,000 pounds of relief cargo to Seward in the first few days following the earthquake. Members of the Civil Air Patrol also airlifted food, medical supplies, fuel, equipment and many passengers to Seward and other towns along the Kenai Peninsula. Those pilots helped evacuate people from Seward, Hope and Portage, too.

In an effort to keep information flowing following the destruction to Seward's Radio Station KIHB, Army personnel and city officials mimeographed a daily bulletin. That newssheet helped keep Seward's citizens abreast of what was happening in their town.

When a Seattle newspaper heard about the Seward radio station's problem, it published a story that led to another radio station donating a transmitter. The transmitter was shipped free via Northwest Orient Airlines to Anchorage, where it transferred to an Air National Guard C-123 that flew it to Seward.

Armed Forces Radio Service loaned a few more bits of equipment, and soon military technicians had KIHB back on the air three days after it went silent. It then served as a Civil Defense communications link.

Even though Seward, the All-America City with a promising future, was blackened by those raging fires, battered by the earthquake, inundated by tidal waves and lost about 95 percent of its industry, the rush of aid from the military and others helped its residents soldier on in the face of adversity.

When Seward city leaders met with Alaska's U.S. Sen. E.L. "Bob" Bartlett on Saturday, they told him that the city needed federal money to help rebuild the city.

"We need a grant … with no red tape," they told him, because if the federal government went the route of giving Seward a loan, the townspeople would have to vote a bond issue to pay it back.

"We couldn't float a bond issue on peanut butter in this town right now," Seward City Manager James W. Harrison said.

After the meeting, Bartlett flew to Washington, D.C., for a Monday meeting to give a disaster report to government officials.

"Well, we've no place else to go but up," was the opinion of most of the people of Seward. In a delayed presentation of the first All-America City award three months after the earthquake, Stanley Gordon, editor of *Look* magazine, who presented the award, said he had been deeply depressed by the earthquake reports at first, for it seemed that Seward was completely destroyed.

"'What will we do about the All-America City award?' I asked myself," Gordon told Seward's citizens. "But, before I could dwell upon the disaster, my mind was relieved by a telegram from the valiant city: 'Doing OK – everything considered!'"

Like the mythical Phoenix, Seward rose again. From the ashes of fire and devastation of flood, in 1965 the city again won an All-America City award, as did Anchorage and Valdez – this time given for a resurrected Seward.

The townspeople built new and completely modern docks, improved the small boat harbor and constructed a marine way and canneries. They'd built new homes and businesses and put in new sewer and water lines. And they promoted Seward's Silver Salmon Derby to perhaps the biggest single sporting event in Alaska – one that attracts thousands of visitors to the city on Resurrection Bay to this day.

As the years march forward, Seward will never forget those who were lost and the courage of those who remained. The Seward City Council established the first Sunday after Easter as "Seward Memorial Thanksgiving Day."

The townspeople of Seward rebuilt their city better than before the Good Friday earthquake of March 27, 1964, as seen in this photo taken in 1968.

14

V<small>ALDEZ</small> W<small>ASHED</small> A<small>WAY</small>

T he Alaska Steamship Co.'s coastal freighter *S.S. Chena* sat tied up at the Valdez dock on that clear, calm Good Friday, March 27, 1964. Many of the community's 1,000 residents had gathered on the dock to watch the longshoremen unload her cargo.

Capt. Merrill Steward, in the dining room of the ship, felt a tremor at 5:36 p.m., followed by some heavy shocks. He ran toward the bridge and reached the shoreward side three decks up about 20 seconds after the first tremor.

He saw the Valdez docks "folding up, collapsing in a tremendous noise," he later told interviewer Genie Chance. He watched crowds of adults and children running and trying to keep their balance as the two-story warehouse and dock buckled and split.

The *Chena* then began to rise on a "tremendous mound of water" that seemed to come in from the Valdez Arm, Steward said, adding that the ship "keeled over to port about 50 degrees as it rose a good 30 feet above the dock, which was rapidly disappearing."

The captain sounded the alarm bells.

The water dropped the ship where the dock once sat. It hit bottom about 50 to 70 feet landward from where it had been docked.

Steward said the giant wave moved into town, smashing over buildings. At the same time, his ship took a tremendous roll starboard

Anchorage Museum at Rasmuson Center, Sidney Hamilton Collection, AMRC-B1976-82-164

Above: The Valdez waterfront was a hub of acitivity before the Good Friday earthquake of March 27, 1964.

Below: The massive quake destroyed the waterfront and most of Valdez.

University of Alaska Fairbanks, Alaska Earthquake Archives Committee Collection UAF-1972-153-254

EARTHQUAKE!

– a roll from which the captain thought the ship could not recover. Before he could react, another wave built up that was filled with broken pilings, pieces of warehouses and other debris. The *Chena* shifted upright and then took another heavy roll to port.

A series of waves washed the ship over the dock, and then over the breakwater into the small boat harbor, where crushed and capsized small boats surrounded it. The *Chena* struck bottom several times with its 20-foot-diameter propeller churning in water one second, mud the next.

One witness living near the dock at the time described seeing the huge waves lifting and dropping the large ship. Unbeknownst to those Valdez residents, a massive underwater landslide caused those first massive waves.

"It picked up the *Chena* and tossed it like I used to toss boats in the bathtub," Helen Irish, 14 at the time, recalled in a 1964 *Life* magazine article. Irish had just arrived home from the dock when the earthquake began.

"People on the dock were running, but the water just rose up and swamped them," Irish said. "Dozens of people just floated away … they just floated away."

When water filled the harbor again, the captain of the *Chena* managed to get the ship headed offshore, scraping bottom as the waves surged up and down. They passed over an area where a large cannery had disappeared moments earlier. The *Chena* crashed through logs, wrecked boats and huge chunks of ice from the beach as it made its way out of the harbor.

Steward said they bounced around in turbulent waves that seemed to build up near his ship, and within seven or eight minutes his red-hot engines, which had filled with mud and debris, had to be shut down for 30 minutes to cool.

The ship continued to "wallow around in oscillating waters – extremely rapid rise of about 20 feet and drop every half-hour." The *Chena* drifted for four hours around the Valdez Arm, and then dropped anchor about a half-mile off the visible shoreline.

It did not take long for fire to consume a large portion of Valdez after oil tanks ruptured.

Between 10-10:15 p.m., the captain reported that fire broke out in Valdez. He said about three or four city blocks "burned furiously all night."

The fire consumed Beal's Plumbing, Beal's Hotel, Valdez Transfer and Fuel Co. and Derringer's Propane Station. Then Standard Oil Co.'s pumping control plant caught fire.

Those on shore described violent shaking where the earth seemed to move in waves that reached three feet high at times. Crevices opened and closed all around them with water and silt spurting up like geysers some four to five feet high. Some people reported falling into the crevices and sloshing around in sludge as water mains and sewer lines broke.

George Gilson, in his grocery store at the time, told Chance a continuous roar accompanied the quake. He made his way to his store's front door and noticed the front wall heaving, about to collapse. He then looked down the street and saw the dock "fly through the air" southward and disappear "in an instant" taking 30 men, women and children to their deaths.

EARTHQUAKE!

Within minutes of the first tremor, about three-fourths of Valdez – which sat on a spongy bed of sand, silt and gravel – had been destroyed. The tidal waves wiped out the dock, warehouse, cannery and 40 boats. Falling buildings and utility poles crushed dozens of cars. The east wall of the Alaskan Hotel collapsed, leaving upstairs rooms exposed. And highly flammable oil spilled out of ruptured storage tanks and later caught fire, destroying even more of the town.

Following the quake, Valdez residents made their way to higher ground and spent a sleepless night on the ridges in Thompson Pass in subfreezing temperatures. Tremendous waves continued to roll into town for hours, carrying several feet of water and debris into businesses and homes left standing. The receding waters then carried portions of buildings, boats and possessions back out to sea.

Six U.S. Army Otter aircraft and five helicopters took off from Fort Wainwright in Fairbanks and headed south at 11:30 p.m. They planned to land the Otters at Gulkana, transfer passengers into the empty helicopters and continue on to Valdez.

University of Alaska Fairbanks, Alaska Earthquake Archives Committee Collection; UAF-1972-152-276

Large fissures opened on Valdez streets.

Only one Otter landed at Gulkana at 2 a.m., however. The other five were forced to fly to Fort Greely due to bad weather. The choppers landed on frozen lakes near Gulkana to wait out the weather, according to a report in a military document titled "Operation Helping Hand."

The helicopters made it into Valdez at 7:30 a.m. Saturday morning, and the survey party saw the devastation firsthand.

"Valdez had taken a desperate beating," the report stated. "The waterfront was a tangle of smashed timbers, boats and debris of all sorts."

No waterfront installations remained, the Union Oil tank farm was ablaze, the electricity was out, the water system inoperable and the sewer system was damaged beyond use.

The Army team met with Valdez Mayor Bruce Woodford, the state trooper and a doctor. They all agreed with the mayor's decision to evacuate the city.

All but 40 men and five women left Valdez that Saturday. Some traveled to Fairbanks, in Alaska's Interior, and many piled into cars and drove more than 100 miles over the crevice-lined Richardson Highway to Gulkana and Glennallen, where they found the U.S.

U.S. Army photo

Within minutes, the massive quake destroyed three-fourths of Valdez on March 27, 1964.

EARTHQUAKE!

Three Alaska Overland buses drove 115 Valdez residents to Fairbanks following the earthquake and tidal waves on Good Friday 1964.

Army supplying cots and C-rations. Teams had set up a dining hall at the Glennallen High School and identified available living spaces for the 500-plus evacuees in schools, lodges, private homes, garages and warehouses.

U.S. Army helicopters and Air Force transports flew out remaining townspeople, including 53 patients from Harbor View mental hospital to the Alaska Psychiatric Institute in Anchorage.

More Army troops from Wainwright arrived in Valdez via convoy. They set up a mess hall to feed themselves and those remaining in town and brought in a water purification unit.

Soldiers then began handpicking through debris on the beach as they searched for the missing citizens of Valdez. Military aircraft assisted in the search by flying over the city and surrounding area for a few days.

U.S. Air Force transports flew some earthquake victims to Anchorage.

Army engineers and signalmen worked with Valdez public utility workers to get telephone lines and electricity working in a limited capacity. Other soldiers and civilians worked together to clear the devastated town of debris.

Another work party collected all perishable food from homes and commercial buildings and stockpiled it at the evacuated hospital. There the Valdez postmaster, who was a cook as well, set up a community kitchen to feed those left in town.

Stray dogs became a nuisance and a danger, according to military records. Someone suggested they all be shot, but the Army commander thought most were pets of those who had evacuated and did not agree with the suggestion. Instead, he appointed a crew of dogcatchers. They corralled the animals and put them in a secure location, fed and watered them, By the end of two weeks, most animals had been reclaimed.

Alaska Gov. William A. Egan, one of the community's most famous residents, arrived with other state officials to survey the damage on Sunday afternoon. As their plane approached the airport, they saw tons of debris floating on an oil-covered bay. A house drifted a half-mile offshore. Overturned boats and dead fish were everywhere, according to a newspaper story of the governor's visit.

Above: Military troops helped clean up the debris after the earthquake and tidal waves hit Valdez on March 27, 1964.

Right: GIs rounded up stray pets and kept them safe until their owners could return to Valdez.

Valdez businessmen told Egan and his entourage that nothing would stop them from rebuilding their city.

"We are down on one knee, but we're going to get back up," Mayor Woodford said, adding that he thought it would be several months before residents could return home. He had no doubt, however, that the good people of Valdez, who suffered more than $20 million in property loss, would rebuild.

To make that happen, the town of Valdez – which had been hastily thrown together during the 1898 Klondike Gold Rush era – had to move. Its original settlers had chosen the site, which sat in the middle of the outwash delta of a glacier, over higher ground a few miles west because it was closer to the Valdez Glacier and a trail that thousands of stampeders used to get through Alaska's Interior to the gold fields in Canada.

The U.S. Army Corps of Engineers researched the area and chose the delta of Mineral Creek for the new townsite. It had stable ground with dense, medium-size cobblestone gravel that went down about 100 feet. Planners then laid out the new town – ironically, in the same place that those original settlers had rejected.

Homeowners paid a fee of $400 for their lots and the Corps, along with Urban Renewal funds, replaced the public utilities. Soon dozens of buildings that hadn't been too badly damaged were hauled to the site and new buildings were constructed.

One by one, Valdez businesses and families moved to the new town and old Valdez became a ghost town.

In 1965, the National Civic League recognized Valdez – along with Anchorage and Seward – as an All-America City for its exceptional recovery after the earthquake.

This aerial photograph shows the layout of the new town of Valdez, about four miles inland from the original town. Valdez received an All-America City award in 1965, which recognized its residents for how they faced adversity and rebuilt their community.

15

CHENEGA DESTROYED

For the 68 residents of Chenega, the oldest Native village on Prince William Sound, the Good Friday earthquake on March 27, 1964, started slowly. The floors of the 20-some homes, mostly frame and sitting on pilings, began to roll and walls creaked. Then violent shakes rocked houses, most of which had no electricity, running water or sewer systems.

P.S. Hunt, Crary-Henderson Collection; Anchorage Museum, Gift of Ken Hinchey, B1962.001A.171

Most of Chenega, seen here in 1912, was swept away by tidal waves following the 1964 earthquake.

The people, a mix of Aleut, Yupik and Athabaskan ancestry, dashed out of their homes. About 90 seconds after the onset of the quake, water rushed halfway up the beach. It then rushed out, leaving the entire bay dry.

Villagers knew that water going out so fast would be coming back fast. They raced toward higher ground.

Eyewitness Joe Komkoff told interviewer Genie Chance that he saw a wall of water about 300 yards offshore. The 35-foot-high wave struck Chenega, which means "beneath the mountain," with a roar about four minutes after the quake began.

"There was no warning whatsoever," said Natasha Ruppert, a seismologist with the Alaska Earthquake Information Center, in a 1964 documentary produced by the San Francisco television station KPIX-TV.

Survivor Margaret Borodkin, 35 at the time of the quake, recalled her experience in *The Day That Cries Forever*, a book written by John Smelcer, that reveals how the lives of those with ties to the village were altered forever on that day.

"After a few minutes I began to hear a loud sound," Borodkin said. "I couldn't see because I was trapped on the floor, but it must have been the giant tidal wave."

When the wave struck the house, it felt as though a bomb was going off.

"Everything was crashing and rolling and smashing," she recalled.

Borodkin lost consciousness. Then the receding water washed her out into the bay. When she awoke, she found herself floating on what she thought was the wall of a house.

The three giant waves generated from the massive earthquake killed 23 villagers, more than one-third of the settlement's population. Chenega suffered the highest percentage of loss of life of any community in the Good Friday earthquake.

And their village was destroyed. The waves wiped out the oldest continuously inhabited Native community in the area – a place where the Chenega people had lived, fished and harvested the land for more than 10,000 years. They swept away everything in the village,

The schoolhouse, seen here up on a hill, was one of the few structures that survived the tsunami that hit Chenega.

including sturdy log structures like the Russian Orthodox Church, a store and the Bureau of Indian Affairs building. Three fuel tanks and the schoolhouse, which sat about 90 feet up on a hill, remained – although water did enter the schoolhouse basement.

Survivors, who spent the night huddled in the snow around a campfire high on a hill overlooking their ruined village, had no choice but to move away from their beloved village.

They spent the summer in government-issue tents in Tatitlek, on the coast south of Valdez. Then the Bureau of Indian Affairs built some small houses, which were dubbed "Chenega houses." But many Chenegans were not happy there and began moving – some to Cordova, Anchorage and other Alaska towns. Others moved south to the Lower 48.

They maintained a village council, however, and a group returned to the old site in 1976 to place a memorial plaque listing the names of those lost above the doorframe of the village corporation office.

That's when the survivors decided they needed to resettle the area

This aerial view shows the new Chenega Bay Village on Evans Island Sept. 28, 1989.

and chose a hillside above Crab Bay on Evans Island, about 20 miles south of the old village.

After a few years of negotiations with the government, Chenegans began building their new community in 1984 and named it Chenega Bay. Although many survivors did not move to the new village, those who did still try to continue to keep their ancestor's traditions and culture alive ... while incorporating modern comforts that include electricity and running water.

16

CORDOVA AND OTHER SMALL TOWNS

Although Cordova lies on the waters of Prince William Sound, it did not suffer as much from the great quake or tsunamis as its sister cities. It did see damage to its waterfront, and the nearby Million Dollar Bridge collapsed.

USGS photo

The Miles Glacier Bridge, also known as the Million Dollar Bridge, across the Copper River about 50 miles from Cordova collapsed during the 1964 earthquake.

Buildings along Cordova's main street, seen here after the 1964 earthquake, did not suffer any great damage. Although the tides did come in quite high the night of the quake and washed out some homes and boats near the shoreline.

C.B. Sanders, on duty at the Cordova Airport Federal Aviation Administration station, told interviewer Genie Chance that he saw ground waves when the earthquake hit.

They "looked like ocean swells," Sanders said, and occurred at about 30-foot intervals. These waves rocked the control tower so hard that he had to sit down to keep from falling.

Ray Goodman watched as a wave, which he thought was about three feet above the Cordova dock, lifted the dock up and set it off to the side of the pilings where it had originally stood.

Cordova merchant and fisherman Melvin Soder reported the quake lasted about five minutes, and during the violent shaking he saw the water in the harbor move about erratically. Soon after, the tide receded and grounded the boats in the small boat harbor.

Others in Cordova said they saw ground swells 4 to 4-1/2 feet high. They also watched the ground split open and close again as buildings rocked and trees swayed, as if in a strong wind. The power lines also snapped, disrupting electrical service.

Cordova historian Virginia Lacy said she had just arrived home from Cordova Insurance when the earthquake began. She grabbed her 6-year-old grandson and ran outside to join her son, Mike, and his wife, Shirley.

She remembered standing on the hillside on Second Street watching the mountains roll and telephone poles shake. Then the power went out.

"I had a fireplace, I could still cook," she recalled, so she made hotdogs and salad and invited people to spend the night at her home.

Bob Reed, manager of KLAM radio, was broadcasting music when the station building began to shake at 5:36 p.m. The Anchorage station he was monitoring went off the air, so he turned off his transmitter to reduce the danger from high voltage.

Reed then joined his family in an adjacent room and rode out the quake while watching the radio tower on the tide flats whip back and forth. At 5:45 p.m. he put the radio station back on the air, and then went to check the damage in his community.

He found downtown Cordova "practically untouched by the quake," but the city dock had been "shaken considerably." He noted loose pilings leaning askew, and canneries and other buildings adjacent to the dock had been pulled 6 to 12 inches away from the dock.

The veteran radioman sent his family to higher ground, while he stayed at the station to man the radio and watch the water.

"The water rushed out and stayed out," Reed later recalled. "It did not come back for many hours. You could hear it whistling down the channel sounding like Niagra Falls."

Water rushed into shore around 11 p.m. It reached half of high tide, and then went out again. It rushed in again at 12:15 a.m. about 4 feet above the high tide line.

The high water carried away several houses along the shoreline,

The U.S. Coast Guard Cutter *Sedge* rode out the earthquake in Cordova and then set sail for Valdez that night.

including an abandoned house just below the station that knocked the radio tower off its pedestal as it went by.

But all in all, Cordova was spared major destruction.

Since the crew of the U.S. Coast Guard cutter *Sedge* was not needed in Cordova, Lt. Cmdr. Dan Jones received orders to go to Valdez. By 7 p.m. the ship was under way, heading into Cordova's 60-foot channel. It began slowing down and at 8:19 p.m. it ran aground near North Rock Light.

"Our fathometer just kept dropping," crewmember Pete Corson recalled. He added that he noticed the tide was being sucked out of the channel and thought it was strange.

"It was incredibly dark outside, and these giant snowflakes were falling so it was very hard to see, but we could hear this loud clapping – which were halibut flapping on the seabed."

The cutter ended up on the bottom of the dry channel. By 8:24 p.m. the ship was afloat again.

"We rode it out under anchor and then went on our way," Corson said.

The *Sedge* was offshore on Sunday, March 29, just after midnight when crewmembers heard a sound like an underwater explosion, commander Jones told Chance.

"Similar to a depth charge or torpedo," he recalled, and added that the crew felt three minor tremors within the next few minutes.

The Homer Spit and mainland dropped between 2 and 6 feet from the massive earthquake on March 27, 1964. The spit and some buildings, like the Salty Dog Saloon, seen here, flooded.

Homer

The March 27, 1964, earthquake shook Homer for about 3 minutes, according to U.S. Geological Survey records, and dropped the mainland and Homer Spit between 2 and 6 feet. There were a few landslides and minor fissures in the ground, along with one or two submarine landslides at the end of the spit. Some wells had a temporary loss of water.

While the community only saw slight damage, one submarine landslide did take out most of the harbor breakwater so the harbor and dock had to be replaced.

Some buildings on the end of the spit had to be elevated due to higher tides following the quake. Construction crews raised the highway and parts of the spit above high tides by adding fill.

Seldovia

The waters around Seldovia have long been home to Alaska Natives. The area was a meeting and trading spot for the Tanaina Kenaitze of Cook Inlet, the Chugach people from Prince William Sound, the Aleuts from the Aleutian Chain and the Kodiak Koniaqs.

The settlement of Seldovia grew up along the waterfront in Kachemak Bay in the early 1900s as canneries settled in the area. Residents could only access homes and businesses by walking the beach at low tide. By the 1930s, a wooden boardwalk had been built so villagers could walk from one end of town to the other no matter what the tide was doing

The earthquake on March 27, 1964, changed all that when an underwater landslide dropped Seldovia 4 feet. Seawater flooded over the boardwalk at high tide and water poured into town.

After much discussion, the residents passed a referendum to accept an offer from the Alaska State Housing Authority to rebuild their homes and businesses on higher ground.

The main street and its boardwalks flooded when the ground on which Seldovia sat dropped 4 feet during the earthquake on March 27, 1964.

Kenai-Soldotna Area

The massive earthquake on Good Friday March 27, 1964, came on with a rumble and gave the residents around Kenai and Soldotna a good scare as the ground rolled, cracked and shook their homes and businesses.

U.S. Geological Survey scientists said that since the Kenai area is mostly made up of sandy soil, the ground shook a great deal but was spared the devastation suffered by other comunities.

Except for air travel, the Peninsula was cut off from the rest of the state, however. The heaving of the ground caused crevices to split the road in many places and broke bridges along the Seward Highway.

The giant earthquake on March 27, 1964, compressed and buckled many railroad bridges, like this one on the Kenai Peninsula that buckled laterally.

Above: The bridge at Cooper Landing collapsed during the earthquake.

Below: The U.S. military brought in a Bailey bridge, commonly used during World War II, to connect the people of the Kenai Peninsula to the rest of Alaska.

17

TIDAL WAVES OVERTAKE KODIAK

Sixteen minutes before the Good Friday earthquake, the Rev. Donald Bullock watched as carpenter Louis Horn selected two small eye bolts to hang a new cross from the ceiling above the altar in the sanctuary of Kodiak's St. James the Fisherman Episcopal Church. The men shared their conversation in the church, which sat atop the hill above the harbor, for an *Anchorage Daily Times* story two weeks after the massive shaker.

"Do you think these will hold it, Louis?" the minister asked.

"Sure, Father," Horn replied.

"What if we have an earthquake?" Bullock asked, and then chuckled.

"Even in an earthquake," the carpenter assured him.

Eyewitnesses said they heard a rumbling sound five seconds before feeling the first tremor. At 5:36 p.m. on March 27, 1964, the ground slowly began to shake. Within a minute of the initial tremor, the shaking grew more intense.

Chuck Powell, chairman of the Kodiak Island Borough Assembly, raced out of an office on the second floor of the bank building. He hurried downstairs and out into the street. The shaking became so severe that most people had to hang on to something to stay standing, he remembered.

"Power lines snapped, poles whipped back and forth, and buildings swayed with cracking noises," he later told interviewer Genie Chance.

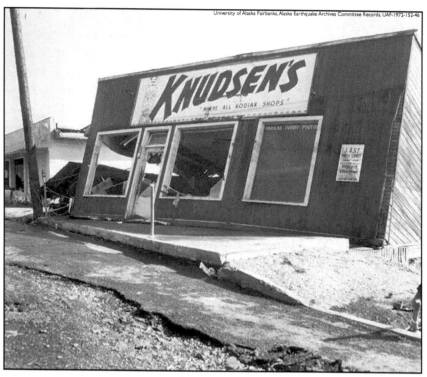

The 1964 earthquake and tidal waves knocked Knudsen's store in downtown Kodiak right off its foundation.

"The shaking was violent for about one minute and trailed off for about two to three minutes," according to Kodiak city engineer Jim Barr. The city's electrical power went out at 5:40 p.m.

Kodiak Island Borough tax assessor Howard Fremlin said the hard jolt and shaking sent everyone in the waterfront Elk's Club toward the front door. The floor moving up and down in waves made walking difficult.

"When you took a step, your foot was still on the floor instead of up in the air," Fremlin told Chance. "We fell and stumbled, waded through the broken glass and falling bottles, and finally made it outside."

Once out in the street, he saw ground waves, utility poles "fanning in the breeze," telephone and power lines snapping and glass store fronts "popping out."

Fremlin said he noticed wooden frame buildings "rolling and swaying." But none collapsed.

He jumped in his car and quickly drove to his house on a bluff overlooking the small boat harbor, about half a mile from the Elk's Club. From this vantage point, he and his wife watched as water rose to the top of the pilings. It came up so fast that most boats were not able to cut loose in time to escape as part of the breakwater broke away and swept the dock and boats into town.

The water then receded rapidly, leaving the small boat harbor almost dry.

"It was just sucking right out of the harbor," Fremlin later recalled.

Pharmacist Kelly Boyd, who ran out of the downtown drug store as merchandise crashed to the floor around him, said sirens began to wail about 30 minutes after the quake to warn of tidal wave danger.

University of Alaska Fairbanks, Alaska Earthquake Archives Committee Records, UAF-1972-152-219

Witnesses on Pillar Mountain watched as a tidal wave swept into Kodiak following the 9.2 temblor that struck Southcentral Alaska on March 27, 1964.

The Fremlins packed their car and drove through the business district en route to Pillar Mountain. They noticed several people milling about as though nothing had happened.

But most of Kodiak's residents instinctively knew that they had to head to higher ground. They believed a tidal wave would strike at any minute. And they were right.

Rev. Bullock's family joined a stream of vehicles heading up Pillar Mountain.

They stopped about a mile up and settled in to wait. That's when they heard an announcement come over a shortwave radio that Kodiak was sinking into the sea.

At 6:30 p.m. a wave surged in like a fast-rising tide and struck with such force it tossed buildings and boats around – making a complete mess of the waterfront.

Mrs. Fremlin described it as a "big, foaming wave" before it struck the outlying islands. It then swamped Mission Road and surged around the shoreline into the small boat harbor where it "foamed and boiled and bubbled."

"It all happened so fast that very few of the boats were able to get out of the harbor," said assemblyman Powell, who was watching the devastation from a safe distance on a hill. "I've shot the Snake River in a sea skiff, and I wouldn't have wanted to be out there (in the channel)."

He saw the water carry away boats, a plane, buildings and the channel's buoy marker.

"And you know what the anchor is on those (buoy markers)," Powell said. "And they made about four or five passes up and down the channel."

This wave, which crested at 23.5 feet 15 minutes later, knocked the King Crab Cannery into the water. While floating intact, it crashed into the bulkhead. The Donnelly Atchison store also broke loose and picked up a hangar with a Grumman Goose in it – both were swept away as the water withdrew.

Another eyewitness reported a massive wave rushed in at 8:30 p.m., crested at 24.5 feet, and took out the pile driver. The sound of the waves was "half roaring and half hissing," he recalled.

This aerial photograph shows the devastation caused by several tidal waves that swamped Kodiak following the record-strength earthquake on Good Friday 1964.

EARTHQUAKE!

The water again withdrew from the shore.

Powell said the first two waves "loosened things," but caused little damage to downtown Kodiak. It was the third wave at 11 p.m., reaching an elevation of 25.5 feet, and the fourth wave, topping off at 26.5 feet that arrived at 12:30 a.m., which dealt the most destruction.

Mrs. Fremlin said the water withdrew between Kodiak and Near Island after each wave and stayed out for a long time. Then it returned – each time traveling faster and farther inland.

The tidal waves killed 14 and caused around $24 million in damage. They destroyed more than 100 homes, as well as the telephone utility, movie theater, grocery store, dry goods store, bars, fish canneries, boats and docks.

The Armed Forces Radio at the Kodiak Naval Station fell off the air after the first wave struck as water inundated that building and

University of Alaska Fairbanks, Alaska Earthquake Archives Committee Records, UAF-1972-152-18

This view of the wreckage suffered by Kodiak's residents includes smashed buildings and boats all across the downtown area.

Tidal waves carried many boats in Kodiak's fishing fleet into various sections of the mainland.

the power house, leaving the station without heat or power for five days. The waves finally subsided enough by 7 a.m. on Saturday that workmen could begin clearing the road to the nearby U.S. Navy base, which also sustained heavy damages and dropped 5.5 feet.

As residents made their way back into town, they found everything topsy-turvy. A home filled with mud sat in the middle of the main street. Cars had been dragged out to sea, while boats had landed all over town. One boat, the *Selief*, made the news after State Trooper Don Church, attempting to locate all the missing fishing boats, called out on his radio.

"*Selief, Selief,* where are you?"

"It looks as though I'm in the back of the Kodiak schoolhouse, five blocks from the shoreline," came skipper Bill Cuthbert's reply.

The U.S. Army and Air Force arrived to help the Naval base and residents of Kodiak get back on their feet. They provided equipment and technicians to furnish the town with a temporary telephone system and installed telephones in businesses and strategic spots like the fire department and civil defense headquarters. Since poles had been toppled, heavy field wire stretched across the ground connecting the system.

A 150-man Seabee disaster team, equipped with tools, rations and cold-weather clothing, arrived the day after the quake and tsunamis, according to military reports. They immediately started repairing the power plant, roads and river crossings. Welders and pipefitters repaired the city's main crab freezing plant. Crane operators cleared demolished and damaged buildings.

One building would not need to be razed, however. The Episcopal Church up on the hill made it through the earthquake and tsunamis just fine.

Rev. Bullock's wife, Evelyn, wrote about the family's experience through the whole ordeal in an article published in the *Spokane Daily Chronicle* a few weeks after the disaster. She said the quake had "shaken, cut, dropped, heaved and twisted the earth in many places, but in the little church overlooking Kodiak harbor, it had failed to shake loose Father Bullock's new cross."

Other structures did need replacing, though. But rebuilding in the same location was not feasible since the center of town, along the northeast end of Kodiak Island, had sunk nearly six feet and flooded with seawater every day at high tide.

Townspeople, business owners and the city of Kodiak obtained low-interest loans through the federal Urban Renewal program to replace houses, fishing boats, commercial buildings and the boat harbor.

They cleared the debris out of Old Kodiak, then flattened hills and excavated gravel from the base of Pillar Mountain to fill the low-lying center of town. Their original town – a mix of small houses and stores, cottonwood trees and winding gravel roads – turned into a modern city filled with commercial buildings and wide paved streets.

Hundreds of fishing boats and numerous fish processing plants now make Kodiak one of the most productive commercial fishing ports in the nation.

18

VILLAGES NEAR KODIAK IN RUINS

T he ancient Alutiiq village of Afognak, located on an island about three miles north of Kodiak Island, suffered greatly from the devastating Good Friday earthquake and tidal waves that followed. Once it had been a large village, with more than 1,000 inhabitants. But by March 27, 1964, only 190 remained, according to a U.S. Census Bureau report.

The villagers made their living from the sea, just as their ancestors before them, and lived in small frame homes that stretched four miles along the lowlands facing the sea. The village also boasted a community hall, store, schoolhouse and lumber mill.

Enola Mullen, owner of the village store, and her husband were in the store when they felt a "long, steady shaking." It knocked merchandise from shelves and made cars parked outside rock back and forth at 5:36 p.m.

Alfred Nelson, sitting in a rocking chair in his home, thought at first that his children were rocking his chair. Then he saw the ceiling light swaying and a bucket half-full of water sloshing.

"That's when I knew it was an earthquake," he later told interviewer Genie Chance. "I was wondering when it was going to quit."

He then heard a report on his shortwave radio that Seward had been wiped out. Nelson looked out in the bay and saw the water

Alaska State Library, Alaska Territorial Department of Education, ASL-MS146-07-53A-1

Following the Great Earthquake of 1964, a series of high waves inundated Afognak Village, seen here in 1934. The damage was so extensive that the village had to relocate.

higher than normal, and told his wife to put the children in the car and head up the mountain. He then followed in his truck, picking up several other people along the way.

Peggy Needham, one of three schoolteachers, heard a radio report around 6:30 p.m. from the Kodiak Naval Station warning of an approaching tidal wave 15 feet high and advising people to go to higher ground.

She and other villagers tossed blankets, food and warm clothes into their cars and trucks and raced up the mountains behind the village. The first wave caught several people in the lower part of the village as they were trying to run toward higher ground. They managed to wade through the waist-high water to safety.

Needham and her neighbors watched as monstrous waves surged over their homes, smashing them like kindling wood. They saw several homes and the community hall sucked back into the sea when the water withdrew in a mad whirlpool of debris. Soon other buildings were swept off their foundations and moved inland; automobiles and trucks washed into small lakes behind the village; and ice in the lakes carried out to sea.

"They weren't standing waves – not a wall of water – as you'd expect," said Needham as she described the waves to Chance. "But rather the water rushed in like a high tide, only 10 times faster and a good 15 to 20 feet higher than normal."

All night long the ocean surged and receded. The villagers huddled in the snow and cold while tremors sporadically shook the earth beneath them. When they finally came down the mountain, they found 23 of their 38 homes were destroyed.

The Mullens discovered the waves had deposited their store one-third mile inland. Two of its exterior walls had been demolished and the remaining portion of the building was lodged among some trees. They salvaged what merchandise they could and gave it to the villagers who had lost everything.

One woman told Chance that the waves had lifted her house and its foundation right out of the ground and washed it about one-

The villagers of Afognak rebuilt their community and named it Port Lions, seen here in 1968.

EARTHQUAKE!

quarter mile inland. Although the floors were damaged by water and mud, none of the windows had broken and the knickknacks still stood on the windowsills where she had placed them before the quake.

Two days after the tsunamis, a radio report warned that another 90-foot wave was to be expected at any moment. The villagers again fled to the safety of the mountain. They returned to the village during daylight hours, Needham said, but continued to sleep on high ground for several nights.

No one at Afognak died in the earthquake and tsunamis that followed. But skipper John "Sut" Larsen, returning from Kodiak on board his fishing boat *Spruce Cape*, must have run into trouble on the sea. His body later was found, ironically, at Spruce Cape, the landmark after which his boat was named. Harry Nielson, another Afognak villager, also died on that boat along with Theodore "Ted" Panamarioff of Ouzinkie.

It was decided that rebuilding the village at that same location was not feasible. Not only had the majority of the homes been destroyed, but the tectonic subsidence at Afognak had brought saltwater into the wells.

A new site was selected on Kizhuyak Bay on Kodiak Island. The site choice wasn't popular with some villagers, so they instead chose to move to Kodiak, other towns in Alaska or the Lower 48.

The philanthropic Kodiak Island Lions Club helped those who wanted to establish their new village on Kodiak Island. And soon a new identity began to develop, according to the village website – that of the people of Port Lions. There the villagers continue to pass on to new generations their ancestors' traditions and culture.

Old Harbor

Another community, Old Harbor, sits on the southeast coast of Kodiak Island about 70 miles southwest of the city of Kodiak. It has been inhabited for around 2,000 years by Alutiiq people. Most residents, like the Shugaks, were living a subsistence lifestyle when the Good Friday earthquake hit.

Young Tobias Shugak was lying on a bed in his family's home at 5:36 p.m. His sister stood nearby holding a baby sister. At first he thought his sister was shaking the bed.

"But it got harder, and my sister said 'earthquake!' and we ran outside," he told interviewer Genie Chance.

The children said the "huge snake" made all the buildings in the village weave back and forth as the ground moved in waves. They added that the dock pilings began "twirling in the air" and then the water "went way out – farther than light tide."

Villagers fled to the mountain, even though rocks, dirt and snow were sliding down toward the village.

Janet Tunohun remembered her father saying a tidal wave was headed their way. The family immediately joined other villagers in climbing to higher ground.

"And a wind came up," Tunohun said, adding she saw the "big, ugly wave come in and hit the houses."

Residents of the village of Old Harbor gathered for evacuation at the school, one of two buildings left standing following the earthquake and tidal waves of March 27, 1964.

The schoolhouse and church, seen in this photo of Old Harbor taken in the 1950s, were the only buildings left intact following tidal waves on March 27, 1964.

Some of the houses broke apart, and others just floated away. She remembered a lamp burned brightly inside one house as it floated out to sea like a boat.

"Some houses went around in a circle and landed on the land again," Shugak recalled.

His father and another man were aboard the fishing boat *Alexander* in Old Harbor bay when the quake struck. Shugak told Chance that an incoming wave swept the boat into the village, "almost to the schoolhouse," and then receding water carried it seaward again until it became stranded on the dry bottom of the bay. The men jumped overboard and ran to the mountainside and joined the other villagers.

In the bright moonlight, the villagers watched as the water came and went all night and destroyed all the homes in their village. Only the school and church were left standing. One witness, who entered the church the next day, reported that the high water mark inside the missionary's house was six inches from the ceiling. The waves had destroyed the chapel, along with all records, books and the organ.

The villagers rebuilt their community in the same location, and incorporated their city in 1966.

Ouzinkie

Tidal waves also inundated Ouzinkie, located on the west coast of Spruce Island about 12 miles north of the city of Kodiak, following the Good Friday earthquake. Originally established in the mid-1800s as a retirement community for the Russian American Co., the Russians referred to the settlement in 1849 as "Uzenkiy," which means "village of Russians and Creoles." Other sources say, however, it means "rather narrow."

By the time of the 1964 earthquake, the village existed for the fishing industry and its more than 150 residents were a mixture of Russian and Alutiiq people.

Some who went through the quake described seeing ground waves as long as 30 feet cross the village when it hit at 5:36 p.m. on March 27.

Earl and Merrle Carpenter had arrived in the village the year before to serve as cannery storekeeper and postmaster for the Ouzinkie Packing Co. cannery. They later said in an article for the Alaska Historical Society that the earthquake did not cause much structural damage.

Merrle Carpenter quickly started snapping photographs to show her boss what had happened. She did not know at the time that she was capturing photos of the bay going dry.

The villagers told her and her husband to get to high ground because all the water that had left the bay was going to all come back.

"And it's going to come back fast," the villagers said.

The Carpenters joined the rest of the village climbing up Mount Herman above the cannery store. They remembered everyone was concerned for those still out on fishing boats who had not yet returned to Kodiak Island. They could hear them on the radio, calling for help – then the radio went dead when a huge wave covered the store.

Records later showed that five men aboard the F/V Spruce Cape, heading toward Ouzinkie, lost their lives to the tsunamis that followed the quake.

After a series of tsunamis washed through the cannery, the Carpenters made their way down to the severely damaged store and salvaged some supplies to help feed the villagers. Although the labels had been washed off the tin cans, the food inside was fine.

The couple later managed to save the cannery safe, as well, and dried out $4,000 in waterlogged bills on top of their stove.

They found the back half of the store had washed out to sea along

Massive tsunamis destroyed the Ouzinkie Packing Co. on March 27, 1964,

with most of the cannery building. The livelihood of most of those in Ouzinkie washed away, too.

The U.S. Postal Service commended the Carpenters, who left the village in May 1964, for "the unselfish devotion to the public service that was so amply demonstrated by postal people during the disastrous earthquake."

They also received a personal note of thanks from Alaska's U.S. Sen. E.L. "Bob" Bartlett.

Following the disaster, Columbia Ward bought the remains of the store and rebuilt it and the dock, but not the cannery. Then in the late 1960s, the Ouzinkie Seafoods cannery was built. That operation sold out to Glacier Bay, but it burned down in 1976, shortly after the sale. No canneries have operated there since.

Kaguyak

Another community, Kaguyak, located at the head of Kaguyak Bay on the southeast coast of Kodiak Island, was a happy Alutiiq-Russian village with about 20 residents on the afternoon of March 27, 1964. The Good Friday earthquake and resulting tsunamis changed it forever.

Renee Alexanderoff, 22 and pregnant at the time of the earthquake, told Genie Chance that her husband, Chief Simeon "Simmie" Alexanderoff, helped her and their three children escape up the mountain following the initial earthquake. He and three other fishermen – Zaedar Anakenty, Victor Melovedoff and Max Shelikoff – then returned to the village to help rescue Donald Wyatt, a geologist from Los Angeles, and his wife, Joyce, who were camping outside the village.

The men loaded them and clothing into a dory and then pushed it over a small hill between the village and the lake. The group almost made it across the lake to safety when a huge wave burst across the shore, through the village, over the hill and across the lake.

The water swamped the dory and three of the men lost their lives. Alexandroff was last seen clinging to the dory. His body was never found. They later found Anakenty's body on the beach and Wyatt floating in the lake.

Kaguyak sat on a strip of land by a lake, as seen in this photograph taken prior to the earthquake and tsunamis of March 1964.

EARTHQUAKE!

Walter Meloeoveoff, Renee's 61-year-old father, told Chance they were getting dinner when they heard a "kind of whistle." He said he'd had a premonition earlier that day that something might happen.

"Then come the earthquake," he said.

The family ran outdoors as the shaking got worse. They looked at the bay and noticed the tide had receded an unusually long distance.

They knew a wave would be coming and fled with several villagers toward the mountain. Meloeoveoff stopped to assist an elderly woman, recuperating from illness, so he trailed the others. He looked back and saw a huge wave heading toward them.

"Oh, boy, that big swell was coming about 20 feet behind us, just rolling in, and all the woods and ice in it," he recalled. "We just made it."

The water receded and the "big bay" went totally dry.

Another wave, bigger than the first, swept in and washed away the buildings and killed the men attempting to cross the lake in the dory.

The villagers stayed on the mountaintop where the temperature registered 18 degrees that clear, still night. The next morning, they were evacuated.

Dories carried them through choppy, debris-filled waters to the large crabber *Fern* anchored offshore in low tide.

Once aboard the ship, the villagers learned that skippers Fred Ogden and Wayne Mathewson had been just off the southern coast of Kodiak Island when the quake struck. The men said that the boat jerked and bounced as if striking bottom, but they just thought they were in rough waters.

It wasn't until they heard a radio report about the earthquake and tsunamis that they realized what had happened. They then dumped their boatload of crab overboard so they could maneuver the boat better and settled in for a long night.

At daybreak, they motored toward nearby Kaguyak and Old Harbor to see if anyone needed assistance. When they arrived at Kaguyak, they found no houses left. So they anchored and rescued the villagers.

The people of Kaguyak relocated to other villages, including Old Harbor and Akhiok, seen here, following the 1964 earthquake.

They loaded about 100 people on board the vessel and then headed for Kodiak, making a few stops en route to help villagers salvage art treasures and icons from their church that were floating in the ocean.

The *Fern* finally made it to Kodiak. But while unloading the passengers and gear, a high tide came in. Soon people were wading in waist-high water on the dock as they retrieved bundles of clothing and the paintings from the Russian Orthodox Church that had been rescued on the way.

Kaguyak never was rebuilt. Some of the villagers settled in Akhiok, some relocated to Old Harbor.

19

Alaskans Learn They're Not Alone

In those first hours after the devastating earthquake and tidal waves of Good Friday 1964, the overwhelming emotion for many Alaskans was one of isolation. In most of the stricken towns, local radio and television stations dropped off the air when electricity went out. No one knew what was happening in other parts of Alaska, nor if their family and friends were dead or alive. Alaskans felt alone and cut off.

Some people picked up news reports from the Lower 48 on transistors and battery-powered radios, and slowly Alaskans learned about the damage done to the state. They also learned that people across the globe were concerned for the people of Alaska.

One of the first messages heard came from Britain's Queen Elizabeth, who had expressed her sympathy to U.S. President Lyndon B. Johnson. So before they tried to rest that long, dreadful night, many Alaskans did not feel so alone anymore. They knew the world cared about them just as they cared about each other.

"Alaska was one big family," Mrs. Ross McCoy told Alaska historian Phyllis Downing Carlson in the late 1960s. Her husband had been lost when the Valdez dock collapsed, but "everyone was wonderful – if they had and you didn't, they shared with you – clothes, food, money."

Many Valdez refugees evacuated to Fairbanks, which hardly felt

More than 100 refugees from Southcentral Alaska were taken to the Interior town of Fairbanks following the devastation of the 1964 earthquake.

the quake. Some learned firsthand the generosity of people from the Golden Heart City when three men entered a hotel that lodged refugees.

"Are you from Valdez?" they asked, and then passed out $50 bills from their pockets to each Valdez family staying there (about $380 in 2015 dollars).

The refugees praised the kind hearts of those who lived in that Interior town.

"Here in Fairbanks, we don't need money," one refugee said. "Anything we need, somebody helps us with."

Other towns and villages across Alaska pitched in to help, too. Around 200 laborers, 30 carpenters, 31 carpenter helpers, 32 heavy equipment operators and 32 truck drivers from Kotzebue, Point Hope, Kivalina, Kiana, Shungnak, Noorvik, Noatak, Selawik and Buckland offered to help rebuild the stricken areas. Barrow, the nation's most northern community, quickly began raising a disaster fund. And from undamaged Juneau, Ketchikan and other Southeast communities came an overwhelming flood of concern and offers of assistance.

Alaskans learned there were no rich or poor. The earthquake not only leveled buildings, it also leveled distinctions, political as well as financial and social. Politicians forgot their differences and all Alaskans were united in their misfortune.

Americans everywhere moved rapidly to help their northern brothers and sisters. The Salvation Army kept a steady flow of supplies on the way to displaced families. And using Seattle as its base, the American Red Cross immediately organized their facilities.

"I've never seen anything like this," said Seattle Red Cross chapter manager Joseph Hladecek in the days following the disaster. "Everyone wants to do something to help out in some way."

The hearts of people all across the nation especially went out to those from Seward, selected that year for the All-American City

University of Alaska Fairbanks, Alaska Earthquake Archives Committee Records, UAF-1972-153-196

Seward's All-American sister cities created a campaign, Save Our Seward, to help the townspeople recover.

award. Seward, one of the smallest cities ever to receive the honor, had planned to celebrate the distinction by inviting the public to two days of festivities on April 4 and 5.

The disaster that shattered the little city on Resurrection Bay changed all that, but at the suggestion of one of Seward's All-American sister cities, Allentown, Pa., a trust fund called SOS – Save Our Seward – was established. Other All-American cities rallied around, including Alexandria, Va; Woodstock, Ill.; Roseville, Calif.; Gastonia, N.C.; and Woodbridge, N.J. Missouri's town of Neosha, named an All-American City in 1957, sent a check for $1,000 to help rebuild.

"One of the things that brought us up from nearly a knockdown was your wonderful wires," responded Seward's mayor Perry Stockton to all the well wishes and assistance. "We have just postponed our All-American celebration."

Seward's residents agreed – their city had suffered a great deal, but Seward's spirit remained unbroken.

The spirits of all Alaskans who lost loved ones, homes, businesses and prized possessions on Good Friday were heartened by the good will of their fellow Americans, including a few young people from Hawaii and New York.

Three youngsters at Kailua, Hawaii, staged a backyard play, sold tickets and turned over their entire proceeds of 83 cents to the Red Cross to help the earthquake victims.

John Loeb Beaty, almost 7, of Port Jefferson, N.Y., also sent some money to Anchorage.

"Dear Mr. Mayor," read the printed letter addressed to mayor George Sharrock. "I feel so sorry about your earthquake. I wanted to send you my Easter basket, but Daddy said the eggs wouldn't last. I'm sending you one dollar, instead."

Some New York teens collected 1,000 new dresses made by youngsters participating in the Mobilization for Youth Inc. vocational training program. The boys and girls voted to give the dresses to Alaska kids, and they drove to Washington, D.C., to present the gift to the Alaska Congressional delegation.

People and businesses around the world sent money to help towns like Valdez, pictured here, recover from the Good Friday earthquake in 1964.

Oregon lumbermen donated 3 million to 5 million board feet of lumber to help rebuild Alaska. The government provided the ship and the longshoremen donated their time and labor in packaging and loading it. The Carpenter's Union contributed $50,000 to the disaster fund and the AFL-CIO turned over $25,000 to Red Cross and Salvation Army officials. Employees at Sicks Rainier Brewing Co. asked that company funds, normally used for their annual picnic, be donated instead to needy Alaskan families.

The International Telephone and Telegraph Corp. contributed $5,000 immediately to the city of Valdez, and said that more would be forthcoming when they had a better picture of the city's needs. National businesses from across the United States increased deposits and opened new accounts in Alaska banks to aid in making funds available for reconstruction work.

Jose Iturbi, famous Basque conductor, harpsichordist and pianist, offered to give a benefit concert to help disaster victims, and light

Tons of supplies from the Lower 48 arrived in Alaska and were quickly unloaded and distributed to communities in need.

heavyweight boxer Eddie Cotton of Seattle offered to fight a charity bout with proceeds to go to the quake victims.

Civilian, Army and Navy planes airlifted tons of supplies from heavy-duty machinery to newspapers. Sweating loadmasters performed amazing feats loading planes in a short time working 12-hour shifts without let up.

On April 3, a wrong-way Santa Claus traveled north in a jet instead of a reindeer-drawn sleigh. On board was the first of 10,000 pounds of toys destined for Alaska children. The project snowballed after it was started by a disc jockey in Seattle. Toys poured in from far and wide across the state of Washington.

While the generosity of Alaska's fellow countrymen was overwhelming, people from other countries sent help and sympathy, as well.

The residents of Skopje, Yugolavia, who had previously gone through an earthquake, recalled with gratitude the help extended them at that time and the town's mayor cabled a message of sympathy to Alaska Gov. William A. Egan.

The Japanese government donated $10,000. Its people knew firsthand the devastation wrought by earthquakes. Messages of sympathy also were sent to President Lyndon B. Johnson and Secretary of State Dean Rusk from Asian, African, European and South American countries. Canadian Prime Minister Lester Pearson sent a letter, as well.

"... I should be grateful if you would convey our deep sympathy to those in Alaska who have suffered such heavy and painful loss ... I know I speak for all Canadians when I assure you that we stand ready to do whatever we can to assist the people of Alaska at this tragic time."

A gift from a Canadian child, Wendy Loydhouse of Queensland Road in Vancouver, B.C., heartened Gov. Egan as he struggled to cope with all the disaster problems.

"To the dear children. This money is for you," said the message in childish handwriting on a note wrapped around a Canadian $1 bill.

Anchorage Museum at Rasmuson Center, Ward Wells Collection, AMRC-wws-4176-84

Alaska Gov. William A. Egan surveyed the damage at the Anchorage Turnagain-By-The-Sea subdivision following the earthquake on March 27, 1964.

The Apostolic Delegate to the United States, Egidio Vionozzi, had last visited Alaska in 1961 when he laid the cornerstone for the new Catholic Junior High School in Anchorage. He visited the state soon after the earthquake to bring a $10,000 check for the disaster fund, and to convey the Pope's blessing to all Alaskans. Vionozzi told Alaskans that Pope Paul asked them to have confidence in Divine Providence in their hour of trial and said that they were showing the true spirit of pioneers in refusing to be overcome by adversity and misfortune.

Alaskans showed the pioneer spirit that carved a state out of a wilderness, and there were many stories to show that they did not allow misfortune to overwhelm them.

For instance, Anchorage city employee Patricia Mayo, who worked long overtime hours and refused to fill out a time ticket, instead wrote on its back: "This is my city. I do not expect to be paid for helping to bring it back to life!"

Hundreds of Alaskans showed their best sides as they picked themselves up, brushed off the dust and set about to make Alaska whole again. Volunteer nurses, some of whom had not worked at their profession for 20 years, left their homes and families to fulfill the mission for which they had been trained. City crews worked around the clock to restore power, water, phone and sewer services as rapidly

Edith and Edward Lindsay papers, Archives and Special Collections, Consortium Library, University of Alaska Anchorage

Business owners offered space to other businessmen whose buildings were damaged during the earthquake, like this one in downtown Anchorage.

EARTHQUAKE!

as possible, while volunteers searched through tumbled houses and swaying buildings for survivors and to carry out people's keepsakes and valuables. And many people whose world looked pretty dark with loss of homes, life savings and livelihood, volunteered to help with the rescue and rehabilitation work.

Businessmen, whose stores and facilities were usable, generously made room for those in need, even their competitors. R.E. Grier, manager of quake-ruined Anchorage J.C. Penney, sent letters to all Penney charge customers directing "those unable to make their payments because of earthquake losses or the need to divert finances to emergency needs to postpone payments until your affairs have improved."

A similar notice was sent to patients of the Holmes Johnson Clinic in Kodiak: "If you have extensive property loss due to earthquake, please contact us, and we will hold your statement."

Perhaps the story of Sister Phillias, nursing supervisor at Providence Hospital in Anchorage, best epitomizes the selflessness and devotion to duty displayed by Alaskans following this tragic event.

Recovering from major spinal surgery when the quake struck, the nun saw the double glass window in her room lurch from its frame and felt her bed slide five feet across the room. She was convinced that her services were needed to pitch in with the others. Even though she was not able to be back on nursing duty, she did her bit by standing in the lobby directing visitors and answering questions.

"Alaskans and Providence Hospital proved themselves worthy of each other," said Sister Barbara Ellen on Easter morning. "Both performed nobly. Nothing less than a superlative effort would have succeeded."

Nothing less than a superlative effort, indeed. The earthquake dealt a staggering blow to Alaska's economy. A few days following the disaster, experts estimated the new state had suffered between $350 million to $750 million in damages. And no one knew what effect it would have on the fishing industry, tourism or other sources of income for the new state.

Officials in Washington, D.C., immediately moved to provide long-term reconstruction funds. President Johnson, both parties and houses within Congress and the American people supported using federal money to rebuild Alaska as soon as possible.

"No community, no state, no corporation, can meet such a calamity," stated an editorial in the *Pittsburgh Press* four days after the quake. "This, then, is a legitimate role for the federal government. It is legitimate because no one else has the capability. And whatever the government does can be justified because some of its citizens are in grievous need. Moreover, rubble and wreckage pay no taxes – the sooner the energetic Alaskans get back in business, the sooner they will repay Uncle Sam."

With well wishes from so many people all around the world, and financial assistance from the federal government, Alaskans did, indeed, get back to business. The motto across Alaska became, "Better than before."

Military Lends a Helping Hand

Alaskans' grit and determination helped the 49th state rebound from the largest earthquake to hit North America in recorded history. But the military effort, code named Operation Helping Hand, made it happen.

The Office of Emergency Planning – predecessor of the Federal Emergency Management Agency – immediately worked with the U.S. Army Corps of Engineers to jump into action.

Less than 10 hours after the initial shake, emergency teams in small aircraft were assessing damage. Within a few days, a special projects office had been established in Anchorage, Valdez and Seward to award contracts for demolition and clearing debris, as well as repairing water supplies, sewer systems, power sources, fuel supplies and communications systems.

Hardhats and helmets replaced Easter bonnets that first weekend. And the Corps of Engineers made clearing roadways a priority.

University of Alaska Fairbanks, Alaska Earthquake Archives Committee Collection, UAF-1972-153-298

Operation Helping Hand delivered many supplies, including food, clothing and medicine, to Alaska towns devasted by the Good Friday earthquake and tsunamis of March 27, 1964.

"It took us 12 hours to cut through the biggest slide," one bulldozer operator later said. "And when we got through, there was another just ahead."

Alaska, which became a state five years earlier, had limited disaster-response capabilities. But it did have military bases loaded with highly trained troops. U.S. Navy and Coast Guard personnel were stationed at Kodiak; Army troops at Fort Greely; Army at Fort Richardson and Air Force at Elmendorf in Anchorage; and Army at Fort Wainwright and airmen at Eielson in Fairbanks. Alaska National Guard troops, in Anchorage for an annual two-week training program, were kept in town for an extra three days to protect businesses and homes from looters.

The day after the earthquake, 17 C-123 Providers took off from Elmendorf Air Force Base and carried equipment and supplies to Kodiak, Valdez and Seward. Operation Helping Hand delivered 3.7 million pounds of cargo to several devastated towns during the first three weeks of the operation.

The massive airlift operations by the Military Air Transport Service shattered records during this time, flying more than 1,300 hours to haul in more than 2.5 million pounds of cargo — from baby food to heavy equipment — from Lower 48 bases, according to military records. More aircraft arrived from McGuire Air Force Base in New Jersey with electric generators and vans on Easter Sunday.

The largest project during this time involved the Military Air Transport Service, the Alaska Air Command and the Air National Guard when they combined forces to move a 520,000-pound Bailey bridge from Elmendorf to the Kenai Peninsula to replace the bridge destroyed at Cooper Landing on the lower end of Kenai Lake. This type of bridge, frequently used during World War II, is built on site from a kit.

Army engineers trucked the bridge in sections from Eklutna, 25 miles north of Anchorage, to Elmendorf. Then it took five days and about 60 flights to get all the pieces of the bridge and installers on location.

Military pilots also flew hundreds more hours in small aircraft to photograph and film the massive destruction to help responders and geologists learn the extent of the damage.

Reconstruction averaged $1 million a month in Anchorage alone during the first year after the earthquake, according to Corps of Engineers' records. Altogether, the Corps spent more than $110 million on salvage, rescue and rehabilitation efforts.

20

REBUILDING BETTER THAN BEFORE

Alaska's Good Friday earthquake was ranked No. 4 on the list of major news stories of 1964 in a poll conducted by The Associated Press of the nation's news editors. It was beat out of first place by the campaign and landslide election of U.S. President Lyndon B. Johnson. The ouster of Russia's Nikita Khrushchev ranked No. 2, and the continuing civil rights struggle came in at No. 3.

But Alaska's newspapers put the Great Alaska Earthquake as the top story of the year. The comeback from calamity from the second-mightiest quake in recorded history to a heady new growth became the second big story for the fledgling state.

When "nature lost her sanity," as some residents thought, more than the landscape of Alaska changed. The massive tremors that hit the Southcentral coastline altered the entire outlook of the nation's newest state – the devastation set loose a new spirit in a state already overflowing with hope and plans.

Alaskans immediately rolled up their sleeves and began rebuilding their communities. Undaunted by the incredible destruction and the enormous job ahead, Alaskans looked to the future as they had in the past with their faith in Alaska.

Although no one knew how much federal assistance ultimately would be made available to help with the estimated $400 million to $700 million dollar loss – more than $2 billion in today's dollars –

Alaskans did receive some immediate financial help. U.S. President Lyndon B. Johnson made $5 million in federal funds available within days, and then Congress quickly and unanimously appropriated $50 million in federal disaster relief.

President Johnson also appointed an Alaska Reconstruction Commission, and Congress worked to obtain retroactive disaster insurance to cover private and personal property losses for Alaskans. The Small Business Administration made low-interest loans available, too.

The state Legislature stepped up right away, as well. At the request of Alaska Gov. William A. Egan, it authorized a $50 million general obligation bond – the limit of Alaska's ability to offer public reconstruction aid or matching funds.

People around the world sent money, food, lumber, clothing and equipment to help out the devastated state. And engineers, financial experts and government officials offered their expertise, as well.

Citizens of Alaska did not wait for all the financial pieces to fall into place before fixing their broken state, however. Power workers

Anchorage residents went right to work rebuilding their city, as this photo taken on C Street soon after the 1964 earthquake shows. Bulldozers cleared debris, and businesses began opening.

immediately went to work repairing power poles and snapped lines; gas company crews supplied fuel needed to power generators; radio operators got their stations back on the air; utility workers repaired water and sewer lines; and telephone companies got phone service back on line.

Shopkeepers hurried to clear out debris, repair wrecked stores and get their businesses up and running. J.C. Penney in Anchorage, which had held its grand opening in March 1963 and whose department store in Anchorage suffered devastating damage, quickly assured Alaskans it would rebuild. That vow showed the retailer's confidence that Alaska would rebound and come back strong.

Oil companies quickly found new offices, if theirs had been damaged, and were ready to begin the new exploration season in record time.

And federal officials' decision to green light a multimillion-dollar project to rebuild the Alaska Railroad's port facilities and terminal yards at the quake-shattered port of Seward bolstered the economy even more.

To aid fishermen of Prince William Sound, Alaska Gov. William A. Egan in mid-July agreed to let the Japanese enter the Sound to buy fish, a move that resulted in some controversy at the time. Another bright note appeared in late September when Pan American Petroleum Corp. announced two giant finds: the discovery of one of North America's largest iron ore deposits and an immense oil field.

As 1964 came to a close, Gov. Egan predicted that 1965 would be better for individuals and business. He also said it would see the birth of many small industrial efforts.

"In the discussions of what happened after the March 27 earthquake, much has been said of the federal and state help extended to victims of that disaster," Egan said in an *Anchorage Daily Times* article recapping the year on Dec. 31, 1964.

"Too little has been said of the spirit and the determination of Alaskans, of their faith in the future, exemplified by their immediate reaction in applying for aid to rebuild their homes and their businesses and to root themselves more deeply in Alaska."

Walter J. Hickel, who became Alaska's governor in 1968, believed in Anchorage. He built the Captain Cook Hotel, seen in the background, on land that had been damaged during the great quake. The first tower opened in 1965. Two more towers followed in the 1970s.

He stressed, by all accounts, 1964 saw major developments in the oil and gas industry, hard-rock mining, timber, fisheries and tourism, despite the earthquake.

"All of these things have made for the biggest year Alaska has had, development-wise and business-wise, since statehood," Egan said. "All in all, Alaskans have the best year ever to look forward to in 1965."

Historians agree that although the 1964 earthquake brought Alaskans to their knees, it actually helped the state's economy by flooding federal dollars north for recovery. By summer 1965, the majority of what had been destroyed had been rebuilt so quickly that the National Civic League awarded Anchorage, Seward and Valdez the title of All-America City for their speedy recoveries.

Alaska also saw a spike in its population. It grew at a rate well above the national average – 14.4 percent compared to 8.1 percent – and had the fifth-highest state growth rate in the United States, according to the U.S. Department of Commerce.

With Alaska well on its way to a full recovery, state lawmakers once again turned their attention to choosing 103 million acres of federal land per the Alaska Statehood Act. After all, those federal dollars weren't going to flow north indefinitely, and the Legislature needed to build the state's treasury. Once they chose land, it could be sold to provide funds to run the new state government.

But the question, "Who owns what?" soon became a major issue.

ALASKA LAND IN DISPUTE

21

HOMESTEADERS HEAD NORTH

A couple of months after Alaska officially became a state, an intrepid band of Michigan folks, dubbed the "59ers," left Detroit bound for Alaska. The caravan, consisting of 17 cars, six camper-trailers and a 1936 moving van named "The Monstrosity," headed north on March 5, 1959.

Most of these adventurers had blue-collar jobs and hoped the grass might be greener in the Last Frontier. The group included bricklayers, carpenters, mechanics and other tradesmen who felt they had no future in Detroit with its stagnant economy and double-digit unemployment numbers.

They thought Alaska held more promise. For a filing fee of just a few dollars, they could claim a homestead and carve out fruitful lives for themselves and their children on the Kenai Peninsula.

The U.S. government first

Known as the "Monstrosity," this van was among the caravan of vehicles bound for Alaska that left Detroit, Mich., in March 1959.

encouraged homesteading in the Continental United States during the mid-1800s when economic and social changes gripped the developed Eastern states. People looked to the west and the vast underdeveloped lands with a rather romantic vision for new opportunities.

In 1862, President Abraham Lincoln signed the Homestead Act with the idea that free land would help develop this unpopulated area. The act took effect on Jan. 1, 1863.

"An allusion has been made to the Homestead Law. I think it worthy of consideration, and that the wild lands of the country should be distributed so that every man should have the means and opportunity of benefitting his condition," Lincoln said at the time.

Special legislation extended the provisions of the act to the territory of Alaska in 1898. General homesteading requirements from the Bureau of Land Management were to:

1) Be age 21 or older, or the head of a household, or served in the military

2) Be a U.S. citizen or filed a declaration to become one (had to be a citizen before the homestead could be patented)

3) Live on their claimed land for most of five consecutive years (after June 6, 1912, it was decreased to three years)

4) Never borne arms against America or aided its enemies

5) Live in a habitable dwelling (a tent would not count)

6) Cultivate at least one-eighth of their land (grain or vegetable crops were typical, but raising hay for horses was allowed since it was a commercial crop)

But homesteading in the remote territory didn't catch on much due to poor weather and poor soils. Less than 200 homestead applications had been filed in Alaska by 1914.

Alaska homestead applications increased after World War II and the Vietnam War, however. Those 20th-century pioneers were looking for the same land ownership opportunity that had lured settlers out to the Western states during the previous 100 years.

Alaska newspapers touted the benefits of homesteading to lure people north after statehood. And Alaska's new U.S. Sen. Ernest Gruening often was quoted as saying, "We need people."

Homesteaders used horses and wagons to haul supplies to their land on Cache Creek.

So the Detroit 59ers sold their homes, packed their belongings and headed toward a chance at a brighter future. And the press picked up on their plans.

"We are pooling all we know how to do in this cooperative venture that probably none could do alone," 59er spokesman Ronald Jacobowitz said in an interview. "Everything we are doing, every plan made and carried out has been done by the vote and consent of all."

The day of their departure, hundreds of people turned out to cheer them on their way – some gave them food and money. The *Detroit News* assigned a reporter to accompany the group and send updates from their journey. *Life* magazine sent photographer Bill Ray to capture their trials and tribulations.

Newspapers couldn't get enough of the new stampeders. They churned out updates as the caravan made its way toward the Last Frontier.

"A cold expanse of snow and ice lies ahead," reported one paper. Another said the north was a "wild country that will separate the men from the boys." Yet another claimed the venture was "a test of men against virgin soil."

By March 10, after driving along fog-shrouded and slippery highways, the group reached Fergus Falls, Minn. Three cars and two trailers became separated from the caravan during a heavy snowstorm. One station wagon got stuck.

The Michigan 59ers reached Mile 0 of the Alaska-Canada Highway at Dawson Creek on March 15 – 10 days after leaving Detroit.

The journey proved too much for nine families. They dropped out before reaching the border and returned to Michigan.

The rest of the group reached the Alaska Highway and Dawson Creek on March 15. Twelve days later, the 59ers pulled into Palmer after traveling 4,500 miles. Enthusiastic well-wishers greeted the bunch and welcomed them to the new state. Then the Alaska State Troopers escorted the caravan from Palmer into Anchorage, where a raucous celebration in their honor exploded along Fourth Avenue.

Sgt. Gardner B. White Jr. of Elmendorf Air Force Base entertained them with a song he had written in their honor, titled "My New Alaska Home." Anchorage Mayor Hewitt Lounsbury welcomed them, too.

"You are the first pioneers of the new state," Lounsbury told them.

The Hofbrau then treated the state's newest pioneers to dinner.

"It's great to be in Alaska," said spokesman Jacobowitz in an interview for the *Anchorage Daily Times* on March 27.

Another 59er, Bertha Donaldson, said she was eager to get to Kenai and starting building a cabin. She was tired of traveling, boiling water over a campfire and sleeping in a trailer. But even though she and the other three-dozen 59ers were tired from their long drive north, they were glad to be in Alaska.

"We'd do it again," Donaldson said, and added she had high expectations for the upcoming summer and had packed a swimming suit. She said more Michigan homesteaders might head north in the summer, too, if they were assured of a parcel of land measuring 10 square miles each.

Robert "Bob" Atwood put in his two cents, as well. Atwood, editor and publisher of the *Anchorage Daily Times*, had been a major supporter for the push toward statehood and hoped Alaska might grow to more than a million people in the not-to-distant future.

"Success of these people is important to every Alaskan," he wrote in an editorial that welcomed the 59ers. "They are symbolic of the thousands of others who want to come here and make a home."

The 59ers drove to Kenai on March 28. But once they arrived there and looked the area over, they did not find it to their taste. They decided instead to settle in the Susitna area where they thought the climate better for farming and larger tracts of land were available.

However, the Bureau of Land Management would not guarantee them contiguous blocks of land in Susitna – or anywhere else.

This winter view along the Kenai River in 1956 shows a small homestead on the right bank. When the 59ers finally arrived in Kenai, they decided they didn't want to settle there and moved on to the Susitna Valley.

Between 1898 and 1903, people could claim up to 80 acres for a homestead. That acreage increased to 320 acres during 1903 to 1916. Then the Alaska homestead plan was revised so people only could claim 160 acres.

The requirements for living on the land changed from five years to three years in 1912, and in the 1950s an amendment changed allowable short leaves of absence so homesteaders had to live on their claims not less than seven months per year.

Other amendments followed for Alaska homesteads because cultivating land for crops was hard or impossible in the soil found in many areas of the state. Homesteaders faced other hardships, too, including remoteness, severely cold weather, short growing seasons, high cost of supplies, no market for crops and lack of roads.

New amendments also allowed people to claim up to five acres without cultivating the land if they lived on the land and built a habitable dwelling. They then had to pay $2.50 per acre at the end of the proving up process. These homesteads could be increased by another five acres if claimants showed that they needed the additional acreage for a business.

Some of the Michigan homesteaders claimed land around Talkeetna. And on June 25, another caravan with 76 new 59ers left Detroit and headed north to join those in the Susitna Valley.

Life in Alaska proved harder than most expected, though. They encountered many of the same hardships as their homesteading brethren of the 19th century, such as lack of transportation, harsh weather and the dangers posed by wildlife. Of the 21 families that originally came north from Detroit, only four earned their homestead patents by clearing, improving and living on their parcels of land.

One of those four, the Don Devore family, staked out land five miles north of Talkeetna at Mile 232 on the Alaska Railroad. At the time, Talkeetna was little more than a fishing village with no water, sewer or paved roads. The only access to the area was via train or air.

The Devores cleared their land during summers and put up firewood, preserves and food from their garden and canned salmon to get them through the long winters. They also hunted for wild game.

The Davore family, one of the original Detroit 59ers, built this homestead at Mile 232 along the Alaska Railroad route near Talkeetna.

"We would often down a moose in summer, and without a way to refrigerate the meat, we'd wrap the quarters in muslin and hang them high in a tree where the bears couldn't get them," Don Davore said in an email interview. "The outside two to three inches would crust over and be covered in white fly eggs – but once you cut into the heart of the meat, it was good eating!"

Life in the wilderness was not for the faint of heart. It took courage, determination and stamina.

"As a family, we learned self-reliance and survival on the barest of necessities," Davore said. "Our nearest neighbor was four miles down the tracks toward Talkeetna. Our mail was thrown from a speeding train."

When his father died suddenly in 1961, Don Davore said he and brothers Dennis and Gayland left the homestead to find work to help support their mother and younger siblings, Susie and Bruce, who stayed on the property.

He and Dennis found work on the railroad's extra gang, and Gayland went to work on a farm in Palmer. Eventually, the entire family left the homestead.

Don Devore and his wife, Mavis, now live in Talkeetna. They built a rustic lodge called Denali Fireside, where travelers can stay in suites or cabins and enjoy "one of Alaska's friendliest villages."

The old Devore homestead cabin, one of the only remaining 59er cabins left in Alaska, still can be seen from the railroad. The deteriorating building also can be reached by hiking five miles up the railroad road tracks from Talkeetna. The area is considered "off grid" as it still has no roads, power or infrastructure and is serviced by the last "flag stop" train in North America.

Other areas of Alaska were settled as homesteaders made their way into the wilderness and claimed land in Southeast, Fairbanks and the Matanuska Valley. Homesteaders settled places near Knik, Takotna, Chickaloon, Seward, Homer and Bear Cove on Kachemak Bay. An article in the July 1959 *Alaska Call* describes how homesteads near Ninilchik on the Kenai Peninsula grew.

"Eight miles from Ninilchik on the way to Homer is a new settlement of homesteaders. There are 12 people: Rex Hanks, Ray Marx, Clyde Tomas, Vernon McMillan, Bill Nutte, Jim Nutte, George Welch with his wife and three children, and Joe Hoffman."

And three miles up the beach from Ninilchik another group was carving out a living in the wilderness.

"Deep Creek has a small settlement that may grow in the future. Ed Nickolay, Bill Kashenko and Robert Morris live there. Roy Erickson, Polly Odman and her two sons, and Seymour with his wife and their child. ..."

About two miles from Ninilchik and left of Deep Creek a new community called "Little Kansas" also sprung up.

"... a few young couples came into this area where probably no man ever lived before. Now there is a trail road for jeeps which leads to the homes ... Their life is full of toil and hard work, but they are proud of their efforts and results are noticeable already. Their cabins, their gardens, their wells with modern pumps, their machinery for work on the land and with timber, and even their livestock indicate that they are serious about their permanent stay in the settlement."

The *Call* article stated that all of the homesteaders are "newcomers from the Continental states, although some of them have spent considerable time in Alaska prior to taking homesteads. ..." It also pointed out that the homesteaders had to find work off their claims in order to survive.

"... not one of those homesteaders was able to make any living on the homestead, but had to work in fishing, on the road, or make his living expenses in some other way."

Homesteads were not only carved out of the remote regions of Alaska, either. Several homesteads in the Anchorage area were made possible when Congress passed Public Law 82 in 1947. It permitted veterans with at least 90 days of service to substitute up to two years of their military service to satisfy homestead residence and cultivation requirements.

Active duty servicemen could commute between Fort Richardson and their homesteads to prove up on their parcels of land. Others worked jobs in Anchorage and then returned to their families on the weekends to work on their homesteads.

Some early Anchorage homesteaders grew crops and others raised livestock. Hog farmer Tom Peterkin has a street named for his family in Mountain View.

Names of main thoroughfares like Muldoon, Boniface and Tudor pay homage to some of those early homesteaders. Other areas like the Hillside, Sand Lake, Eagle River and Chugiak began as homesteads where pioneers farmed potatoes and raised poultry and pigs.

The Federal Land Policy and Management Act of 1976 repealed the Homestead Act in the Lower 48, but it granted a 10-year extension on claims in Alaska. When homesteading ended in Alaska on Oct. 21, 1986, few parcels of land had been available for the program for more than a decade. Tens of millions of acres of federal land had been withdrawn from homestead entry to allow the state and Native corporations to select land under terms in the 1958 Alaska Statehood Act and the 1971 Alaska Native Claims Settlement Act.

The last homesteader in the nation, Kenneth Deardorff, received patent to his Alaska claim in the late 1980s. The Vietnam War veteran from California had long dreamed of a life in the Far North, fueled by subscriptions to outdoor magazines from an uncle. He originally made his way to Alaska looking for work with the U.S. Geological Survey, but once in the Great Land, decided to homestead.

National Park Service photo

Kenneth Deardorff, seen here on the porch of his cabin on his homestead near Lime Village in western Alaska, was the last person to receive a patent under the 1862 Homestead Act in 1988.

ALASKA LAND IN DISPUTE

Deardorff filed for an 80-acre parcel on the Stony River in Southwestern Alaska in 1974. Transportation to and from his homestead, about 200 air miles west of Anchorage, was via boat or dog team. He first pitched a small nylon tent in February and lived in that while building a small cabin. When his wife arrived, the couple began constructing buildings from white spruce trees on their land south of McGrath.

To help support his homesteading lifestyle, Deardorff opened a small general store on his property that catered to those traveling the Stony River. He also trapped for marten during the winter when temperatures often dipped to 65 degrees below zero.

He had fulfilled all the legal requirements of the Homestead Act by 1979, but the wheels of bureaucracy moved slowly. It took another nine years for him to receive the patent to that land.

In an interview published Sept. 1, 2012, with the *Beatrice Daily Sun* of Nebraska, Deardorff talked about his homesteading experience. Turns out the first homesteader in America, Daniel Freeman, applied for title to a 50-acre claim in Beatrice in 1863.

"I have a lot of mixed emotions about that time," Deardorff said in the interview about his time in Alaska. "It was certainly enjoyable and certainly frustrating, but all in all absolutely rewarding and something I would do again."

By the time Deardorff, who eventually moved to McGrath, received his patent on May 5, 1988, BLM had conveyed 3,277 homesteads in Alaska that equaled more than 360,000 acres – or less than 1 percent of the total land in the Last Frontier.

It took many years for the federal and state governments and the indigenous people of Alaska to settle once and for all the issue of who owned the remaining available land.

22

WHO OWNS THE LAND?

Alaska Natives, the first to settle the vast unoccupied wilderness of the Great Land thousands of years before Europeans spotted its shores, fought to hold onto their way of life for generations. Most had no knowledge that Russia had claimed ownership and named it Russia America when fur traders landed in the Aleutians in the 1700s.

Russians rarely traveled into the Interior or along the western and northern coasts where about 20,000 Eskimos and Indians lived, according to a series about the Native land claims that appeared in the *Anchorage Daily News* during 1978. The series' author, Robert D. Arnold, reported that the other 10,000 Eskimos, Indians and Aleuts were unaware that Russia had sold its interests and land to America in 1867. They lived in the southern coastal regions and would not see any representatives from the United States for a few years.

Alaska's First People were considered "uncivilized Native tribes" in the Treaty of Cessation, excluded from citizenship and "subject to such laws and regulations as the United States may from time to time adopt in regards to aboriginal tribes of that country."

When Tlingit chiefs learned that Russia had sold Alaska to the United States, they immediately voiced their opinion that Russia had no right to do so. They also told a U.S. Treasury Department agent that Russians had lived in their country only because the Natives had given them permission to do so.

"The dissatisfaction among the tribes on account of the sale of the territory did not arise from any special feeling of hostility, but from the fact that it was sold without their consent, they arguing that their fathers originally owned all the country, but allowed the Russians to occupy it for their mutual benefit, in that articles desired by them could be obtained from the Russians in exchange for furs; but the right of the Russians to sell the territory, except with the intention of giving them the proceeds, is denied," the agent wrote in 1869.

Some historians say the extra $200,000 included in the $7.2 million payment that America gave Russia was intended as a payoff for Alaska's Native people but was pocketed by Russian hierarchy, instead.

There were several incidents between the U.S. Army and the Natives during the next few years, most of which were provoked by the Army when the War Department was in charge of Alaska's affairs, according to historian C.L. Andrews. After the Army was withdrawn to battle Nez Perce Indians in Idaho, things quieted down. In fact, the Army's departure prompted the Natives of Southeast to think that America no longer had an interest in their country.

Alaska State Library, William H, Partridge Collection, ASL-P88-013

Most Alaska Natives were not aware that Russia sold their homeland to America in 1867. The town of Sitka, seen here a few years after the transfer occurred, shows many Tlingit clan houses built with sawed lumber, which replaced the traditional post-and-beam architecture beginning in the 1870s. This photo, shot northwest from the top of Castle Hill, also shows the parade ground, cannery, governor's house, Russian blockhouse, Native cemetery and the Native village, which white people called "The Ranche."

"The Russians have stolen this country from us and after they have gotten most of the furs out of the country, they have sold it to the Boston Men (what the Natives called Americans) for a big sum of money, and now the Americans are mad because they have found that the Russians have deceived them, and we are glad to say that after so many years' hard fight we get our country back again," Sitka chief Alexis Annahootz said at the time, according to historian Ted Hinckley.

Congress had not adopted any laws to allow people to get title to land in the new possession, so there really was little interest for Americans to venture north to settle the wilderness. And since the government hadn't faced the need to give title to land that settlers occupied, as it had in the American West, it did not make any treaties with the Natives. Instead, it designated Alaska "Indian Country," which did not extinguish the Natives' title to the land.

The U.S. government handed the baton of governing Alaska to the Navy in 1877. Within a few years, the Navy became involved with aiding the settlement of Southeast Alaska by threatening the Chilkats.

Following discoveries of gold in the 1880s, many prospectors began arriving in Southeast. At first the Chilkat Tlingits refused to allow travel through their territory to the gold fields, but the Navy convinced them otherwise by sending a warship equipped with a Gatling gun to escort several sailboats carrying armed prospectors into the Chilkat area.

A modified Gatling gun, which had six rifled barrels around a central revolving cylinder, became common on naval ships around the world between 1880 and 1910. It was operated by turning a hand crank at the side of the weapon and could fire 200 rounds per minute.

When the Natives learned what the Gatling gun could do, and received assurances that the miners would not interfere with their fur trade, the Tlingits agreed to open Dyea Pass into Canada to prospectors.

Soon the Natives found themselves on the losing end of property rights as U.S. government officials began recognizing gold claims staked by miners under the first land law established for Alaska in the 1884 Organic Act.

University of Alaska Fairbanks, R.C. Force Collection, UAF-2003-174-219

Gold miners and merchants quickly claimed land in St. Michael when gold was discovered in Northern Alaska in the late 1890s. This wood frame building with glass windows and a shingled roof, which belonged to the U.S. Land Office, ushered in a new era where Native subterranean buildings once had been the norm.

It gave protection to miners' claims and lands used by missionaries – but only a promise of continued use and occupancy of lands to holders of aboriginal rights, according to the Alaska Native Foundation.

Historians say the intention of the act, which provided the first civil government for the new possession, was "to save from all possible invasion the rights of Indian residents of Alaska" until such time they could "ascertain what their claims were."

U.S. Sen. Preston B. Plumb of Kansas eloquently stated his opinion during debate on the act.

"I do not want to impose a government on several thousand Indians, for the purpose of assuming to consult the convenience of about 400 white people, which shall do the Indians more hurt than it will do the white people good. I propose that the Indian shall at least have as many rights after the passage of this bill as he had before."

And even though the 1884 Organic Act did not have any provisions for Alaska's Natives to gain title to their land, it did contain language that would provide for the settlement achieved 87 years later:

"Indians or other persons in said district shall not be disturbed in the possession of any lands actually in their use of occupation or now claimed by them but the terms under which such persons may acquire title to such lands is reserved for future legislation by Congress."

Following passage of the Organic Act, white settlers began streaming into Alaska. The white population grew from 430 in 1880 to 6,700 in 1890.

Alaska Natives soon became a minority in their own land. Miners staked gold claims on their land, canneries denied them fishing rights, lawmakers banned them from voting, people discriminated against them in public, and yet others claimed Native land for their own purposes, including homesteading. They also saw reduced subsistence marine and game populations due to outside companies harvesting for profit.

About 50 years later, Tlingit and Haida Indians from Southeast Alaska took the first legal step to gain control of their land – they filed suit against the federal government for taking land that belonged

U.S. Forest Service photo

Natives in Southeast Alaska filed suit against the federal government in 1935 for taking land near Ketchikan that belonged to them. This photo shows a logging operation in the Tongass National Forest.

to them. In 1935, they asked for $35 million to pay for the land and hunting and fishing rights that had been taken from them by the U.S. Forest Service. That legal battle lasted for the next three decades, until judges sided with the Natives in the late 1950s. The U.S. Court of Claims early in 1968 awarded the Tlingit and Haida Indians $7.5 million for claims against land within the Tongass National Forest, Glacier Bay National Monument and the Annette Islands Indian Reserve.

Around the same time that the lawsuit in Southeast was filed, Congress passed legislation attempting to preserve large areas for use and occupancy for Alaska Natives. The Indian Reorganization Act, enacted in 1934, allowed the Department of the Interior to establish reservations in Alaska. This would not mean giving Natives title to land, but instead the department would hold title in trust for them.

Even though non-Natives in Alaska feared this move would lock up lands, and Natives feared they would be confined to small areas with limited resources like the Indians in the Continental United States, the Interior Department established seven reservations between 1941 and 1946.

The largest encompassed 1.4 million acres and included the villages of Venetie, Arctic Village, Kachik and Christian Village.

Alaska's Native people historically traveled between seasonal camps, like this summer village at Point Belcher in northern Alaska, to subsist off the land. This photograph shows tents, dog teams, sleds and drying racks made of driftwood for fish with the ocean in the background.

Unalakleet, the smallest, contained 870 acres. Other reservations included Akutan, Diomede, Hydaburg, Karluk and Wales, although a court later ruled the Hydaburg reservation wasn't legally established.

Secretary of Interior Harold L. Ickes explained that creation of reservations would preserve Native land from the ever-growing non-Native population and military influx during World War II.

"The large influx of population into Alaska as a result of war activities, and the growing encroachment of the whites upon the land and resources of the Indians and Eskimos have served to emphasize the most serious problem confronting the Natives – the protection of the ancestral hunting, trapping and fishing bases," Ikes said.

Eighty more villages had submitted petitions requesting reservations of 100 million acres by 1950. But by then the fervor to create reservations had waned, most likely because public opinion deemed them as examples of racial segregation and discrimination, according to Arnold in his 13th article in the Alaska Native land claims series printed in the Anchorage Daily News on Nov. 18, 1978.

Another man was thinking about land for Alaska's Natives in the mid-1950s. When Alaska's Constitutional Convention met in Fairbanks in 1955-1956 to draft Alaska's constitution, delegate Col. M.R. "Muktuk" Marston of Anchorage brought up the issue of Native land claims. He wanted to grant to each Native household a home site and a campsite "in the spirit of recognition of past advancement and a token of future participation in future developments." Marston's proposal went nowhere and the convention's 55 members – which only had one Native delegate, William Paul Sr. of Ketchikan – dropped the issue.

The territory owned less than 1 percent of its 375 million acres of land at statehood, and less than 1 percent of Alaska had been surveyed. But language in the Alaska Statehood Act, making Alaska a state in 1959, included a promise that would provide funds for the new state well into the future – Alaska could chose 103.5 million acres from federal lands, an amount larger in total area than California, to build its economy. This land was categorized in three types of grants: Community (400,000 acres); National Forest Community

(400,000 acres); and General (102,550,000). Additional territorial grants of 1.2 million acres for school, university and mental health purposes were confirmed with statehood. All grants combined gave the State of Alaska about 105 million acres, according to the Alaska Department of Natural Resources.

But the act also had a disclaimer that said the new state and its people disclaimed all right or title to lands that "may be held by Eskimos, Indians or Aleuts" or held in trust for them. That language set the stage for a land rights battle and settlement of mammoth proportions.

University of Alaska Fairbanks, Ernest H. Gruening Papers, UAF-1976-21-55334

Laura Mae Beltz jumped for joy in the arctic village of Kotzebue when she learned that Alaska had become a state. Many Alaska Natives believed statehood would be the key to solving the land claims issue.

That long-delayed lawsuit against the federal government by the Tlingits and Haidas, ruled in the Natives' favor in 1959, bolstered the position that Alaska's First People owned the land. The judgment stated, in part, that the Tlingits and Haidas had established their use and title to the lands and waters of virtually all of southeastern Alaska.

– "That they were using and occupying that land according to their Native manner of use and occupancy in 1867 when the United Sates acquired Alaska from Russia ...

– "That such use and occupancy was not interfered with by the United States or its citizens until 1884;

– "That beginning in 1884 and continuing thereafter, these Indians lost most of their land ... through the government's failure to protect the rights of such Indians in such lands and waters through the administration of its laws and the provisions of the laws themselves."

Following that ruling, other Native groups began pressing their rights to ancestral lands.

One example of their unity in the early 1960s stemmed from the new state's plan to create a recreation area in the Minto Flats region, which was an important Athabaskan fishing, hunting and trapping area. Alaska's Interior Natives joined the people of Old Minto to stop the state's plan to take their land.

Natives faced another challenge when the state proposed to build the largest dam in the world at Rampart Canyon on the Yukon River, about 100 miles northwest of Fairbanks. The plan called for flooding 10,000 acres of the Yukon Flats, which the Natives claimed would destroy one of their primary subsistence areas.

In this case, others joined the Natives in their opposition to the plan. The U.S. Fish and Wildlife Service claimed there would be an overwhelming loss of fish and wildlife from the flooding. Conservationists said more than 1,200 Natives would be displaced and the livelihood of nearly 10,000 in Alaska and Canada would be affected by the reduction in the salmon run. The government later scrapped the dam idea.

The state had assumed it could choose any 103 million acres of land not taken by the federal government. But when advisors to Gov. William A. Egan encouraged him to select the land around Prudhoe Bay, Alaska's Native people decided it was time to get serious.

That selection of land, over which a battle to build the largest pipeline in human history later raged, triggered Natives across Alaska to unite and demand their rights. They began fighting for their homeland in Congress, federal and state courtrooms and in the court of public opinion. And one man played a huge roll in helping them organize into one giant unifying voice.

23

ROCK, NATIVE UNITY AND LAND CLAIMS

Near the village of Point Hope on a finger-like peninsula called Tikigaq by Inupiats, Howard Rock's shaman grandmother, Sigvaun, predicted that he would become a great man following his birth in 1911. More than 50 years later, the prophecy came true. Rock, small in stature, became a giant among men when he helped organize Alaska's Natives to receive the largest land settlement for American Indians in U.S. history.

Chosen by the Native community in 1962 to head up a newspaper to address his people's issues, Rock had no journalism experience. Yet his paper grew into the voice for his people.

Raised in the traditional Eskimo way, Rock learned to hunt with his father and embraced his culture. But he also had a foot in the western world.

Like many Native children of the time, Rock had to leave his village at the age of 15 to continue his education past the eighth grade. He studied at White Mountain Vocational School near Nome, where he became interested in sketching and oil painting.

Rock traveled to Medford, Ore., when he was 22 and served as an apprentice to Belgian artist Max Siemes. He later studied art at the University of Washington.

When World War II erupted, Howard joined the U.S. Army and was sent to North Africa to serve as a radio operator. He returned to Seattle at the end of the war and worked as a jewelry designer for

the next several years before returning to Alaska in 1961 for a vacation.

While visiting his family in Point Hope, Rock learned that his relatives and friends were worried about a U.S. government plan to detonate a nuclear blast and create a harbor in the Arctic for shipping minerals and other goods from northwest Alaska. Members of the Atomic Energy Commission thought an underwater nuclear explosion at the mouth of Ogotoruk Creek near Cape Thompson was an ideal place to test the peaceful use of atomic power.

"There were attempts to lull us, the people of Noatak, Kivalina and Point Hope," Rock later told author and historian Lael Morgan in an article titled "Tundra Times: A Survival Story," which appeared in the Alicia Patterson Fund Newsletter dated July 15, 1972.

Born on Aug. 10, 1911, the son of Sam Weyahok (Uyagaq) and Emma Keshorna Rock was baptized with his Christian name after a man named Howard Caldwell arrived at the Episcopal mission following Howard's birth. The Rev. Frederick W. Goodman also anglicized Weyahok to Rock, which is the English translation.

"We were wheedled with rewards of acclaim from science and the peoples of the world if we would agree to go along with 'Project Chariot.'"

Alaska Natives' opposition to Project Chariot led researchers to compile "Project Chariot Marine Mammal Study, Cape Thompson, 1960-61," a study of the effects a nuclear blast might have on marine life in the area. This is the cover of the study and the arrow at the top left shows the location of Point Hope.

Project Chariot

Edward Teller, known as the "Father of the H-bomb," made several trips to Alaska during the late 1950s to gain support for a deep-water harbor near Point Hope. The Atomic Energy Commission had approved plans to set off five nuclear explosions in Ogotoruk Creek in order to create a harbor and show the world that nuclear energy could be used for peaceful purposes.

Teller traveled the territory promoting his dream of "engaging in the great art of geographical engineering, to reshape the earth to your pleasure."

He told Alaskans that the energy department could "dig a harbor in the shape of a polar bear, if required," according to Peter Coates in his 1989 article titled "Project Chariot: Alaskan Roots of Environmentalism," which appeared in the fall issue of *Alaska History Magazine*.

"If your mountain is not in the right place, just drop us a card," Teller said.

After the bombings of Hiroshima and Nagasaki that ended World War II, worldwide pressure built to ban testing of nuclear weapons. So in 1958, the Atomic Energy Commission announced the "Plowshare Program," an effort to harness nuclear energy and transform it into peaceful uses for humanity.

Codenamed Project Chariot, the harbor planned for Cape Thompson was the first operation under this program and would serve to provide scientific and engineering data for future excavation projects – including a new, sea level Panama Canal.

Edward Teller, seen here in 1958 when he was director of the Lawrence Livermore National Laboratory, wanted to experiment with nuclear blasts in Alaska's Arctic to prove how thermonuclear energy could benefit mankind.

The atomic blast at Cape Thompson, north of Kotzebue, would create a channel 270 yards by 1,000 yards wide and provide an excellent harbor for the area, according to an article in the *Anchorage Daily Times*. Experts estimated it would take three blasts to do it, each about the force of the bombs exploded over Japan.

"Of course, the blast would take place 400 feet beneath the sea, and that should prevent any radioactive fall-out," the *Times* article reported.

The Atomic Energy Commission's plan to blast a harbor near Kotzebue caught a wrinkle in May when it admitted that the shock waves might break windows in Siberia, 300 miles away.

Teller arrived in Anchorage in June 1959 to discuss the projected atomic blast at Cape Thompson with state and local officials. He said the new deep harbor would be used for transporting coal from deposits on the north side of the Brooks Range.

As the meeting progressed, Alaska business leaders began questioning the nuts and bolts of the harbor-coal operation. When they informed the scientist that the frozen Chukchi Sea would make the harbor ice-locked for nine months each year, Teller reasoned that warehouses could be built to store the coal until the harbor cleared. When asked how the coal would be transported from the coalfields to the harbor, Teller said a railroad would be built.

It became clear that Teller had no idea how much money would be needed to make a coal operation commercially viable in the Arctic. And, in fact, when asked that question, the scientist changed the subject and asked where he might purchase souvenirs, according to historian Dan O'Neill.

Teller apparently did not concern himself with how the Alaska Native people might feel about a nuclear explosion in their backyard, either. Neither he nor any other AEC representatives associated with the project had consulted with the people who lived in the area up to that time.

"It is a wilderness with no trees, no nothing," said *Anchorage Daily Times* editor Robert Atwood. "Nobody would want to live there."

Alaska State Library, Project Chariot Marine Mammal Study, ASL-PS61 - photo No. 3

Atomic engergy scientists thought Point Hope the perfect place to test nuclear bombs as it was so remote, as seen in this 1960 aerial photograph.

The Inupiat people of Point Hope lived partly in the modern world and partly in the past as evidenced by this home that consits of both woodframe and sod.

But people did live there. The Inupiat Eskimos have occupied the area around Point Hope for about 2,000 years, and 45 miles southeast in Kivalina, people have lived and hunted for centuries.

The AEC built housing for laboratories, quarters for staff and three gravel airstrips during the summer of 1959. During the next three years, it conducted more than 40 bioenvironmental studies. The final product, titled "Environment of the Cape Thompson Region Alaska," became the first true environmental impact statement.

AEC representatives finally traveled to Point Hope in 1961 and played an 11-minute film showing what the lower Ogotoruk Valley would look like after the detonation of one 1-megaton and two 200-kiloton thermonuclear bombs.

Officials told the Natives that they would get front-row seats for the blasts, which would be equal in energy to 160 Hiroshima bombs, and would be offered jobs as railroad and harbor operators and coal miners.

The people of Point Hope, Kivalina and Noatak were told that they would be relocated to Nome and Kotzebue following the detonations, and then moved back in a year – but not to their original homes. Instead, the Natives would receive modern, new houses located near the new Ogotoruk Valley harbor.

The villagers became quite concerned following this meeting. With the help of Howard Rock, they organized and began their vocal opposition to the project. They also sent a letter to President John F. Kennedy and told him that the nuclear project was too close to their homes and hunting and fishing areas.

Other opinions across the territory were mixed.

"We think the holding of a huge nuclear blast in Alaska would be a fitting overture to the new era which is opening for our state," wrote George Sundberg, editor of the *Fairbanks Daily News-Miner*.

Conservationists voiced concern over the blasts' effects on wildlife roaming the tundra and whales at sea. Alaska's Natives voiced their concerns to Gov. William Egan. And the Russians, just 50 miles across the Bering Strait, also needed to be considered – officials had to weigh what the propaganda value to them would be from the blasts.

Soon tests showing high levels of harmful radionuclides in Natives subsisting on caribou began sending up warning flags. It appeared that worldwide nuclear testing fallout was being absorbed by lichen, a rootless tundra plant that caribou eat in abundance. The fallout, retained in the caribou's bones and tissues, entered the bodies of those who consumed the animals.

Alaska State Library, Project Chariot Marine Mammal Study, ASL-PS61 - photo No. 37

Residents of Point Hope gathered in 1960 to help haul in and butcher a whale for the village just as their ancestors had done centuries before them.

Protests from scientists finally joined the voices of Alaska's northern people against the continuation of the project, and in the fall of 1961, Project Chariot was abandoned after expenditures of nearly $4 million. Its demise marked the first successful opposition to the American nuclear establishment and ushered in the era of environmentalism, wrote Dan O'Neill in "Nuclear Excavation" in *We Alaskans Magazine* in December 1989.

The AEC decided to conduct its cratering test in the Nevada desert in July 1962, instead, but it did not forget about Alaska. It decided to bring fresh radioactive fallout from the Nevada nuclear explosion to the Ogotoruk Valley to answer a question it had posed to the U.S. Geological Survey: Would the bombs contaminate local drinking water?

The USGS had said in some situations "it could be a substantial and a serious handicap to man's activities." The AEC wanted proof.

And so the USGS applied radioactive fallout to plots of ground in the valley, watered it and collected runoff to test in a lab. At the end of the experiments, all the materials used and all contaminated soil, rocks and plants were collected. This debris was removed from the plots, put into 55-gallon drums and taken to the lower end of Snowbank Creek where the drums were emptied into a burial site and covered with four feet of dirt.

When Alaska Gov. Walter Hickel and U.S. Sen. Frank Murkowski visited Point Hope in September 1992, they surveyed the burial mound just north of the abandoned Project Chariot base camp. The politicians promised the people of Point Hope that they would make sure any residual waste would be removed and the site cleaned up by March 1993, according to a newspaper article.

True to their word, on Feb. 10, 1993, the headlines of the *Anchorage Daily News* reported, "Feds tap $3 million to clean up nuke site." Although the Department of Defense said it was "99 percent sure" the waste did not pose a danger to the people of Point Hope.

AEC faced more controversy when opponents tried to stop Project Long Shot in 1965 and Project Milrow in 1969, but those Defense Department detonations went on as planned on desolate Amchitka Island, about 1,400 miles southwest of Anchorage.

Alaska officially entered the nuclear age when an 80-kiloton device — four times more powerful than the bomb dropped on Hiroshima in

A Point Hope man hauls a skin boat via dog team to the water's edge to embark on a whale hunt in the early 1960s. Although the Inupiat helped to squash plans for a deep-water port made by nuclear detonation, some radioactive debris remained buried from tests done in the area.

World War II – was unleashed 2,300 feet below the treeless Aleutian island on Oct. 29, 1965, according to the *Anchorage Daily Times*. The stated purpose of the explosion was for seismic test detection development, according to the Department of Defense.

Although Defense officials said there would be no need for further testing, they decided to detonate another nuclear device on Amchitka four years later, despite opposition from Alaskans, conservationists, state representatives and national politicians. Many thought the blast would cause an earthquake and tsunami.

With millions of dollars invested in the Milrow project, the AEC sent scientists to Anchorage to assure people the device would create neither a huge quake nor tidal waves. They said the blast could trigger an earthquake "waiting to happen," but such an earthquake would be less severe than if natural pressures within the earth discharged on their own, according to a newspaper article. The Atomic Energy Commission mentioned it would establish a "safety area" around the remote island.

And so on a clear, bright Oct. 2, 1969, the AEC detonated its 1.2-megaton device equivalent to 1 million tons of TNT on the island in the Aleutians in order to check calibration. The aftershocks created a 6.5 seismic shock, but no major earthquake, tsunami or "unforeseen event" occurred.

Scientists said they did not detect any radiation from the device detonated 4,000 feet in the ground on the tiny island. One newspaper article claimed that initial surveys "showed but one deaf sea otter, some cracking of pavement and minor damage to a building at ground zero."

Another project code named "Cannikin," rumored to be five times larger than Project Milrow, reared its head two years later. It turns out the nuclear test in 1969 was, in part, to ensure that the Cannikin test could be contained, according to Department of Defense records.

Gov. William A. Egan and many public officials opposed the test, which was part of the Operation Grommet nuclear test series, and national environmental groups battled all the way to the U.S. Supreme Court in an unsuccessful drive to stop the third Amchitka blast, according to newspaper reports. Protestors also demonstrated around the world.

But on Nov. 6, 1971, the world watched as the AEC detonated

Atomic Energy Commission photo

a five-megaton nuclear warhead designed for the LIM-49 Spartan anti-ballistic missile on the barren, rocky 42-mile-long island. Buried at the bottom of a 6,000-foot shaft, "Cannikin didn't vent radiation, produced no destructive earthquake and spawned no tidal waves," according to the *Associated Press*.

The test was the largest underground explosion ever detonated by the United States.

Atomic Energy Commission workers lower the canister into the test shaft on Amchitka prior to the Cannikin project blast in 1971.

ALASKA LAND IN DISPUTE

Jay Hammond, then an Alaska state senator, turned his penchant for homespun poetry into a protest of the Amchitka test blast. The *Anchorage Daily News* printed his letter to the AEC on the day of the massive explosion.

Open letter to the AEC

Alaskans are told there's no reason for panicin'.
Just 'cause you're pushing the button on Cannikin.

Despite even the efforts of Senator Mike,
Who protested with picket sign during a hike.

Past that White House which takes a dim view of his capers
(Like his lachrymose leak of the Pentagon Papers).

Our distress, unlike some, is caused by the fact
That endangered Sea Otter might suffer impact.

We'd rather instead you'd trigger The Bomb
In some area where we knew without qualm

Unendangered species were found to abound.
We suggest Manhattan Island as prime "zero ground."

While we've been told many times there is no need to fear
A boot to Alaska's ecological rear

One thing still puzzles and so I demur:
If you know exactly what's sure to occur

Please ease my intellectual indigestion.
Tell me: If you know all the answers —

WHY THE HECK POP THE QUESTION??????

But the people of the region chose to protect their way of life and heritage instead. Eskimo leaders from 20 villages met in the fall of 1961 to discuss strategy. They called the meeting "Inupiat Paitot," which means "The People's Heritage."

Environmental studies began to show that fallout from radiation after test blasts contaminated lichen, which caribou eat, and it was finding its way into humans who consumed the caribou.

With opposition growing ever stronger, the AEC backed down and shelved the idea in 1962.

That's when the Arctic Slope Native Association asked Rock to start the *Tundra Times* newspaper. The association saw it as an avenue for Alaska's Native people to be part of their own destiny.

The paper, financed by philanthropist Henry S. Forbes of Milton, Mass., changed the way many Natives saw themselves.

Along with journalist Tom Snapp, Rock covered issues that affected Alaska's Native people and encouraged them to have pride and respect for their heritage and cultures – and to fight for them.

The first issue, released on Oct. 1, 1962, promised unbiased reporting.

"Long before today there has been a great need for a newspaper for the northern Natives of Alaska. Since civilization has swept into their lives in tide-like earnestness, it has left the Eskimos, Indians and Aleuts in a bewildering state of

University of Alaska Fairbanks, Alfred R. Ketzler Collection, UAF-1992-202-12

Association on American Indian Affairs Director Laverne Madegan, seen here with Howard Rock and a man identified only as Fergus, convinced philanthropist Henry S. Forbes of Milton, Mass., to finance the *Tundra Times*. Forbes, a retired physician, was a descendent of Ralph Waldo Emerson and a champion of aboriginal rights.

Tundra Times editor Howard Rock, left, and journalist Tom Snapp, center, show visitor Theodore Hetzel the tools of their new trade, including printer's type blocks and plates.

indecision and insecurity between the seeming need for assimilation and, especially in Eskimo areas, the desire to retain some of the cultural and traditional way of life," Rock wrote in his first editorial.

"With this humble beginning we hope, not for any distinction, but to serve with dedication the truthful presentations of Native problems, issues and interests."

Journalist Tom Richards, who worked at the *Tundra Times* from 1968 to 1974, later said that Rock had a gift for explaining complex issues.

"He was the most soft-spoken man," Richards said. "But he had tremendous impact with just a few words."

After taking on the U.S. Atomic Energy Commission to prevent its Arctic atomic project, Rock used the *Tundra Times* to fight the federal government on behalf of Aleuts virtually enslaved in the Pribilof Islands working for in-kind wages in the seal harvest.

Through his newspaper, Rock unified Alaska Natives by "knowing the hearts and minds of the people," Alaska leaders said.

With help from new Native activism and the *Tundra Times*, Natives realized that state selections of 103-plus million acres of land granted under the Alaska Statehood Act, plus federal withdrawals and uses, soon would result in appropriation of most of Alaska's more desirable land, leaving them with little good land.

In 1962, the U.S. Interior Department received one of the first organized appeals for land on the North Slope. The next year, Native groups asked the department to close land around Native villages to state selection until claims were resolved. And by 1965, the Bureau of Land Management had received Native claims for 15.7 million acres, including 9.8 million on which the state had applied. In 1966, the claims covered 122 million acres.

Alaska Natives began filing protests on a staggering amount of land. Some groups filed on land that other groups filed on. Secretary of the Interior Stewart Udall, in charge of conveying lands to the state through the Bureau of Land Management, was in a bind. He also was the trustee for Native American interests. He issued an injunction in 1966 that tied up transfer of title from federal to state ownership until the Native land claims issue was settled. The state had chosen only 12 million acres by this time – 1.5 million on the North Slope.

Udall's freezing of land

Courtesy Tuzzy Consortium Library

U.S. Secretary of the Interior Stewart Udall, seen here later at an annual awards banquet for the *Tundra Times*, froze Alaska's land selecions in 1966 until the Native land claims issue was settled.

ALASKA LAND IN DISPUTE

selections not only stopped the state from choosing land, it also stalled non-Native homestead applications and disrupted business plans for many companies.

"If it was an Indian problem, we'd still be working on it," said Native leader Emil Notti later. "When it became a problem for the state of Alaska, homesteaders, oil companies, cities, it became everybody's problem."

The state wanted the issue settled fast, because without land, it could not develop its economy. The Native people wanted it settled, too, but not at their expense.

At a time when there was often disharmony around the state, Rock used the *Tundra Times* to push for the formation of a statewide gathering of Natives. Native groups in Southeast Alaska had been politically organized since 1911 when they formed the Alaska Native Brotherhood, and the Tanana Chiefs had banded together in Alaska's Interior in 1915, but these groups had little in common with Natives in Barrow or Wales until the statehood land claims issue heated up.

Rock helped set the stage for the first Alaska Federation of Natives convention in October 1966. More than 400 Alaska Natives representing 17 Native organizations met for three days in Anchorage to address their aboriginal land rights.

"Perhaps more than anyone else, he (Rock) helped weld together the frontier state's 55,000 Natives for their successful years' long fight to win the largest aboriginal land claims settlement in American history," wrote Stan Patty of the *Seattle Times*. He added that Rock was their voice, at times about the only calm voice when crescendos of dissent threatened to tear Alaska apart.

The fledgling AFN operated on a shoestring budget, according to an article in the *Juneau Empire* titled "The Struggle For Land" found online at the Alaska History and Culture site.

"Villages held bingo games and raffles to raise cash for the cause, and AFN borrowed money – $100,000 from Natives in Tyonek who sold oil leases on their reservation, and $200,000 from Yakima Indians in Washington," according to former AFN attorney Don Mitchell.

Native leaders like Emil Notti, pictured here in the 1960s, spread the word about Alaska's land claims issue.

Alaska Gov. Walter J. Hickel created the Alaska Rural Affairs Commission in order to help AFN leaders with expenses so they could travel and meet to discuss negotiations. They only had enough money to meet in Anchorage once a year, however.

"But we could only afford one hotel room," former president of NANA Regional Corp. John Schaeffer told the *Juneau Empire*. "So all 15 of us stayed in one hotel room."

As Natives began working together toward a common goal, Alaska's land claims issue started making news across the United States.

"We had people on Johnny Carson explaining it, we had people on talk shows, late night talk shows, 'Good Morning America,' wherever and whenever," Emil Notti, a former Alaska Federation of Natives president, later told KTUU Channel 2 News.

When Alaska Natives were not invited to attend meetings to discuss a settlement in Washington, D.C., in May 1967, two Native leaders decided to crash the party to present the Native point of view.

Notti and Democratic State Rep. Willie Hensley, a Kotzebue Eskimo, flew to the nation's capital to join in discussions about Native land claims that originally only included Gov. Hickel, Interior Secretary Udall and other officials, which also may have included President Lyndon B. Johnson, according to an *Anchorage Daily Times* article.

One state task force offered a settlement proposal of 40 million acres of land and royalty from both state land and federal outer

Native leaders met with then-Interior Secretary Walter J. Hickel during the fall of 1970 in Washington, D.C. Clockwise from left: Walter Hickel; Tim Wallis, president Fairbanks Native Association; Charles (Etok) Edwardson, executive director Arctic Slope Native Association; Eben Hobson, Barrow; Emil Notti, president Alaska Federation of Natives; attorney Barry Jackson, standing; state Sen. William Hensley, Kotzebue; Alfred Ketzler, Nenana; Barbara Trigg, Nome; Delois Ketzler; Harvey Samuelson, Dillingham; George Miller; unidentified; state Sen. Ray C. Christiansen, far right; Frank Degnan, Unalakleet; Moses Paukan; Morris Thompson; and John Borbridge, back to camera.

continental shelf land. But the Interior Department rejected the royalty idea, saying it probably was illegal and Congress would not approve it.

The Interior Department proposed $180 million, or $3,000 per Alaska Native, and grants of not more than 50,000 acres to each of the 200-plus Native groups.

Natives countered with $500 million cash and millions of acres of land.

Many proposals were suggested and rejected by the state and federal officials and the Alaska Native community. The claims issue lagged on.

But who owned what land came to a head with a major oil

discovery on Alaska's North Slope in 1968. Soon the oil industry became a major player. It wanted to make sure its early leases at Prudhoe Bay were good and that they had rights of way to build an 800-mile pipeline to get oil to market from the North Slope.

Oil companies met with leaders of the AFN in 1968 in an attempt to sway them into settling with the state and federal governments. Robert Willard, a leader in the claims battle from Juneau, later told a *Juneau Empire* reporter how he remembered what Arctic Slope Native Joe Upicksoun told oil company executives at that meeting.

"Not one drop of oil, not one inch of pipe will come from the Arctic Slope until the Native claims settlement act is settled," Upicksoun said.

Willard said the oil executives told the AFN board that nothing would stop the building of that pipeline. They would take the Natives to court if they had to – even if that process took 100 years.

"We can wait," came Upicksoun's reply.

Big oil could not. The industry threw its weight behind the Natives.

During the next three years, the federal government, the state

University of Alaska Fairbanks, Atlantic Richfield Company Collection, UAF-1982-146-3

and the Native community – along with oil companies, environmentalists, sportsmen groups, chambers of commerce and mining interests – offered and rejected numerous settlement proposals.

By late 1971, both houses of Congress had agreed on a compromise solution and sent the final settlement

Oil companies joined Alaska Natives' calls for settling the land claims issue following a major discovery of crude oil at Prudhoe Bay. The discovery well is seen here, enclosed in a metal building in 1969.

document to Alaska so the Natives could analyze it. The Alaska Federation of Natives convened in Anchorage on Dec. 18, and after discussions, voted 511 to 56 to accept the bill, reported the *Anchorage Daily Times*.

The federation had set up a phone link between the convention hall and the White House, so word was sent immediately following the vote tally. Then the delegation waited.

Finally, they heard U.S. President Richard M. Nixon's voice.

"I want you to be among the first to know that I have just signed the Alaska Native Claims Settlement Act," Nixon said.

Some Native sources dispute the newspaper account and say that the AFN meeting happened after the president signed the act into law.

Recognizing that nearly 78,500 Aleuts, Eskimos and Indians had valid claims to the land, had never signed any treaties and never had been defeated in war, Congress awarded Alaska's aboriginal people 44 million acres of land and $962.5 million – the largest settlement the U.S. government ever had made with Native Americans.

In exchange, Alaska's Natives gave up their aboriginal land claims, which ended the land freeze and opened the door for the oil pipeline on the North Slope. They also surrendered their aboriginal hunting and fishing rights.

However another provision that mandated establishment of conservation units in Alaska to reserve another 104 million acres – Alaska National Interest Lands Conservation Act, passed by Congress in 1980 – guaranteed Natives access to traditional subsistence resources across the new conservation areas.

In hearings before the Subcommittee on Indian Affairs before the U.S. Congress in October 1969, Rock put into perspective why Alaska's First People wanted millions of acres of land returned to them.

"We continually hear people from other states say something like this: 'Why do you need so much land?' To ask a Native person this question is akin to an insult," Rock said. "It is a silly question, an uneducated question as far as the Native man or woman is concerned.

THE OLD STYLE HUNTERS COSTUME.

Alaska State Library, Talmage Family Collection, ASL-P345-444

Alaska's Native people have subsisted off the land for millennia. The land provided for their existence, and they used all parts of animals they killed for food, clothing and tools, wasting little.

The Native person knows the meaning of his land and how much land his village needs to keep it going."

When the Alaska Native Claims Settlement Act was signed into law, Rock hailed its passage as "the beginning of a great era for the Native people of Alaska."

The act established 12 regional corporations to serve the diverse nations and language groups in Alaska. The 221 Native villages within these regions, as well as Natives in the cities of Juneau, Sitka, Kenai and Ketchikan, were required to form corporations, funded by the large monetary settlement.

If Natives lived in urban areas, the Natives had to sign up "at large" to a region. Those living outside Alaska joined a 13th corporation.

The huge job of conveying the land to the new corporations began soon thereafter. Alaska's First People had to learn how to organize, enroll shareholders and run businesses. Tlingit John Hope, a Juneau resident involved in the land claims issue, later summed up the years of Native adjustment to a corporate world in an article in the *Juneau Empire*.

"It's like you and I never saw a baseball game in our lives," Hope said. "We'd never seen mitts or bats or baseballs. All of a sudden you were told, 'Here's your mitts. Here's your bats. Here's your balls. Tomorrow you play the Yankees.'"

The for-profit corporations for each region soon began venturing into businesses to make money for their shareholders. The region owning the land also would receive 30 percent of all income from timber and minerals and 70 percent would be divided among all regional corporations proportionately.

Settlement money was not to be used for nonprofit human resources, so the regions established nonprofit corporations in the villages to take care of health, welfare, housing, education, social services and political needs of the Natives within the corporations' boundaries.

Grants from federal, state and private groups fund the nonprofits.

In 1975, Rock's leadership was recognized with Alaska's Man of the Year award, which he shared with U.S. Sen. Ted Stevens. That same year, the newspaper was nominated for a Pulitzer Prize for meritorious public service.

Rock died of cancer on April 20, 1976.

"I've never seen anybody die the way Howard died – he went in a blaze of glory," Tom Richards said. "His eyes had a burning light."

A granite headstone and the rib of a giant bowhead, which typically pay tribute to a mighty hunter, mark his final resting place in the Tikigaq tundra about a mile from Point Hope. Rock's legacy – Native unity and activism – lives on.

But even though Rock's efforts helped Alaska's Native people settle claims to their land in the Last Frontier, it was just the beginning of the fight for many to get the land that was theirs.

24

NATIVES MUST PROVE LAND USE

The millions of acres granted to Alaska Natives under the Alaska Native Claims Settlement Act of 1971 had to be adjudicated and surveyed by the Bureau of Land Management. The bureau was inundated with requests for land claims – and much land was selected by more than one entity, village corporation or regional corporation.

Another wrinkle in the distribution of land was that the settlement act repealed the Alaska Native Allotment Act of 1906, which had allowed Natives to acquire title of up to 160 acres of nonmineral land. While thousands of individual Native allotment claims survived the repeal, many claims were amended and others stayed pending.

Alaska's Natives had to show that their ancestors used lands in order to get allotments under the settlement act. This often proved a difficult task, as most of their history was not written down – it passed orally through the generations.

When Natives petitioned for land, they had to write detailed accounts of how the land had been used and submit paperwork to the BLM. One such account, recorded by Kenaitze Indian tribe member Alexander Wilson in 1967 and later transcribed and given to this author, described his people's history along the Kenai River.

Wilson said the Kenaitze lived in a village called Ch-kee-took, upriver from the Kaknu, or Kenai River, where the Federal Aviation

Administration and a cannery later stood. He described a place farther upriver where the Natives lived both summer and winter, as well as Portage, which was called Cook-ul-detht.

"Indians used to portage their canoes over this place," Wilson said, adding that Cook-ul-detht means "climbing up."

Wilson said the Kenaitze then carried their canoes and hunting equipment for 20 minutes on the portage and came out up river and got back on the river at Ch-kildeth, which means "going down." They then moved across the river at Big Eddy, or Bun-toon-chkee-layshet, which means "going through lakes."

Alaska Natives did not view the land as real estate. As the Indian names show, they saw every trail, creek and bend in the river as an individual entity and their connection to the earth ran deep.

Wilson's account follows the trail used by the Kenaitze all the way to Skilak Lake, which was called Ka-stu-dee-lint-buna, and Kenai Lake, whose name was Ski-lyank-bunn-a, where his ancestors hunted

Alaska State Library, Clinton H. Bentz Collection, ASL-P448-71

Kenai Lake, seen here in July 1943, was called Ski-lyank-bunn-a by the Kenaitze.

Native Alaskan Girls Drying Salmon
John Urban Collection/Anchorage Museum. B1964.001.783

Alaska's First People taught their children to dry salmon just as their ancestors before them, as seen in this photograph of young girls helping to dry salmon on racks in northern Alaska during the 1930s.

and fished all winter. He said white men changed the names to Kenai Lake for the upper body of water and Skilak Lake for the lower.

Wilson's account described how his ancestors fished the rivers and hunted for seal and sea lion, which were preserved in blubber or dried.

"There were skirmishes with the Aleut when the hunters ventured too far toward the Alaska Peninsula or toward Seward and Prince William Sound," Wilson said. "Although the Aleuts are friendly now, they still have the dislike instilled in them from centuries back because of these encroachments and skirmishes."

He described many villages, tribes and languages in dozens of areas along the Kenai Peninsula. He also shared several stories of how his people used the land all over Cook Inlet, as well.

"The beluga whale was hunted in these parts," he said. "All kinds of berries were harvested and put up in oils or dried."

He said moose first were seen and taken at Nikiski.

"Indians were fearful of the animal for a long time," Wilson said. "They'd rather tackle a bear with a spear, than a moose with a gun."

Wilson gave many examples of life in the past and the traditions and culture of the Kenaitze. Only men hunted, parents or guardians chose mates for their children and women had to remain away from camp during menstruation.

"Food was handed to her, but no article of any kind accepted from her, especially by any male, which was a bad omen," he said. "She had to stay put until her period was over."

He also wrote that Indians began moving to Fort Miklas, or Kenay, in the 1880s. He then described a hunting party that returned to its village after a weeks-long hunting trip to find a devastating illness had claimed all lives except three small children. The children had walked the beach toward Kasilof, where other people took them in.

In his effort to prove how his ancestors had used the land, Wilson also explained why so many Alaska Natives did not know how to write their history to prove their claims.

University of Alaska Fairbanks, Sheldon and Lorena Turner, Alaska Survey Expedition Collection, UAF-1994-193-37

Natives, like this man on the Alaska Peninsula, were adept hunters in their seaworthy bidarkas. Note the gut parka – a waterproof garment.

"The reason so few Indians know their background is they were discouraged early in school," he said. "We were broken away from our way of living."

He went on to say that White teachers did not allow the children to speak their Native language, or Russian, in the schoolyard.

Teachers punished those speaking anything other than English by scrubbing their mouths out with soap, making them eat cayenne pepper or whipping them with a green birch rod.

"I should know what these were like, as I got two kinds – the birch rod and cayenne pepper," Wilson said. "With so few of the older ones left in this village of Kaknu, it is difficult to gather the information needed direct from the older individuals."

Wilson died in 1968, but his family carried on with their attempts to claim their ancestral land. Family members applied for one 63-acre piece in the Kenai Lake area and marked the boundary by tying pink fluorescent tape around trees. They then nailed metal screw tops to trees, slipped a paper listing the name of the applicant and the allotment number into a jar, and then screwed the jar onto the nailed lid.

Wilson's family only received 13.3 acres of that piece. They found the state had given 50 acres to a homesteader, who claimed he did not see any markers. One of Wilson's nieces later investigated and found the remnants of shattered glass jars and pink tape buried in a pile along the property.

Alexander Wilson's family wrote the information about their Native land allotment on a piece of paper, put it into a Mason jar and then nailed the jar to a tree on the land that had been used by their ancestors for generations.

Even with detailed accounts such as Wilson's, and claimants walking the land and placing markers to show borders, it sometimes took years for Alaska's Native people to get their Native allotments – if ever. They had to attend hearings and justify their requests. Some people spoke against them at these hearings. Many Natives credit the late U.S. Sen. Ted Stevens with helping them resolve disputes and getting them title to their land.

Not all land claims have been settled as of 2015. Myriad appeals, lawsuits and legal interpretations among the state, corporations, the public and Interior Department all contributed to delayed conveyance. The Bureau of Indian Affairs has this disputed property classified as "Restricted Status," so it still is under federal government control.

Passage of the Alaska Native Claims Settlement Act did, however, allow the state to move forward with its land selections and allowed oil companies to begin building the largest pipeline in human history.

Alaska's Only Reservation

The Metlakatla Reservation on Annette Island in Southeast Alaska was the only Alaska reservation or reserve not extinguished by the 1971 Alaska Native Claims Settlement Act, because the community decided to remain a reservation. It received no benefits from the act and is the only reservation in Alaska.

The community began when a group of Tsimshian people left their homes in British Columbia and followed William Duncan, a lay missionary in the Church of England, from Old Metlakatla to Alaska in the late 1880s. The Church of England originally had sent Duncan to Christianize the Tsimshian in Fort Simpson in 1857, as it believed it needed to indoctrinate aboriginal people with Western culture.

Duncan immersed himself in the culture and language of the Tsimshian and taught them about Christianity and modern ways of life. But the group decided to find a spot where they could build a religious community away from the doctrines of the church, which was insisting that Duncan administer certain rituals and ceremonies to the Tsimshians that Duncan felt inappropriate for the Natives.

Alaska State Library, Alaska Division of Tourism Collection, ASL-P22-06-074a

The town of Metlakatla featured boardwalks and buildings near the waterfront and the church in the center.

The missionary met with U.S. President Grover Cleveland in Washington, D.C., who told Duncan he and his group could choose land in Alaska for their new home. A small group of men traveled by canoe around islands in Southeast. The majestic beauty, sheltered bays, gently sloping beaches, nearby waterfall and abundance of fish on Annette Island amazed them.

On Aug. 7, 1887, Duncan and 826 Tsimshians arrived and proclaimed the birth of New Metlakatla. Residents of the community still celebrate this day as Founders' Day to remember the courage and foresight of the original pioneers.

Duncan drew up plans for streets, homes and public buildings. Within two years, he and the people had built a combination church and day school.

Following Duncan's death in 1918, the town's government took charge of managing the community, economic and social affairs. Today, a 12-member tribal council, mayor, secretary and treasurer govern the now-incorporated entity, called Metlakatla Indian Community, according to the community's website.

PRUDHOE BAY OIL

25

BLACK GOLD FOUND ON NORTH SLOPE

As prospectors searched for gold in the northern wilderness during the late 1890s, some sourdoughs stumbled across enough black goo along the Klondike River to spark the interest of reporters Outside.

"What is said to be the greatest discovery ever made is reported from Alaska. Some gold prospectors several months ago ran across what seemed to be a lake of oil. It was fed by innumerable springs, and the surrounding mountains were full of coal. It is stated that there is enough oil and coal in the discovery to supply the world," reported an *Associated Press* dispatch on July 13, 1897.

But it took 60 years and 10 days of oilmen punching more than 100 holes in the frozen ground to find commercial quantities of crude. Then on July 23, 1957, Richfield Oil Co. struck black gold with a test well in the Swanson River region on the Kenai Peninsula. It pumped 900 barrels of oil per day on a short test.

News of the first tanker, *F.S. Bryant*, leaving the Kenai Peninsula filled with thousands of barrels of oil bound for the Lower 48 may be compared to the news of the *SS Portland* leaving St. Michael with its ton of Klondike gold in 1897. It had the same effect. Instead of miners looking for gold, though, it brought prospectors searching for oil.

Prospects for the petroleum industry in Alaska by 1966 looked bright. Alaska ranked 11th nationally in proved oil reserves and eighth in proved gas reserves.

Oil companies were producing oil and natural gas in the Kenai Peninsula and Cook Inlet, with 15 offshore oil platforms, onshore oil and gas wells, and large processing, refining and transportation facilities. They also were providing Alaskans with gasoline, diesel fuel, heating oil and jet fuel. And they built a pipeline beneath Turnagain Arm that carried natural gas from the Kenai Peninsula to heat Anchorage homes and businesses.

In September 1967, Cook Inlet monthly production surpassed that of Swanson River for the first time with 1,186,414 barrels compared with 1,090,528 for the Swanson. Experts believed the oil industry would continue to increase its activity in Alaska following its profitable production from the Swanson River and Cook Inlet areas and favorable results from seismic and geological exploration on the North Slope of the Brooks Range.

Alaska State Library, Alaska Division of Tourism Collection, ASL-P22-06-069

After crude was discovered near Kenai, oil companies began finding more deposits in Cook Inlet, as seen by this offshore rig near Anchorage. By late 1960, Alaska had 19 producing oil or gas wells and 18 major oil firms located in the state – 17 in Anchorage.

PRUDHOE BAY OIL

Based on recommendations in 1964 of Tom Marshall, the state's only geologist, Alaska had selected 1.5 million acres of the Arctic coastal plain bordering the Beaufort Sea between Naval Petroleum Reserve No. 4 and the Arctic National Wildlife Refuge as part of its land entitlement of 103 million acres granted under the Statehood Act. Marshall had recognized some general geological similarities of the Arctic Slope to areas in the Rocky Mountains that were producing petroleum. Even though the U.S. Navy and U.S. Geological Survey had been test drilling in the Arctic for decades with no commercially significant discoveries, Marshall believed the Arctic Slope probably held the richest oil land in Alaska.

USGS geologist Marvin Mangus spent nine field seasons working for the government and other parties between 1947 and 1958 on expeditions in the North Slope. But he did not find any deposits that would be commercially viable. He did discover a small field at Umiat, two small gas fields at Gubik and Barrow, three prospective gas fields at Meade, Square Lake and Wolf Creek, and two minor gas deposits near Cape Simpson and at Fish Creek, according to a recent article in *Petroleum News*.

But after 30 years of exploration in the reserve, at a cost of $50 million to $60 million, the federal government finally said enough in 1953 after drilling 75 test wells near Umiat. Congress no longer would appropriate money for a program that was not producing economically viable results.

Five years later, the government opened parts of the North Slope outside Naval Petroleum Reserve No. 4 to simultaneous filing of oil

Top left: Following a major discovery of crude in 1957, Standard Oil Co. built Alaska's first oil refinery at Nikiski, near Kenai. It opened on Oct. 10, 1961.

Bottom left: A pipeline linking the Swanson River Field with a marine tanker facility at Nikiski was dedicated on Oct. 1, 1960. Alaska's U.S. Sen. Ernest Gruening stands to the far left of the group attending the ceremony. The Standard Oil Co. of California tanker *W.H. Berg* took on the first load of crude from the Nikiski terminal one month later on Nov. 12.

The Kenai Peninsula saw tremendous growth as workers and their families followed the drilling activity and homesteaders used oil well roads to access new lands.

Aviator Noel Wien took this aerial shot of the U.S. Navy exploring for oil near Umiat.

and gas leasing. That spurred oil companies to conduct geophysical and geological studies.

In December 1960, the government made the area for finding commercial deposits of oil even smaller after it established the Arctic National Wildlife Refuge, which covered almost 19 million acres. Between the refuge and the naval reserve, the oil industry now was limited to exploring acreage lying between the Colville and Canning rivers.

Exploration moved slowly due to problems with drilling and production in such a remote, frigid region.

In spite of the obstacles, several companies – including British Petroleum, Colorado Oil & Gas, Sinclair, Richfield Oil Co., Standard Oil Co. and Pan American Petroleum – were making exploratory drill tests in the vast area of 45 million acres lying north of Alaska's Brooks Range by 1965, according to newspaper articles of the time.

"Everything was confidential," said Mangus, who then worked for Richfield. "We didn't trade maps unless we were partners with a company. Even then there was some secrecy."

Geologists believed that Alaska's Arctic Slope held the greatest petroleum potential of any geological province within the United States, however, because of its vast basin with tremendous thickness of marine sediments. Drilling done on Naval Petroleum Reserve No. 4 had shown those sediments contained both oil and gas. Experts just did not know if the area had "favorable reservoir conditions which are so essential for major accumulations of oil or gas," said Rollin Eckis, president of Richfield, in a speech to the Greater Anchorage Chamber of Commerce in September 1964.

Transportation to the remote region was problematic, as well. There were no roads to the potentially oil-rich land, and passage via ship to Point Barrow was limited to a few weeks a year due to sea ice.

John C. "Tennessee" Miller decided to prove the feasibility of transporting men and equipment overland for the oil industry and convinced Richfield to let him try during the winter of 1964. Miller planned to take a caravan of Caterpillar tractors loaded with seismic exploration equipment from Fairbanks north through Anaktuvuk Pass, a low altitude pass that cuts through the Brooks Range from Bettles in the Yukon drainage to the Arctic Slope.

Miller, founder of Frontier Companies of Alaska Inc., spent two weeks staging supplies needed to establish a second Richfield Oil geophysical crew on the North Slope. He then set out on his quest, facing frigid temperatures, frequent equipment breakdowns and dangerous river crossings. It took 40 days to reach his destination – only 18 days were actual travel days, however. The rest were spent repairing equipment, waiting out bad weather and dealing with other hazards.

The Cat trip proved that the pass could be used to link to the Alaska Railroad, which increased the timeframe for shipping items to the North Slope to about seven months per year instead of a few weeks by sea. It also proved the versatility of the D7 Cat. The weight of the D8 was found to be dangerous on river crossings and the D6 too small for pulling sleds, according to a special publication from *Petroleum News* titled *Harnessing a giant: 40 years at Prudhoe Bay*.

Atlantic Refining and Richfield merged early in 1966 to become

John C. "Tennessee" Miller proved that Caterpillar tractors could travel from Fairbanks to the North Slope through Anaktuvuk Pass in 1964.

ARCO. Soon after the merger, ARCO district manager Harry Jamison persuaded Alaska Gov. Walter J. Hickel to make leases available near the Prudhoe Bay area for oil and gas leasing. Jamison thought if oil companies could lease land adjacent to Naval Petroleum Reserve No. 4, then exploration could go forward. Hickel agreed and opened seven critical tracts.

Before 1966 closed, however, the federal government put a stop to Alaska choosing any more land from the 103 million acres granted it under the statehood act. U.S. Interior Secretary Stewart Udall imposed a "land freeze" on the transfer of lands claimed by Alaska Natives until Congress sorted out their claims.

"In the face of federal guarantee that the Alaska Natives shall not be disturbed in the use and occupation of lands, I could not in good conscience allow title to pass into others' hands," Udall said in a statement. "Moreover, to permit others to acquire title to the lands the Natives are using and occupying would create an adversary against whom the Natives would not have the means of protecting themselves."

The seven tracts opened by Hickel had already been selected by the state, so those lease sales were not affected by the freeze. And a multitude of companies filed for leases on nearly 7 million acres in January 1967. As Jamison had predicted, exploration then began in earnest – although most companies drilled dry hole after dry hole, according to *Petroleum News*.

But even though they were feeling discouraged, the experts at ARCO would not give up.

"Once we asked the governor to put up those tracts, to me that was a clear signal," Jamison later recalled. "You don't renege on that obligation. Though it wasn't a legal obligation, it was a moral one."

ARCO partnered with Humble Oil, and the companies then shared maps and expertise to decide the most promising spots to sink test wells. Then 11 years after hitting its first producing well on Swanson River, ARCO hit the mother lode of crude along the Beaufort Sea coast on Alaska's North Slope.

It happened the day after Christmas. When the crew opened a rig to check the results, they were surprised by natural gas bursting into the air. When it was ignited from a 2-inch pipe, it flared 50 feet in a 30 mph wind.

"In December (1967), we hit the oil, but they did not call the official discovery date until February or March of 1968," Mangus recalled of the spudded Prudhoe Bay State No. 1 well that had been started in April 1967. "You didn't want everyone to know."

And so ARCO began 1968 with an understatement about its discovery. The company reported publicly that its State No. 1 well had a gas flow in "not a small amount."

On Feb. 17, ARCO announced that its well had struck oil and "looks extremely good." By March 13, the well had flow-tested at 1,152 barrels per day. In June, it tested at rates up to 2,415 barrels per day, and ARCO announced that its confirmation well at Sag River, seven miles away, was an oil producer, as well.

Communication between the drill site, offices in Anchorage and headquarters in the Lower 48 were rudimentary at best. Most messages were relayed via single sideband radio on a public frequency in the early days. Sometimes, when they couldn't get through on the sideband radios, the drilling team used a ham radio operator in the camp to send messages via shortwave to another operator, who then placed collect telephone calls to relay messages to management. Secrecy at that time was not a priority.

But the ARCO discovery changed the way the crew communicated. Daily updates were relayed from geologists who flew from the North Slope to Fairbanks or Barrow to give daily drilling reports over secure phone lines.

"As a result, I, or one of the other well-site geologists, had a daily round trip commute of close to a thousand miles, just to make a couple phone calls and mail two or three letters," said C.G. "Gil" Mull, who served as well-site geologist for Humble Oil on the Prudhoe Bay State No. 1 well, in a *Petroleum News* article titled "Talk far from cheap in early days."

Eventually, ARCO set up a telephone relay system in camp to

University of Alaska Fairbanks, Atlantic Richfield Collection, UAF-1982-146-12

The oil industry pumped into high gear on the North Slope after it discovered a massive oil field at Prudhoe Bay in 1968. This drilling rig is sending out a spray of steam during exploratory work in 1969. Additional wells were needed to define the limits of the field.

send secure messages. British Petroleum used a system akin to one developed during World War II to keep messages secret: code talkers. It sent one Welsh-speaking geologist to the drilling rig camp and another to its Anchorage headquarters to exchange messages in their native language.

The 1968 bonanza, with an estimated capacity of 10 billion barrels of recoverable crude, was heralded in an engineering report that stated the North Slope discovery "appears to be one of the largest known petroleum accumulations in the entire world." It covered 88,000 square miles, an area slightly larger than Idaho.

"This well was the last well that will probably be drilled on the North Slope, because everything had been dry holes," Magnus later explained about what he was thinking before that well struck oil. "And by God, when I hit it, here comes this discovery well."

Several more oil companies soon hit large pools, too, including BP Oil Corp., Mobil Oil and Phillips Petroleum.

Thus Prudhoe Bay was born. Soon the state would have nearly $1 billion in its coffers from lease sale No. 23. The total net received from the previous 22 lease sales during the state's 10-year history had amounted to $97.6 million, according to *Petroleum News*.

Oil industry experts and executives from around the world converged on Anchorage in early September 1969. They crowded into hotels and motels across the city.

Most had spent considerable time that year secretly compiling information to make the best decisions on which parcels they wanted to lease. Reports of industry espionage ran rampant, including sightings of mysterious helicopters flying over test wells on the North Slope.

Oil companies, investors, state officials and more than 150 accredited newsmen representing newspapers, magazines, radio and television from all parts of the world filled the Sydney Laurence Auditorium on Sept. 10. State troopers and armed guards stood close by, as bidders handed over sealed envelopes that contained their bids for the tracts they believed held the most promise for big oil finds.

When the 164 bids on 179 tracts were opened that morning, it became apparent that many of the bidders had formed alliances to better their chances for successful bids. And prior bids for leases on the first 22 lease sales that went anywhere from $1 to around $50 per acre were eclipsed by bids in the thousands.

The highest bids came in for Tract 57, the closest land to the Prudhoe Bay oil discoveries. The Mobil-Phillips-Standard Oil of California group bid $72.1 million and was thought to be the winner by most in the auditorium. Until the Amerada-Getty Oil envelope revealed a bid of $72.3 million, the highest bid ever offered for a U.S. lease sale. That winning bid brought in $28,233 an acre for the state, which at the end of the day collected more than $900 million, or an average of $2,132 per acre for its 23rd lease sale that totaled 412,453 acres, according to the *Anchorage Daily Times*.

The 23rd oil and gas lease sale for drilling on the North Slope was held inside the Sydney Laurence Auditorium in Anchorage and brought more than $900 million to the state. Alaska Gov. Keith Miller, holding the microphone, and Department of Natural Resources commissioner Tom Kelly, standing far right, attended.

Not all Alaskans were happy about the oil and gas lease sales as seen by this group of protestors carrying signs outside the Sydney Laurence Auditorium while the bids were being opened on Sept. 10, 1969.

"A plane had been chartered to transport the checks to the Bank of America in San Francisco, while bankers were on hand to cancel the checks from unsuccessful bidders," according to *Petroleum News*.

Once the lease sale was completed, the race was on to find the next bonanza. Oil companies used every mode of transportation to get crews and equipment to those high-priced acres – including the "Hickel Highway" out of Fairbanks.

The highway actually was the path bulldozed by Tennessee Miller and others along old Native trails across the tundra. One truck driver described the weather he encountered along the rough route as he drove a 20-ton transport truck in a convoy along that arctic ice road in 1968.

"We needed almost as much fuel to keep warm as to run the rigs," Burn Roper said in a 1970 interview for an internal British Petroleum publication, adding that the temperatures were somewhere around minus 65 degrees Fahrenheit.

"At this temperature, steel was as brittle as candy; human flesh froze in 30 seconds," Roper said. "Engines had to be kept running round the clock – from fall to spring, they never stopped."

The oil drills did not stop either. And once oil in great quantities was discovered, the race to get all the pieces in place to get it to market went into high gear.

Naval Petroleum Reserve No. 4

When Wainwright schoolteacher William Van Valin learned about an oil lake on the Arctic coast near Cape Simpson southeast of Barrow during the summer of 1914, he staked a claim. He became the first wildcatter on Alaska's North Slope, and his claim included seeps about a mile inland from Smith Bay.

Geologist Ernest de Koven Leffingwell traveled north in 1906 and spent seven years mapping the geology of what is now the Arctic National Wildlife Refuge and surveying the Arctic coastline. He shared his information with the U.S. Geological Survey, which surmised that the area might hold a great deal of petroleum, but since it was so remote, probably would be of no value.

Standard Oil Co. of California sent agents to Cape Simpson in 1921. They did find oil seepages, but the company decided other areas of the country were more accessible and decided not to continue efforts in Alaska, according to *Harnessing a Giant — 40 years at Prudhoe Bay* by *Petroleum News*.

Although prospecting permits were filed under the mining laws in 1921, President Warren G. Harding's administration withdrew large areas surrounding the seeps at Cape Simpson all the way south of the crest of the Brooks Range from oil and gas or mineral leasing in 1923. Nearly 23 million acres, or 38,000 square miles, of the Arctic Slope became the Naval Petroleum Reserve No. 4, and its creation was to ensure the World War I-era U.S. Navy would have future supplies of oil to fuel its fleet. Public Order No. 41 put about half of the Arctic Slope north of the Brooks Range off limits to commercial production. Today, that area is known as National Petroleum Reserve-Alaska.

26

Deadhorse Rises in the Arctic

Once the huge oil field was discovered in Prudhoe Bay in 1968, the race was on to build the infrastructure needed to develop the resource.

"It was like being caught completely unawares in a monstrous avalanche," said H.C. "Harry" Jamison, Richfield Oil's exploration supervisor for Alaska, in a paper written for the Alaska Geological Society Technical Conference, April 19, 2008. "We were deluged with orders, directives, requests, demands, obligations and bureaucratic nonsense."

Jamison said it was chaos as he and his crew scrambled to line up all that was needed to get down to business.

"First, we had to meet the immediate demand for action on the Slope, extension wells, airstrip construction and controls, camp expansion, construction equipment, additional aircraft, fuel supplies, seismic crews, drilling rigs, security measures and a hundred other things," he said. "What about housing several hundred, then several thousand workers? What about flying them in and out? What about finding them in the first place?"

The oil companies faced these and many other challenges as they tried to figure out how to set up operations in the frozen north. The land base that grew on the North Slope to house personnel and provide support for drilling operations, 206 miles southeast of

Deadhorse, seen here in 1969, began growing on Alaska's North Slope after oil companies discovered crude in great quantities.

Barrow, became known as Deadhorse. It was a marvel of modern engineering and eventually encompassed 29 square miles of land and 3 square miles of water.

The leaseholders of the rich arctic oil prospects also had another large problem to solve. The State of Alaska required that the Prudhoe Bay oil field be developed as one unit, not individually by the various companies that held the leases.

The 16 oil companies decided to have two companies manage the operations on the North Slope. The unusual agreement between all these companies, called The Prudhoe Unit, formed two areas within the huge oil field – one for gas and one for oil. Most of ARCO and Exxon's leases were over the gas cap and most of BP's were over the oil rim. The group decided to defer how to export and market the gas portion until a later date and concentrate on crude extraction first. This plan allowed all the lease owners to share the costs and benefits of production.

"The basic reason for 'unitizing' the Prudhoe field was to optimize recovery and equitably divide costs among working interest owners and avoid duplication of facilities," said retired BP executive George Abraham in an article titled "Owners work to unitize Prudhoe Bay" published in *Petroleum News*. "By limiting surface facilities you would also minimize possible environmental impacts."

The Prudhoe Unit agreement was so complex it took almost two years to draft. When finalized in April 1977, prior to the first barrel of oil traveling down the pipeline, it filled two volumes that contained 1,200 pages.

The companies agreed that ARCO was to operate the eastern side, and BP would operate the west side. They then developed a plan for six facilities to handle up to 1.8 million barrels per day of oil, according to *Petroleum News*.

About 70,000 tons of supplies and equipment had arrived by barge from Seattle during the summer of 1969. The next year, however, 175,000 tons on 70 barges journeyed to Prudhoe Bay. The largest sealift through icy conditions in the region's history included modules for BP's three gathering centers to separate gas and water from produced oil.

ARCO would build three centers on its side of the field, too.

The companies laid a gravel road from east to west through the heart of the oil field. Extensions off this main road later accessed gravel pads that held development wells that were numbered on the ARCO side and assigned letters on the BP side. These drilling wells would be used to drill down through 2,000 feet of permafrost and then another 6,000 feet to tap into Prudhoe's rich oil reservoir.

The population to man the wells and build the complex in Deadhorse reached 8,000 by the mid-1970s. Early residents lived in trailer units, but later moved into a permanent base camp made from modular units shipped north on barges. Two turbine generators were installed in the Central Power Station on the BP side, as well. The companies later added five more generators, which made the station the second-largest single power station in Alaska. They also placed diesel generators throughout the camp for backup.

A three-story center, often called the BP Hilton, was built and then expanded in 1976 from 90,000 to 137,000 square feet. It provided living and workspace for about 265 people. Another two 500-worker camps accommodated contractors developing the field.

Since all the pieces for the arctic city arrived on barges in stages, the residents in the northern oil field had no clue what the finished project would look like.

"They were like jigsaw pieces of a bigger whole that we never saw until it was completed," said longtime BP construction veteran Bill Lorenz in an article titled "BP, ARCO prepare to tame an elephant," in *Harnessing a Giant: 40 Years at Prudhoe Bay.*

Anchorage engineer Robert "Bob" Bell, of Bell & Associates, was hired to oversee construction of the ARCO complex at Prudhoe Bay. Bell worked closely with engineering firms to build the facilities and infrastructure, including roads and a causeway that jutted into the Beaufort Sea so cargo could be offloaded.

University of Alaska Fairbanks, Atlantic Richfield Collection, UAF-1982-146-19

A support helicopter hovers over a "cat train" making its way to Deadhorse with modular buildings in 1969.

The construction crews had to work fast due to weather and a short summer season. Temperatures in the winter could dip to more than 100-degrees-below zero wind chill factor.

"We'd finish a section of roadway and the engineers wouldn't have designs ready for the next section," Bell said in an article for *Petroleum News*. "We would build a mile of road, praying our work would be close to the designs, and a week later, we'd get the drawings."

Six months after the Prudhoe Bay discovery, Landon Kelly, an oilfield services veteran, joined ARCO to oversee building of production facilities to process the billions of barrels of oil that would be coming out of the wells. One of two production engineers who shared the job of North Slope coordinator, he made sure the eastern half of the field ran smoothly.

"If anybody had a problem, they'd let me know about it, whether it was injuries or bears, whatever," Kelly later recalled.

But the actual pipeline could not be built until the Alaska Native land claim issue was settled. The oil companies began putting pressure on government officials to settle those claims.

"Suddenly, the game changed," said Byron Mallot, Alaska's first Native lieutenant governor, in a PBS documentary about the pipeline days. "The Alaska Native community went from the prospect of settling our land claims for mere pennies an acre and no land, to very quickly what we were able to ultimately achieve – 44 million acres of land and a billion dollars."

But even after the Alaska Native Claims Settlement Act was passed in 1971, it took a few more years for the dust to settle between Congress, federal agencies, the state and environmentalists before the oil industry actually began construction on that project.

People headed north by the droves, however, in anticipation of work on the pipeline. The *Anchorage Daily News* reported on a dire labor problem in November 1969.

"The alarm was sounded again on the job situation with labor officials reporting an unemployment crisis forecast in October developing with a continued influx of out-of-state laborers," the paper stated. The article added that unemployment numbers were up 20 percent from the year before as workers were "lured north by a 'boom' initiated by the developing North Slope oil fields."

Following the passage of the Alaska Native Claims Settlement Act in 1971, planning continued for the construction of the trans-Alaska oil pipeline. But it took another three years for Congress to approve its construction.

University of Alaska Fairbanks, Atlantic Richfield Collection, UAF-1982-146-17

The Lockheed Hercules C-130, seen here landing at Prudhoe Bay, soon gained a reputation for being one of the most highly desired planes for use on Alaska's North Slope. By the end of 1968, there were 11 C-130s operating from Fairbanks to the North Slope, routinely carrying 24-ton loads at a cost of $4,500 per trip.

27

PLANS FOR A PIPELINE PROGRESS

Once the largest oil field in North America was discovered, the big question became how to get that oil to market. Some thought it could be transported by giant tankers or oil-carrying submarines. Some thought a 2,900-mile pipeline across Canada to the Midwest might be the answer. Yet others believed an 800-mile line south to an ice-free port in Southern Alaska, where ocean-going oil tankers could be filled, would be the best bet.

Humble Oil, BP and ARCO supported the first option. The double-hulled SS *Manhattan* had proved an ice-breaking tanker could travel through the Northwest Passage and Alaska Arctic when it made a much-publicized round trip from the East Coast in the fall of 1969. The 115,000-ton tanker made another successful voyage the next spring. Further analysis proved this method was not commercially viable on a year-round basis, however, due to cost and unpredictable offshore ice conditions.

One company suggested nuclear-powered submarine tankers. Others pitched the idea of building a railroad from Prudhoe Bay to Alberta, Canada, where pipeline facilities already existed. Ideas for tanker aircraft, dirigibles and other airships were floated, also.

When the air cleared, two pipeline ideas proved most popular. One from Prudhoe Bay south to Valdez, or one that ran from the North Slope into Canada, via the Mackenzie River Valley to Alberta, to connect to the existing pipeline system that went over to Chicago and the Great Lakes industrial belt.

Studies showed a hot-oil Prudhoe-Valdez pipeline was the most economical. It crossed fewer permafrost areas, so would disturb the terrain less, and crossed fewer streams and rivers, too. The trans-Alaska route also was half the length of a line to Canada, so it could be built sooner and at half the cost, according to an article titled "Producers weigh many marketing options" in *Petroleum News*.

Alaska Gov. Keith Miller and most Alaskans recognized the benefits for Alaska with building an all-Alaska pipeline south and agreed with the proposal to build a terminal in Valdez. The oil companies all got on board with the idea and focused their energies in that direction. They estimated their proposed plan for a 48-inch diameter 800-mile long line that could carry 1.5 million barrels of oil a day at $900 million – the most expensive project ever proposed by private industry at the time. When completed, the final cost actually came in at more than $8 billion due to the delay in its building, the hurried timeframe to finally construct the line and stringent environmental constraints.

Although oil companies were not given the green light to build the pipeline until 1974, they laid much of the groundwork in advance. In October 1968, three major oil companies formed a joint venture to

After studying several ideas for getting North Slope crude to market, the oil industry decided that building an 800-mile-long pipeline from Prudhoe Bay to Valdez was the best option.

Alaska State Library, Trans-Alaska Pipeline Construction Collection, ASL-P2-5-30 organize, design and plan the pipeline to transport oil from Prudhoe Bay to market as soon as all the legal hurdles had been addressed.

The new enterprise was called Trans-Alaska Pipeline System, and it included BP, ARCO and Humble Oil. TAPS invited other companies to join them, which led to the inclusion of Mobil Alaska Pipeline Co., Amerada Hess Pipeline Co., Phillips Alaska Pipeline Corp. and Unocal Pipeline Co.

Soon after it formed, TAPS faced a few legal issues that slowed its progress on the pipeline. Congress passed the National Environmental Policy Act in 1969, which required an environmental impact statement for major federal actions that might affect the quality of the human environment. At the same time, Native villages filed suit in federal court to halt construction of a haul road to the North Slope, as it and a pipeline would go across land they claimed was ancestral.

"Stevens Village was located directly in the proposed path of the pipeline," said Byron Mallott, Alaska's first Native lieutenant governor, in an interview when he represented First Alaskans Institute. "And the people of Stevens Village said, 'we can't let this happen. That until our claims are settled, until we have certainty about what we own and what we don't own and how this will affect us and our children, we can't allow this to happen.'"

Three conservation groups – Wilderness Society, Friends of the Earth and the Environmental Defense Fund Inc. – also filed a federal suit asking the U.S. District Court to bar construction of the pipeline until Interior Secretary Walter J. Hickel "complies fully with provisions of the National Environmental Policy Act of 1969," according to a story in the *Anchorage Daily Times* on March 28, 1970.

"I saw no recourse," then-director of the Wilderness Society Stewart Brandborg told a PBS reporter in an interview later. "If the environmental movement hadn't challenged the pipeline, we would have ended with damage beyond any description."

A federal judge in Washington, D.C., enjoined both the pipeline and access road in April 1970, ruling neither could be built until the Interior Department heeded the environmental policy act, which required a detailed report on the pipeline's ecological effects before the department could issue a building permit. Interior Secretary Hickel said even without the court order, his department would block the pipeline until it was proven safe.

Gov.-elect William A. Egan visited Hickel in Washington, D.C., in November 1970 and told an Anchorage reporter that Hickel had said Alaska could expect a "significant development" in the pipeline matter within 10 days. A week later, the night before Thanksgiving, President Richard Nixon called his interior secretary to the White House and fired him on the spot.

Popular opinion speculated Hickel had been on the verge of announcing that Alyeska Pipeline Service Co., organized that year from TAPS to oversee construction of the pipeline, had met federal engineering and environmental stipulations for the project. Some concern was tempered when Acting Interior Secretary Fred Russell extended the 1966 land freeze until June 30, 1971, to allow Congress to settle the Native land claims issue and avoid lengthy battles that might interfere with building the pipeline.

Anchorage Museum Rasmuson Center. Steve McCutcheon Collection. AMRC-AMRC-B1990-014-5-Pol-16-4

The land on which the line would go was part of the acreage claimed by Alaska's Native people, so a right of way corridor needed to be settled. Alaska Federation of Natives leaders said they might go to court to protect their rights to the land.

"We don't want to block the pipeline,"

Longtime Alaskan and U.S. Interior Secretary Walter J. Hickel may have been on the verge of giving a green light to the oil companies to build the Trans-Alaska Oil Pipeline when President Richard M. Nixon fired him on Thanksgiving Eve 1970.

Native leaders, like Eben Hopson of Barrow, wanted the Alaska Native land claims issue settled before pipeline construction began.

said then-AFN executive director Eben Hopson in a newspaper article on Jan. 2, 1971. "We're protecting our own rights, which heretofore have not been extinguished by Congress. We've got to protect our own rights – it has nothing to do with the pipeline."

At that time, Native groups claimed 360 million of Alaska's 375 million acres. They also sought a monetary settlement of around $500 million and a royalty from any future gas and oil that came out of the ground.

It took another year, but finally all parties came to an agreement on the land claims issue. Congress passed and President Nixon signed the Native Land Claims Settlement Act in December 1971. That cleared the way for federal and state governments to grant essential licenses and permits. Three months later, the Department of Interior released the final environmental impact statement that stressed the need for domestic and Alaska oil. Then Secretary of the Interior Rogers C.B. Morton declared the trans-Alaska oil pipeline to be in the national interest, which allowed the federal injunction against the pipeline to be lifted.

But an appeals court ruled the proposed right of way and special land use permits for the pipeline did not comply with the Mineral Leasing Act. In some places the proposed right of way exceeded the 54-foot width allowed under the act. Congress would need to approve such a right of way, according to a government document titled "History of Trans Alaska Pipeline System."

So more debate raged over the pipeline for a couple more years while Congress heard from proponents, opponents and environmentalists. And many Alaskans thought the environmentalists from the Lower 48 had gone overboard. Howard Weaver, then a reporter for the *Anchorage Daily News*, summed up the opinion of many who lived in the Last Frontier.

"We weren't hungry for, for vast open spaces. We had them," Weaver told a reporter for PBS in an interview about the pipeline. "You know, that's what we had plenty of. What we didn't have plenty of was decent high schools, flush toilets in bush villages. You know, those are nice things, too."

Environmentalists were worried that the oil industry would dig trenches and bury pipe just like they had all around the world. They believed that approach would harm Alaska's delicate arctic region where permafrost would be melted by hot-oil pipes and cause massive environmental damage.

Hickel, who served as Alaska's governor from December 1966 to January 1969, and then U.S. Secretary of the Interior from January

University of Alaska Fairbanks, James Edwin Morrow Collection, UAF-1977-59-52

Environmentalists and conservationists wanted to limit development in Alaska's northern wilderness, but many Alaskans thought they had enough wilderness areas in the vast state and developing the North Slope could be done in an environmentally responsible way.

1969 until November 1970, assured all that Alaskans would not allow the oil companies to destroy the pristine environment in the north.

"... I can guarantee that we will not approve any design based on the old faulty concept of build now and repair later," Hickel said.

The battle over building the pipeline continued until October 1973 when, in retaliation for American support of Israel in the Yom Kippur War, Arab states declared an embargo on oil shipments to America. That tipped the balance in favor of a new domestic source of oil.

Democratic Sen. Henry Jackson of Washington believed that America was importing too much oil from overseas, which subjected the United States to blackmail.

"... the man in the street wants to ask, 'well, if we can import it from the Middle East and every other place in the world that's substantially insecure, why can't we import it from Alaska?'" Jackson asked in a television interview at the time.

There's no doubt the oil embargo put pressure on politicians to move the pipeline project forward, but oil companies also were more than ready to begin building it. They had spent billions developing Prudhoe Bay and planning for the pipeline. The industry said it was losing $22 million a day in revenue while the oil sat in the ground.

Nixon signed the Trans-Alaska Pipeline Authorization Act on Nov. 16, 1973, after Vice President Spiro Agnew cast a vote for the act and broke a deadlock of 49 to 49 in the Senate.

The act was intended "to insure that, because of ... the national interest in early delivery of North Slope oil to domestic markets, the trans-Alaska oil pipeline be constructed promptly without further administrative or judicial delay or impediment."

The act directed Secretary of the Interior Morton to authorize the federal right of way for the pipeline, which he signed on Jan. 23, 1974. The state followed suit four months later, and issued its right of way lease on May 3.

Now it was time to build a pipeline through one of the most remote and challenging regions in the world.

Workers Blaze Haul Road

Alyeska Pipeline Service Co. needed a road on which to haul supplies and equipment to build the trans-Alaska oil pipeline. So, in anticipation of rights of way being granted, it had tons of road-building equipment and camp units placed along the proposed route in 1969-1970. The road would start at the Yukon River – at the end of the 53-mile Elliott Highway from Fairbanks to Livengood – and go about 360 miles north to Prudhoe Bay. Ice roads were built across the Yukon River each winter to keep supplies moving.

Although the Alaska Native Claims Settlement Act passed in 1971, Congress didn't give the OK to the rights of way permit until the end of 1973. As soon as the permit was received, construction of the road went into high gear.

From late January to mid-April 1974, hundreds of workers moved 34,000 tons of material and machinery into northern Alaska via airplanes and trucks. Five new camps were constructed and seven closed camps were opened. Workers built temporary airstrips on snow and ice, which would be replaced by permanent gravel strips in the spring.

They actually started the haul road in April. With more than 3,400 workers battling temperatures that dipped to minus 68 degrees Fahrenheit, crews built north and south simultaneously from eight sections until they all connected, according to an article titled "Fast and furious construction" in *Petroleum News*. A squadron of more than 60 aircraft, from fixed-wing transports to helicopters, carried supplies across the northern skies to help with the road-building project. Industry records show more than 127,000 flights were logged, an average of 700 flights per day, which carried 160,000 tons of material and 8.5 million gallons of fuel to power construction equipment and camps.

Trucks then carried more than 31 million cubic yards of rock to bring the 28-foot-wide haul road up to state secondary road standards. Completed on Sept. 29, 1974, it took 154 days to build that road through the wilderness – although the $30 million permanent 2,295-foot bridge across the Yukon River wasn't finished until 1975.

"The 3-million-manhour-single-summer project was unprecedented in Alaska history," a *Petroleum News* article stated, and it cost $185 million.

The state renamed the North Slope Haul Road in 1981 for James B. Dalton, a native-born Alaskan and engineer who supervised construction of the Distant Early Warning Line in Alaska during the 1950s. The system of radar stations, which stretched from the Arctic regions of Alaska and Canada to the Faroe Islands, Greenland and Iceland, was set up to detect incoming Soviet bombers during the Cold War era.

Dalton's father, Jack, was an early Alaska pioneer, explorer and adventurer who had established a successful toll road through Southeast Alaska to the gold fields during the Klondike gold rush days.

Anchorage Museum at Rasmuson Center, McCutcheon Collection, AMRC-b90-14-3-701

Road construction crews found more than rocks, dirt and frozen tundra while building the Haul Road. Foreman Pete Peterson holds a mastodon tusk they found in a road cut opposite Five Mile Camp in Alaska's Interior on April 28, 1974.

Right: Construction crews carved a rough road from just outside of Fairbanks to Prudhoe Bay in order to haul supplies for the pipeline through hundreds of miles in Alaska's wilderness. This photo shows the Haul Road dropping from Atigun Pass north to Atigun Valley in the Brooks Range. It later was renamed the Dalton Highway.

Below: Culverts were installed to provide crossroad drainage along the Haul Road, as seen in this photograph near Old Man Camp south of the Arctic Circle near Kanuti National Wildlife Refuge.

Anchorage Museum at Rasmuson Center, McCutcheon Collection, AMRC-b90-14-3-41

Anchorage Museum at Rasmuson Center, McCutcheon Collection, AMRC-b90-14-3-669

Once Congress approved the construction of the trans-Alaska oil pipeline, the oil companies began frantically getting equipment and supplies up the Haul Road to Prudhoe Bay. This line of Caterpillar bulldozers at Galbraith Lake in the Brooks Range were hauled north at a cost of $1.50 per pound, according to information with the photograph. That comes to about $200,000 each.

A convoy of trucks travels along the frozen John River from Bettles just before completion of the Haul Road into Alaska's Interior on March 29, 1974.

Chaining the trucks so they could cross mountainous regions along the Haul Road was not an easy task, as seen in this photo taken near Wickersham Dome on April 15, 1975.

Before the oil industry was given the go-ahead to build the trans-Alaska oil pipeline, it spent several years testing the soil along the route it proposed for the construction. This photo shows a drilling crew testing soil at Chandalar Shelf just south of Atigun Pass, the highest point on the Haul Road.

PRUDHOE BAY OIL

28

PIPELINE SNAKES ACROSS ALASKA

"One of the largest petroleum accumulations known to the world today," newspaper headlines shouted in July 1968, but the oil industry did not receive the official go-ahead to build the Alaska pipeline until spring 1974. It worked tirelessly behind the scenes during those six years, however, to be ready for the green light to build.

Prudhoe Bay is located in the one-third of Alaska that conjures up what most people incorrectly think about the entire 49th state. The Arctic has sub-zero winter temperatures, ice and snow, polar bears, walruses, the midnight sun and a sizeable population of Eskimos. It's not an ideal spot to build anything, let alone the largest pipeline in human history.

The eight-member Trans Alaska Pipeline System created the Alyeska Pipeline Service Co. to oversee construction activities for the massive project. Alyeska then developed the pipeline design and specifications in coordination with many federal and state agencies, including the U.S. Geological Survey, Bureau of Land Management, U.S. Army Corps of Engineers and the Alaska Department of Fish and Game.

They drilled more than 3,000 bore holes between Prudhoe Bay and the ice-free port of Valdez, from which they took 30,000 core samples to study soil conditions along the route, according to oil industry records. Experts studied the best way to cross three mountain ranges – the Brooks, Alaska and Chugach – and hundreds of streams and rivers. The final design made sure the line could withstand a magnitude 8.5 Richter Scale earthquake, too, as the pipe would cross three faults – Denali, McGinnis Glacier and Donnelly Dome.

Alyeska altered its plans as it performed tests on everything from the earthquake zones to permafrost. After its analysis was complete, the industry decided the best route would take the pipeline through Dietrich Pass, later named Atigun Pass, on to Rampart Canyon and Thompson Pass to Valdez.

Along with many other considerations, the planners noted the pipe would be buried wherever possible, bypass geologic hazards and population centers, be raised above permafrost where needed and avoid sites of antiquities and important fish-spawning or wildlife areas, according to a *Petroleum News* article titled "Pipeline tops for moving oil to market."

The pipeline design was unprecedented in human history. Not only did it have to carry 1.5 million barrels of oil a day, the pipe had to fit into three different soil conditions: normal soil where it could be buried normally; discontinuous permafrost where it could be buried if adequately insulated; and continuous permafrost where it would need to rest on an elevated rack, whose pilings were constantly cooled to prevent heating and thawing of the permafrost. Oil, which comes out of the ground at 150 to 180 degrees Fahrenheit, would thaw the frozen soil, cause the pipe to buckle and break, and lead to ecological damage.

The system also had to withstand the combined stress of internal pressure of thermal, bending and seismic forces. Not only that, the pipe required anti-corrosive coating and an outside layer of concrete to anchor it to stream bottoms. All buried sections needed anti-corrosion coating and other protection. Above ground sections required thermal insulation to slow the drop in oil temperature in case the pipeline shut down.

"We have spent tens of millions of dollars in design to meet the stringent challenges of the Alaskan wilderness," ARCO president

Anchorage Museum at Rasmuson Center, McCutcheon Collection, AMRC-b90-14-3-1326

This storage yard at Mile 82 of the Richardson Highway near Fairbanks was one of three that held thousands of pieces of pipe for the massive Alaska pipeline project.

Thornton E. Bradshaw told a Congressional committee in March 1973, prior to Congress approving the pipeline construction. "The trans-Alaska pipeline will be easily the safest and best-engineered pipeline in the world."

The massive pipeline project called for 69,000 lengths of pipe, which cost around $120 million, and came from three different Japanese companies. The strong pipe, with minimum yield strengths of nearly 70,000 pounds per square inch, was stored at huge storage sites in Fairbanks, Valdez and Prudhoe Bay.

Once the federal and state governments had signed off on their rights of way permitting for construction of the trans-Alaska oil pipeline, Alyeska then had to obtain more than 1,300 federal and state permits to construct and operate the pipeline.

The company began hauling in road-building equipment and temporary housing in January 1974, while the ground was still frozen. The tundra would be too soft to drive on in the spring. Convoys of equipment on snow tractors drove north across hardened snow roads and an ice bridge over the Yukon River to reach seven construction camps that had been dormant since 1970. Hundreds of cargo planes landed on frozen lakes and dropped off more material, according to James Roscow, author of *800 Miles to Valdez: The Building of the Alaska Pipeline*.

Left: Prior to the building of the Yukon River bridge in 1974-1975, trucks loaded with supplies for the oil companies drove cross the river when it was frozen. Building a permanent crossing over the Yukon River was a major endeavor finished late in 1975. Named for E.L. Patton, former president of the Alyeska Pipeline Service Company, the bridge carried both the pipeline and vehicle traffic on the Dalton Highway that connects Fairbanks to Deadhorse. It is the only bridge across the Yukon in Alaska.

Below: State highway workers drill to test the depth of the ice along the Yukon River ice bridge in 1970. The crew placed markers along the "bridge" so traffic would not veer off onto thinner ice.

PRUDHOE BAY OIL

Above: Air-cushioned vehicles served as ferries for equipment and personnel across the Yukon River during summer and thin-ice periods.

Below: When not in use, the air-cushioned vehicles were stored on land.

Alyeska awarded contracts to build a 360-mile road, which used 31 million cubic yards of gravel, from Livengood to the North Slope. Contractors began the project on April 29, and at the peak of the effort, had more than 3,400 workers deployed from the Yukon River to Prudhoe Bay to build the road. A massive airlift of 170,000 flights was required to bring in needed materials and equipment before the road was finished on Sept. 29, according to oil industry records.

Then Alyeska appointed two construction management contractors to oversee all the subcontractors on the project. It hired Bechtel Corp. of San Francisco to head up building the pipeline and Fluor Alaska Inc. to manage construction of the pumping stations and Valdez Marine Terminal. These two companies managed a series of subcontractors that had responsibility for separate sections of the pipeline.

Anchorage Museum at Rasmuson Center, McCutcheon Collection, AMRC-b90-14-3-262

Alyeska Service Co. set up 29 temporary construction camps, like this one at Toolik Lake on the North Slope. Each camp was fully self-sufficient with long, modular buildings and laid out on gravel beds that later were removed.

Above: The U.S. Coast Guard Cutter *Soris* broke through the ice to Prudhoe Bay to allow a sealift of barges to bring construction material and supplies for the pipeline project to Prudhoe Bay in 1975.

Below: The Alaska Railroad carried much of the equipment used to build the trans-Alaska oil pipeline to Fairbanks. It then was trucked up the Haul Road to the North Slope.

The pipeline Haul Road had nonstop traffic as trucks carried materials and supplies north to build the trans-Alaska oil pipeline.

Alyeska set up 29 temporary self-sufficient construction camps from Pump Station 1 to the marine terminal in Valdez. Two more camps were added later. The camps consisted of prefabricated modular buildings either flown or trucked in and set atop thick beds of gravel. Pump station camps, which housed more than 250 people, cost $6 million to build. Mainland camps cost $10 million.

The camps had beds for 16,500 people. Workers called the camps collectively "Skinny City," because they dotted 800 miles of wilderness but each camp was only a few hundred feet wide, according to historian Dermot Cole, author of *Amazing Pipeline Stories*. Once the camps weren't needed anymore, the buildings and gravel were removed and the areas re-vegetated.

Three million tons of pipe, machinery, spare parts, fuel and food were hauled in during the two-and-a-half-year construction period. And the haul road had bumper-to-bumper traffic, according to those who drove it.

"It was pretty much insanity," said pipeline truck driver Dave Smallwood in a 2006 PBS documentary by Mark Davis titled "The

American Experience: The Alaska Pipeline." "It didn't really pay to pass the guy ahead of you."

Smallwood said truck drivers basically lived on the road, taking one load after another to the North Slope.

"We didn't have a scale. We didn't have logbooks," he said. "Virtually just lived in the trucks and ate in the camps."

The haul road was wide enough for rigs coming from different directions to barely slide past each other.

"If you met another truck that didn't know you was coming, if you just clicked your mirrors, you'd call that a good pass," Smallwood said. "And the motto was crowd the other guy, not the ditch. Because you'd end up over in the ditch, laying on your side. It was a long way down in a lot of spots."

After waiting so long for all the legal issues to be settled, the oil industry pushed fast and furious to get the pipeline built within the three-year timeframe mandated by Congress. The massive undertaking involved tens of thousands of people working in extreme temperatures and conditions. In an effort to meet the deadline, project managers divided the route into five sections and built them simultaneously.

On March 27, 1975, crews laid the first pipe at the Tonsina River crossing of the Richardson Highway, 75 road miles north of Valdez. Several 40-foot sections of pipe had been welded together and coated in concrete prior to the ceremony.

Anchorage Museum at Rasmuson Center, McCutcheon Collection, AMRC-b90-14-3-1292

The first pipe for the trans-Alaska oil pipeline, seen in this photograph, was laid at Tonsina River near Valdez on March 27, 1975.

Left: This photo, taken north of Mile Five Camp in 1974, shows bulldozers clearing the right of way in order to build the Alaska oil pipeline.

Right: Strings of pipe were laid along the right of way, as seen in this photo taken north of the Yukon River. The pipe then was welded, taped and buried.

The race then was on to weld 800 miles of pipe together, 40 feet at a time.

Laying the pipe took several steps. The right of way first needed to be cleared with chainsaws, bulldozers and scrapers that followed a roughly laid out previously surveyed route. Then a group of surveyors and engineers followed to see if the pipeline could go in that spot or if soil conditions necessitated it be moved to another. They had authorization to move the line 200 feet in either direction if needed.

Once a section was deemed fit, augers and drillers made holes for foundations for supports to hold the pipe if it was to be placed above ground. Other crews filled the holes with water and dirt, which froze solid, to hold the semi-circular supports in place. Next the pipeline

PRUDHOE BAY OIL

Alaska State Library, Trans-Alaska Pipeline Construction Collection, ASL-P2-6-14

Above: Crews lowered sections of pipe into ditches, like here in the Brooks Range about 175 miles south of Prudhoe Bay. They bent the pipe to conform to the contours of the ditches along the landscape.

Right: Eighty check valves were installed at this uphill section of the pipeline laid in the Chugach Mountains on the way to Valdez. The mechanical valves close automatically in the event of pressure loss in the line upstream of the valve to prevent the flow of oil in the wrong direction.

Anchorage Museum at Rasmuson Center, McCutcheon Collection, AMRC-b90-14-3-276

Above: The pipeline was placed on "shoes," or supports, along the above-ground sections of the route from Prudhoe Bay to Valdez.

Below: Sometimes workers had to construct concrete bedding for the pipeline, as seen here in the Atigun Pass of the Brooks Range.

Anchorage Museum at Rasmuson Center, McCutcheon Collection, AMRC-b90-14-3-476

Left: Construction workers put special insulation on pipe sections buried in permafrost areas.

Below: Workers placed elongated supports at the construction site at Denali Fault north of Paxson along the Richardson Highway to prevent earthquake damage to the pipeline.

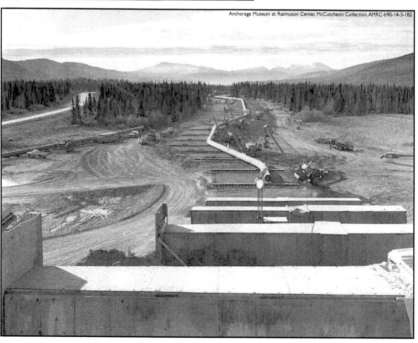

Left: Workers weighted the pipe in some areas so it would not float, as seen in this photograph taken on May 15, 1975, near Pump Station 12 near Mile 64.5 of the Richardson Highway.

Below: "Pigs," like the one pictured here, go through the pipeline to clean and gather information about the condition of the pipe.

Right: Special pipeline bridges, like this one over Hammond River, had to be built. The 800-mile pipeline crosses 34 major streams or rivers and nearly 500 minor ones.

Below: Many pipeline construction camps had landing strips, like this photo shows at Galbraith Lake with a plane taxiing in the distance.

PIPELINE SNAKES ACROSS ALASKA

This aerial view shows Pump Station 5, one of 11 pump stations along the pipeline. It is a relief station with a mechanism to relieve pressure that builds up in the pipeline as the oil descends down Atigun Pass.

sections were carried in 40- or 80-foot segments by crane or sideboom to the location, lowered into place and welded together.

More than half the line was built above ground, and about 380 miles were buried in stretches of varying length in deep ditches, insulated with gravel padding and covered with dirt. In areas where unstable soil was present, but the pipeline had to be buried to accommodate wildlife or road crossings, the pipe was refrigerated to prevent thawing.

Senior project manager Frank Moolin Jr. became known for his work ethic and hard-driving style. Moolin, who had worked on refinery projects in Singapore and the construction of the Bay Area Rail Transit System in California, was the first person on the job in the morning and the last to leave in the evening, according to several sources.

"He demands total dedication, saying, 'Your wife had a baby; so what?'" reported *Engineering News-Record* when it chose him as the construction industry's Man of the Year in 1976.

Moolin initiated a contest, the Alyeska Sweepstakes, where each of the five contractors competed to see how much of their share of the line was completed on time. He also canceled Bechtel's contract as management contractor of the pipeline portion of construction because he thought it was adding too much bureaucracy between Alyeska and the other contractors. It was "one of the most humiliating defeats" in the history of Bechtel, according to historian Dermot Cole.

The massive scale of the project put strains on resources, too.

"Housing, telephones, electricity, everything was in short supply, or no supply," assistant project manager Bill Fowler said in a PBS documentary.

More than 25,000 people were working on the pipeline project by late summer 1975. A *Time Magazine* article in June showed a man holding a check for nearly $1,500 for one week's work on the project, which pushed many people in the Lower 48 to head north in search

Anchorage Museum at Rasmuson Center, McCutcheon Collection, AMRC-b90-14-3-444

Pipeline workers may have earned great wages, but they also endured extremely cold conditions, as this photo of a piece of equipment coated in hoar frost shows.

Workers on the pipeline ate well in the camp mess halls, as seen in this picture with thick steaks on the kitchen grill taken at Prudhoe Bay.

of their piece of the pipeline pie. That was three to four times as much as they could make anywhere else in the country.

The pipeline system was built entirely with unionized labor. Every worker was guaranteed 40 hours per week of pay, even if they couldn't work due to bad weather. And no strikes were permitted by a labor agreement between the unions and Alyeska.

Alyeska not only paid high wages, it provided the best food and housing and other amenities to keep its labor force happy. Those high wages created a boomtown atmosphere in both Fairbanks and Anchorage. Unemployment plummeted to zero in the early days of construction, and many Alaskans also left their old jobs to take advantage of the boom.

Workers on average spent a week on and a week off, or two weeks on and two weeks off, laboring 12 hours a day, seven days a week in a nearly flat, treeless land to build the pipeline. They had to adjust to a totally different environment from their lives before the pipeline. Many could not make the adjustment, and as a result turnover was high. More than 70,000 people worked on at least a portion of the pipeline. Those who managed to hang on had to get used to the extremes of the Arctic.

The sun never rises for 56 days in winter, but twilight does provide enough light to drive without headlights during the day. Winter temperatures drop to minus 60 degrees Fahrenheit, but wind chill can take it to minus 135. Then there is daylight 24 hours a day and temperatures of 70 degrees above and higher from mid-April to mid-August.

When workers went off duty, they headed to the big cities and played hard. They spent their hard-earned wages with abandon, and crime rates increased dramatically.

"It was like a circus every night," Fairbanks police officer J.B. Carnahan later recalled. "People coming to town with three, four, five thousand dollars of cash in their pockets. Suddenly, women that we'd never seen around town before were appearing from places like Florida and New York and suddenly we had reports of gambling going on."

Major organized crime also found its way to Alaska. Newspapers covered many stories about gambling and prostitution.

"We've got 25,000 construction workers earning $100,000 bucks a year in a place where there are 10 men to every woman, you know, you don't

Alaska State Library, Pipeline Impact Collection, ASL-P17-8247

The bar district along Second Avenue in Fairbanks filled with pipeline workers who came to town to spend wages earned on the North Slope.

Fairbanks filled with people hoping to get jobs on the pipeline in the early 1970s. This group of union electricians, standing in front of Union Hall on Sixth Avenue, had traveled together from Boston.

exactly need an MBA to figure that one out," said former *Anchorage Daily News* reporter Howard Weaver in "The Alaska Pipeline," a PBS documentary.

It didn't take long for the number of workers streaming into Alaska to outnumber the amount of jobs available. Reports in newspapers painted a picture of blocks-long lines of men standing outside the Teamster, Labor and Operating Engineers halls. Many had no choice but to return to the Lower 48 when they didn't get hired. Others heard that if they bribed officials they might increase their chances for jobs on the pipeline.

Teamster Al Fleming offered his first two weeks pay to a Teamster insider and within a few days he had a job in the organization's warehouse in Fairbanks. He later told PBS that his new job, which paid $1,000 a week, changed his life.

Gang-style murders also became associated with the Teamsters Union in Fairbanks, which controlled the majority of the labor and supplies for the pipeline. Two Teamster leaders were murdered in

Prices for housing skyrocketed during the early pipeline years as demand exceeded supply. Some Alaska residents cashed in and rented out empty bedrooms, basements, travel trailers and sheds for exhorbitant prices. One two-bedroom home in Fairbanks housed 45 pipeline workers who shared beds on a rotating schedule for $40 each per week, according to Dermot Cole in his book, *Amazing Pipeline Stories*.

1976 while investigating drug activity on the pipeline project.

Harry Pettus and Jack "Red" Martin, employed at the North Star Terminals, mysteriously disappeared about a week apart in late July 1976. They weren't officials of Teamsters Local 959 but were considered top-ranked in the hierarchy of the union, according to an *Anchorage Times* article about the murders.

"Speculation at the time of their disappearances was that both were associated with an extensive drug network thought to serve trans-Alaska pipeline camps," the article stated.

Many people headed north hoping to cash in on the pipeline boom, including these street merchants who were selling pipes, clothes, jewelry and more on College Road in Fairbanks.

"Others thought Pettus' death might have been related to a power struggle over command of the warehouse and its 250 employees at the North Star Terminals."

Martin's badly decomposed body was found in August in a shallow ditch along a highway north of Fairbanks. Pettus' body was found in May the next year only a few miles away from Martin's dumpsite. Both men had been shot in the head.

A three-man taskforce headed by Alaska State Trooper investigators followed up leads, but most led to dead ends. Popular opinion thought the men were involved in the illegal drug trade, even though drugs and alcohol were not allowed in the camps. But no one enforced the rules, and dealing was big business.

Some pipeline workers, like welder's helper Larry Houle,

Mainstream stores like Hoyt's Jewelry on Second Avenue in Fairbanks offered flashy gold nugget and diamond watchbands, money clips, cuff links and rings to those pipeline workers coming to town flush with cash.

smuggled booze in for their own enjoyment and found it was a great source for extra income. Houle said he'd bring it into camp by the truckload and turn a tidy profit from bootlegging his whiskey.

"I kept pretty good records of this, and I might spend six bucks on a bottle of R&R, and I'd turn around and sell that for about $25," he told a PBS reporter. "But the demand was huge, and I took advantage of that."

The Teamsters became quite powerful during the pipeline days. The *Anchorage Daily News* won a Pulitzer Prize for a 15-part series on the rise of Teamsters Local 959 and its influence on state politics. The union, at one point, was banking $1 million a week in dues from a steady stream of workers heading north to find jobs.

"It was like a gold rush," officer Carnahan said in "The Alaska Pipeline." "We had had people from almost every country and from every walk of life. Plus, along with that, you had gamblers and crooks and ladies of the evening. Everybody who could had some piece of that pipeline."

Construction of the pipeline took a little more than two years to complete and came in at $8 billion, almost 10 times the original amount estimated by the industry in 1968. Much of the overrun came from the rushed timeframe for construction, engineering difficulties due to environmental concerns and the harsh conditions found working in remote Alaska.

Project manager Bill Fowler told PBS that he had spent $10,000 to charter an airplane to deliver a $50 part for a Caterpillar tractor to get a piece of equipment back in service.

"How many dollars a day were they spending – $30 million dollars a day, $20 million dollars a day?" Fowler said. "And the production is being held up because of a widget? You know, it doesn't matter what it takes to get the widget, go get the widget."

The highly skilled welders of Union 798 out of Tulsa, Okla., cost a pretty penny, too. The quality of the welding done on the Alaska pipeline had to be perfect as it was inspected more than any other pipeline project in history. The precise work of the "798ers" was legendary.

"A lot of people can weld, but can you make that perfect

Skilled welders set to work welding pieces of pipe together to build the trans-Alaska oil pipeline. Those belonging to Union 798 out of Tulsa, Okla., were considered the best welders in the business.

Cowboy hats on oil workers from Oklahoma and Texas were a common sight in Alaska during the pipeline construction years.

weld, every time, every day, 10 hours a day, month after month after month?" asked pipeline welder Jimmy Pedigo during a PBS documentary on the pipeline. "You've got a lot of people that can write real pretty. And then some people can't. They can just write to get by. That's, that's the difference. To make a good pipeline welder you've got to have that penmanship."

The 798ers were known to be talented, arrogant and "prima donnas." But they also gained reputations as brawlers by tearing up mess halls, fighting with security guards and alienating most of those with whom they worked. Alaska State Troopers sometimes had to be flown to camps to break up small riots. By 1977, toward the project's end, bumper stickers reflected the attitude of most Alaskans toward the pipeline workers in general.

"Happiness is 10,000 Okies going south with a Texan under each arm."

The oil industry tolerated the rowdy welders, however, because the project was moving forward at a good clip. Until early in 1976 when the national media reported that thousands of welds made the year before might be fatally flawed.

In September 1975, a former employee of subcontractor Ketchbaw Industries filed suit against the company saying he had been laid off because he would not go along with a conspiracy to falsify quality control X-rays of pipeline welds.

The Alaska pipeline was unique among pipeline projects in that every one of its more-than 100,000 welds were to be X-rayed, inspected for flaws and certified as part of the process to get the line built. The enormous task quickly overwhelmed subcontractors hired to do the job. Apparently, someone at Ketchbaw got the idea to X-ray a good weld a dozen or more times from different angles, and then to mark those X-rays as coming from separate welds.

The Transportation Department, which set safety standards for all pipelines, opened new hearings on the trans-Alaska oil pipeline to investigate reports of faulty welds on the line.

"Those troubles threaten the fragile Alaska environment, the timetable for delivering oil to the rest of the country, and the price of that oil," reported veteran newsman Walter Cronkite.

Alyeska terminated Ketchbaw's contract. Then a Ketchbaw

Alaska State Library, Pipeline Impact Collection, ASL-P17-8052

X-ray technicians, like Julie Shulenberger seen here, X-rayed the welds where the pieces of pipe were connected to ensure the welds had been done properly.

PRUDHOE BAY OIL

manager was found dead of cyanide poisoning and photographs of welds were stolen from a pump station construction camp, according to historian James Roscow, author of *800 Miles to Valdez: The Building of the Alaska Pipeline.*

Alyeska began a review of all 30,800 welds done in 1975 and submitted its report to the Interior Department in April 1976. The next month it presented its technical analysis and update on repair work under way, according to an industry report.

It found 3,955 questionable welds, or 10 percent of the welds completed in 1975. Many of the questionable welds did not need repair, 1,900 needed minor repair and 37 had to be cut out and re-welded. Alyeska received waivers for three welds, all of which were buried under the Koyukuk River south of the Brooks Range.

The oil companies told the project managers to get the job done, no matter what the cost, according to "The Alaska Pipeline." Alyeska estimated the repair of the welds cost the industry $55 million.

By the winter of 1976, two of the most difficult sections of the pipeline project remained. Workers had to build the line across the rugged mountain passes of the Brooks Range in the north and the Chugach Mountains in the south, where Thompson Pass had a near-vertical 2,800-foot south face to conquer. No one in the pipeline business had ever encountered such steep terrain on which to build.

Engineers finally devised a tower and cable system to fly the pipeline sections onto the face, and cable operators guided the 9-ton pipes into place using radio communications. But project managers had a tough time finding welders willing to risk their lives to complete the sections on the steepest part of the slope. One man already had been injured by a falling rock.

That's when pipeline welder Hugh "Junior" Leslie stepped forward and volunteered. One of the oldest and most experienced welders on the job, Leslie saw this as an opportunity to repair the damaged reputation of the 798ers.

Leslie and another volunteer, Richard Behne, spent a few weeks working in the most dangerous spot where only rock climbers had ventured before, according to "The Alaska Pipeline" documentary.

Preliminary work on rights of way began on Thompson Pass hill on June 15, 1976. A few months later, welders Hugh "Junior" Leslie and Richard Behne volunteered to complete the welds on that section, which is near Valdez and considered by many as the most dangerous spot on the pipeline.

"Snow, wind, rain, anything, sleet, anything you could imagine," Leslie said of those working conditions. "I felt like I was tryin' to wash the windows of the Empire State Building."

The two volunteers completed their welds on Oct. 20, 1976.

"Nothin' can compare with this. No mountain like Thompson Pass," Leslie later said of working on the 55-degree grade. "This is the granddaddy."

While Leslie and Behne completed the pipe along Thompson Pass, other workers tackled Atigun Pass in the Brooks Range, 500 miles north. The highest point on the line at 4,800 feet above sea level, this region also suffered some of the most brutal weather in Alaska.

Between 500 and 700 men were working 24 hours a day on this section, which required the pipe to be buried in heavily insulated boxes filled with concrete because of avalanche threats. Workers soldiered on through heavy snowstorms, high winds and sub-zero temperatures to get the job done by early December 1976.

The last pipeline weld was made at Pump Station No. 3, near Atigun Pass, to finish the project on May 31, 1977. During its construction, 32 Alyeska Pipeline Service Co. employees or contract workers died. Most were killed in 10 aircraft crashes. In addition, three men died when a Hovercraft crashed; two men walked into helicopter blades; one was crushed between a forklift truck and its load; two drowned in the cement they were pouring for a building; and another was killed during a seismic survey.

Many other workers suffered serious injuries from accidents on drilling rigs, through snow blindness and severe frostbite, according to *Harnessing a Giant: 40 Years at Prudhoe Bay*, produced by *Petroleum News*.

When completed, the pipeline crossed 34 major rivers, around 800 smaller streams and three mountain ranges. It also had 11 pumping stations to help move the oil along.

The Valdez Marine Terminal at the southern end of the pipeline, built across the Port Valdez fjord from the town of Valdez, included facilities for crude oil storage and ballast water treatment, as well as fixed-platform and floating berths for oil tankers.

The 800-mile-long pipeline ends at the Valdez Marine Terminal, seen here with the town of Valdez across the water.

The first oil began moving through the pipeline at 5 mph at 10:05 a.m. on June 20, 1977. It arrived in Valdez six days later to be stored in 510,000-barrel tanks to await shipment to oil refineries south via oil tankers.

The *ARCO Juneau*, the first tanker filled with Prudhoe Bay oil, pulled away from its berth at the Valdez Marine Terminal on Aug. 1, 1977.

Byron Mallot, one of Alaska's most respected Native leaders and elected as the state's first Native lieutenant governor in 2014, told a PBS reporter that the pipeline was a mixed blessing for the state and its people.

"Where people lived, the pipeline had a huge impact, and those people suffered a great sense of loss - not just of land, but of place," Mallot said. "But the pipeline pulled Alaska kicking and screaming into the 20th century. And it allowed Alaska's Native peoples to become a social and economic force in ways that I don't think ever would have been achieved, at least not for a long, long time."

The pipeline was raised in several areas along the 800-mile pipeline route to allow wildlife to cross, but near Willow Lake it also allowed homesteaders access to their property.

He added that the pipeline, which has delivered billions of barrels of oil, has had some spills from accidents, vandalism, permafrost thaws and some corrosion due to aging. But overall, it has worked as well as most everyone could have hoped.

"Alaskan oil has been the biggest resource bonanza in U.S. history, transforming Alaska from one of the poorest to one of the wealthiest states in the nation," Mallot said.

Nearly one-tenth of the crude oil consumed in America flowed through that pipeline. It moved its billionth barrel of oil in early 1980, and for decades royalties provided 80 percent to 85 percent of the state's operating budget.

Courtesy Rob Stapleton

Pump Station 8, located 38 miles south of Fairbanks, exploded 18 days after oil began to flow through the pipeline from Prudhoe Bay. The accident on July 8, 1977, occurred when some misdirected oil ignited. One pump worker died and several others were injured in the blast. Oil in the pipeline, which shut down for about a week, was redirected to bypass the damaged station. Crude reached Valdez on July 28, 38.5 days after entering the line on the North Slope.

Investigators ruled the explosion was due to human error.

Some Highlights

29

Iceworm Revives Cordova

Winters in the north can get mighty long, and sometimes people dream up wacky ideas so they don't go stir crazy. That's just what happened in a little town in Alaska's beautiful Prince William Sound.

Cordova's Iceworm, created during the winter of 1960, was a fitting descendent of that famous invention first born full grown from the fertile mind of Dawson City's pioneer newspaper man E.J. "Stoller" White. His invention was the result of a dearth of news and a demand from his editor to go out and rustle up some.

"Get me something that will make headlines and sell papers," the editor of the *Klondike Nugget* told him.

As White pondered what sort of news might attract readers, a huge storm hit the Canadian gold-rush town. That's when a great idea hit the newsman. He announced that new creatures had emerged after the storm: ice worms.

White described them as cold-loving creatures that had crawled out of their holes in a nearby glacier following the unusually chilly storm to "bask in the unusual frigidity in such numbers that their chirping was seriously interfering with the slumbers of Dawson's inhabitants."

Soon the town was abuzz with talk of these worms and sales of the *Nugget* soared. People traveled on expeditions to find the

Iceworms do exist and live in glaciers.

elusive creatures, listening carefully for their chirps. Bartenders also created drinks called Ice Worm Cocktails, complete with ice worms pulled from blocks of ice.

Witnesses reported the crafty barkeeps pulled long, skinny pieces of spaghetti out of these ice blocks as bartenders had been known to make a little cash on the side by selling fake ice worms to gullible out-of-towners.

Ice worms lost their luster as the years went on, and eventually made their way back to the glacier. They became a topic of legend, sometimes seen on local postcards.

Although many people believe ice worms are fantasy, they do, indeed, exist and were first discovered in 1887 on Alaska's Muir Glacier. The tiny black worms avoid the sun and spend their lives in glacial ice. They creep onto the surface of glaciers at night and retreat underneath the ice before dawn.

But Cordova's ice worm, the brainchild of Ohmer Waer, was a gallant effort to attract tourists to Cordova and combat midwinter doldrums. Waer, manager of the historic old Windsor Hotel, looked around the empty lobby one fall morning while drinking a cup of coffee. That's when he had an idea.

"What this town needs is an ice worm," he told his wife.

Waer later said his wife greeted the remark with the scorn it deserved, but his idea was bandied about and interest grew. One evening, Waer got a call from a friend to meet at his house.

"Bob Logan called up and asked me to a meeting at his place," Waer later told Aunt Phil. "When I got there, he, Merle Smith of

Cordova Airlines, Frank Smith and Harold Bonser were sitting around and they asked me about my idea. We kicked it around, and before the evening was over, we had formed the 'Cordova Visitors Association,' and collected a goodly sum to start the ball rolling."

In 1960 just about everyone in town pitched in and did their bit, Waer said. The design of the "Iceworm," of course, was the first matter to be decided. Rosswogs had a supply of plastic hula-hoops that could be used for the framework. However, they cracked in the cold. So Robert Banta, owner of Banta's Builders Supply, fixed new ones of oak that defied the elements.

Banta called Ohmer down to his shop one day to look at some aluminized nine-foot-wide cotton cloth. He said he could supply 150 feet of it, so soon the town women were busy working on the cover for the body of the Iceworm.

"What's the largest length of cardboard you can supply, and how much does it cost?" Waer wrote to Zellerbach, the paper manufacturers. He explained that he needed it for the first-ever Cordova Iceworm.

A 15-foot length came back with a letter from the company.

"You don't owe us a cent; congratulations on a good idea!" it read.

The Iceworm's head was Waer's design. But the creature lost its head several times over the years.

The original one blew off the dock, and

Residents of Cordova, seen here in the early 1960s, rallied around an idea to make an Iceworm and have a celebration to shake off the winter blues.

Cordova's first iceworm wound its way down a street in 1960 with Mt. Eccles in the background.

another burned up in the fire that destroyed Cordova's ocean dock many years ago.

It takes eight legs to carry the huge head – two more every so often and four under the tail. There has never been any problem getting volunteers. Many former teenagers, now grown, point with pride to pictures of earlier Iceworms and can pick out the legs that belonged to them.

While they practiced the Iceworm's ripples and undulations on Lake Eyak airstrip and learned how to wend a sinuous way, the rest of the town's people were busy with their plans for a really outstanding festival. Ideas proliferated, including several contests ranging from beard growing to queen of the festival to floats to crab eating. One enterprising entrepreneur put up cans of water containing plastic worms for souvenirs. Organizers also decided to have a bicycle race from Lake Eyak to town, "cheating and shortcuts allowed."

When the first festival got under way that beautiful, sunny

February, visitors from nearby towns flocked to Cordova. Bill Ekemo, president of the Cordova Chamber of Commerce, and the festival queen led the parade in a Model-T Ford. Children screamed as the multicolored 150-foot dragon-like creature undulated its way down the street, carried by legs belonging to local teens. Then and there, Cordova's Iceworm became an inseparable part of Cordova's history and the annual Iceworm Festival was born.

Over the years the festival has grown and newspapers outside Alaska often pick up the story. An article in a San Diego paper said: "It took many years for the residents of Cordova, Alaska, to come up with an idea for an annual wingding, but when they did, it was a winner – an Iceworm!"

Visitors have come to the winter festival, held the end of January or beginning of February, from all around the world. The "Iceworm coin," a wooden buck accepted in payment for purchases, is now a collector's item found in many European cities – a few have even reached Cordoba, Spain, the city for which Cordova is named.

Cordovans celebrate their Iceworm Festival to this day.

While some people may have thought the idea of creating an iceworm was just plain crazy, it proved so popular that the Cordova Chamber of Commerce formed a permanent committee to handle the basic organization of the festival and patented the words "Iceworm" and "Home of the Iceworm."

30

THE PAINTING PACHYDERM

A pachyderm, who became proficient with a paintbrush and easel, is responsible for the creation of the Alaska Zoo in Anchorage.

It all started when Jack Snyder saw a tongue-in-cheek ad for a Chiffon toilet paper contest for grocers in 1966. The Crown Zellerbach company announced: "$3,000 or a baby elephant" to the winner.

The Anchorage grocer won the contest. Snyder then startled the tissue paper executives when he said, "I'll take the elephant."

One can just imagine the comments bandied about the boardroom after Snyder let his choice be known. Perhaps the executives said something like, "That's right, some crazy Alaskan chose a baby elephant over $3,000 in prize money!"

Those company officials searched until they found an 18-month-old Asian elephant that had worked for a circus. Her name was Annabelle.

Toilet paper reps hustled Annabelle into an airplane and sent her north on July 6, 1966. She stood just 3-1/2 feet tall when she stepped off the plane in Anchorage.

Annabelle, born in India in 1964, was the first pachyderm in Alaska since the ice age. She spent her summer on tour flying around Alaska spreading good will. Alaskans loved her.

Snyder than had to find a suitable winter shelter for his prize. He

Annabelle the elephant, seen here in 1974, was the first animal to live at the Alaska Zoo in Anchorage.

made arrangements to temporarily house Annabelle with Sammye Seawell, owner of the Diamond H Horse Ranch on O'Malley Road. Her Hillside ranch had the only heated stalls in town.

Annabelle had a hearty appetite, and after three months, Seawell asked Snyder about his plans for Annabelle.

"If you want Annabelle, you can have her," Snyder told her.

The little elephant became part of Seawell's family.

Annabelle soon became quite popular with Anchorage residents, which sparked an idea that would secure Annabelle's future. Seawell persuaded Anchorage residents to form a nonprofit corporation to build a place "where the public could visit animals and learn about them."

Anchorage children had asked the city council to think about a zoo back in 1963, when two children – who said they represented 214 other children – presented a proposal to the city.

"We could sell popcorn or hold a carnival to raise money to buy

Pygmy goats had joined the Alaska Zoo family by 1974.

a bison," they said in their petition. "It would be better to have one animal than none at all."

The council set up an advisory board to consider the matter, according to an article in the *Anchorage Daily Times*. The council proposed a zoo be located in the Russian Jack Springs area, but the Anchorage Parks and Recreation Advisory Board rejected that plan several times.

It wasn't until Seawell incorporated her company into the Alaska Children's Zoo on March 28, 1968, that it became a reality. Located on land adjacent to Seawell's ranch off O'Malley, it opened the following year with Annabelle and other donated animals – many of which were orphaned and/or injured.

The 30-acre park's name changed to Alaska Zoo in June 1980 and served as a star attraction to draw thousands of visitors to see various Alaska animals, including grizzly bears, moose and wolverines. A female African elephant named Maggie joined Annabelle as a companion in 1983.

Something magical happened at America's farthest-north zoo when trainers put a paintbrush into Annabelle's trunk in 1991. She started splattering brush strokes across canvas and created paintings in front of cheering visitors. She entertained Alaskans with her artistic skill for many years.

People questioned whether the elephant really could paint and how she could hold a brush. An elephant's trunk has an estimated 40,000 to 50,000 muscles, at least 63 times more than an entire human body. The trunk is sensitive and flexible. Its tip also has a prehensile extension called a finger. That helps the animal perform delicate tasks and pick up small objects.

Elephant trainer David Hall and Annabelle developed her unique technique over time. Hall would load a brush with acrylic paint and hand it to the 8,000-pound artist. She learned to grab the brush with the end of her trunk and make vertical strokes on paper.

Her aim wasn't always on the mark, as she missed the paper about 50 percent of the time and hit the mounting board. Hall had to apply more paint to the brush every few strokes.

But her aim improved over time, and in a few years, people were buying her abstract artwork.

"Annabelle makes her own living – and a living for others," Hall said in an interview for *The Seattle Times* in 1996. He believed she was a 4-ton bundle of talent.

Her prints raised several hundred thousand dollars for the zoo. Her art also graced note cards and coffee mugs.

Annabelle died on Dec. 15, 1997, at the age of 33, following complications from a foot infection. A tombstone embedded with her photograph marks the corner of the zoo where she is buried.

Her companion, Maggie, who was never very impressed with Annabelle's art and usually ate hay while she worked, moved to the Performing Animal Welfare Society sanctuary in San Andreas, Calif., in November 2007. The 35-year-old African elephant is thriving with other elephants in the warm California sun, according to the PAWS official website.

31

BETTY THE FIRETRUCK

Homer residents turned to Betty Crocker when they needed a firetruck in the late 1960s, after they learned about a promotion offered by General Mills. The nationally known company offered a program where people could turn in their coupons for large househlold items. An $800 piano could be purchased with 160,000 coupons redeemed at one-half penny each, according to a 2009 *Homer Tribune* article, titled "Bringing home 'Betty,'" by Naomi Klouda.

How many coupons did it take to get a fire truck? Five million, which equaled about $25,000 in 1969 – more than $162,000 in 2015 dollars. And even though that was an enormous sum, the Homer Volunteer Fire Department women's auxiliary in 1968 and 1969 set out to purchase one on the power of coupons found on items like sacks of flour, cans of Campbell's soup and Betty Crocker cake mixes.

Reporter Klouda found one of the original organizers, Helen Jackson, still had files of memorabilia and documents relating to the effort. In one letter, she thanked an Elmendorf Air Force group that had gathered up a giant garbage bag full of coupons.

"Quite frankly, if it weren't for the warm, genuine, friendly letters and notes of encouragement and interest from literally all over the United States and from all ages and walks of life, we who started the first little snowball on its way would have quit months ago," Jackson wrote. "This is not an easy way to get a fire truck."

But the Homer residents knew it was possible, because another Alaska community had saved General Mills coupons in 1964 for a vehicle. The Copper Valley School in Glennallen organized a campaign and collected 1.5 million coupons to trade in for a new school bus.

When the rest of the nation heard about Homer's effort to get a much-needed fire truck, coupons from all 50 states arrived at the fire department from school children, Boy Scouts, Lions Clubs, military families and locals. By the time they had enough coupons to buy the fire truck, a publicity campaign had let the world know of life in Homer. Somone even wrote the following unsigned poem:

> "In Alaska it's moose, as you all well know
> That's the staple diet of the Alaskan Joe,
> But in Homer, Betty Crocker is on the loose
> That's what we eat, along with our moose.
> We're trying to reach that five-million mark
> To a get a fire truck that does more than bark
> Dog sleds were fine in the old timer's day,
> But not much help when fire holds sway."

A fact sheet shared that Homer's nearest fire department was 80 miles away in Kenai. It also stated that Homer citizens had started the fire department as a nonprofit organization on Feb. 10, 1954, and their equipment included relics from days gone by. Inventory of the small community's fire trucks included a 1946 Mack 750-gallon pumper, a 1953 Jeep pumper with a 375-gallon tank trailer, a 1955 Ford F-100 half-ton that carried a national high-expansion foam generator and accessories, and a 1967 International customized travel-all rescue-ambulance unit.

"All units are in radio contact with each other, the fire house and the dispatcher," read a leaflet handed out in advertising the Betty Crocker promotion. "In case of general emergency or alarm, we have two sirens located at either end of town, which can be activated by pushing a button."

By 1969, the auxiliary had enough coupons to redeem for a firetruck.

- - - - - - - - - - CLIP THIS COUPON - - - - - - - - - -

SAVE 15¢   **SAVE 15¢**

SPECIAL MUFFIN JAMBOREE OFFER!

This coupon

WORTH 15¢

when you buy

1 package Betty Crocker Muffin Mix
and
1 jar any brand of jam or jelly

Mr. Grocer: This coupon if accepted
at your store for merchandise noted
above and in accordance with the
terms of our offer, will be redeemed
at face value plus 2¢ for handling
by General Mills Inc. Send your
coupons to: Coupon Redemption,
P.O. Box 2176, Toronto, Ontario.

SAVE 15¢   **SAVE 15¢**

Homer residents began collecting Betty Crocker coupons in the late 1960s so they could get a much-needed firetruck.

Homer women Edna Morris and Helen Jackson processed most of the coupons. Jackson recalled the many toiling hours spent clipping away excess cardboard from the coupons, then counting them into bundles of 100 points. The final push to the post office involved neatly packaging the coupons into boxes for shipment to General Mills.

"We were not prepared to cope with the avalanche of mail requiring replies, nor did we realize the cost of the postage that would be involved in the project," Jackson later said.

Ray Kranich, one of the volunteers who helped build the fire station on land donated by Hugh Watson, said the nonprofit operated through fund drives and donations before the Great Earthquake of 1964. Following the city's incorporation in 1964, the city issued a monthly check to the fire department for operations, fuel and maintenance. But when the need for a new fire truck arose in 1969, the city didn't have the money to buy one.

"The check would have covered gas, utilities and maintenance, but to hold out our hand to the city to buy a new fire truck – it wasn't going to happen. If people wanted a fire truck, they needed to find a way to get it," Kranich later said. "I don't remember whose idea it was, but the (HVFD) Women's Auxiliary picked up the ball and ran with it."

The "Betty" truck story represented a time of independence in the community, said Kranich, who was serving as the fire chief when the fire truck arrived in Homer.

"In times past, the government didn't do for the people, the people did for themselves," Kranich said. "This is a lost philosophy today."

But the city of Homer may have contributed to the "Betty" truck acquisition after all. Treasurer Helen Jackson found, in her archives, a budget note from the city giving the HVFD a check for $10,100 in 1969.

By Sept. 30, 1970, the auxiliary had mailed all the coupons collected during its 18-month campaign, beating the Nov. 1 deadline.

Anchorage Museum at Rasmuson Center, Steve McCutcheon Collection, AMRC-AMRC-B1990-014-5-TV-074-5

The city of Homer, seen here in 1978 with the airstrip and Beluga Lake, needed a reliable firetruck to serve the growing community.

Pratt Museum Photo Archives, Homer News Collection. PM 1995.029.0141

Homer residents named their new firetruck "Betty."

"This piece of equipment, through its increased fire fighting capabilities, will greatly increase the efficiency of the Homer Volunteer Fire Department," an announcement read.

The bright yellow fire engine, built in Orangeville, Calif., in 1971, arrived just before Christmas that year.

Throughout the years, Engine No. 2, or the "Betty" truck as it was called, responded to numerous fires in the area, the brightest firefighter in the arsenal that included a 1947 World War II vintage Willies Jeep.

The Betty operated for the next 25 years or so. It retired in 1995-96.

32

A GREAT RACE IS BORN

The two legendary visionaries who conceived the 1,049-mile race from Anchorage to Nome hardly could have imagined the success and changes that would happen during the next several decades of the Last Great Race.

In 1964, a history buff who lived in Wasilla had an idea. Dorothy Page, secretary of the Aurora Dog Mushers Club, saw that snowmachines were taking the place of dog teams and mushing. She thought a sled dog race on the historic Iditarod Trail – which originally began in Seward during the gold rush days and stretched to Knik – through the gold camp of Iditarod and eventually to Nome, might revitalize a longtime Alaska tradition.

Anchorage Museum at Rasmuson Center, Ward W. Wells Collection, AMRC-wws-4706-110

Horsepower replaced dog power during the 1960s, as seen by this snowmachine pulling a walrus skin boat up the beach at Gambell on St. Lawrence Island.

Thwaites. 1294.   Alaskan Live Stock.
Value - $100.00 Each.

Good sled dogs were worth their weight in gold when miners first began mushing along the Iditarod Trail. These pups sold for $100 each in 1900 — nearly $2,500 in 2015 dollars.

But Page knew that she would have to find a musher to share her dream before it could become reality.

She endured comments such as "Are you crazy?" for two years, until she talked to Joe Redington Sr. during a break at the Willow Winter Carnival sled dog races in 1966. Page explained her idea to the veteran musher, who had traveled over sections of the historic Iditarod Trail while homesteading near Flat Horn Lake.

His response — "I think that's a great idea!" — has been echoed by hundreds of mushers from all parts of Alaska, the Lower 48 and foreign countries ever since.

Fifty-eight mushers signed up to compete for $25,000 in prize money for the 1967 inaugural race. Since only nine miles of the trail had been cleared, the race ran from Knik to Big Lake on Saturday, and from Big Lake to Knik on Sunday, for a total of 56 miles. Isaac Okleasik, an Eskimo from Teller on the Seward Peninsula north of Nome, won the Iditarod Centennial Race.

Due to a lack of snow in 1968, a lack of money in 1969 and a lack of interest from 1970 to 1972, the race was put on hold. But behind the scenes work continued as volunteers cleared the brush from both the Nome and Knik ends of the trail.

Finally, on March 3, 1973, amid the cheers of hundreds of well-wishers, 34 mushers left Anchorage headed for Nome in pursuit of not only a dream, but also $50,000 in prize money pledged by Redington. They raced across a route that generally followed the trail of a group of mushers who sped diphtheria serum from Anchorage to Nome in 1925.

Dick Wilmarth, a hard-working gold miner and trapper from the Interior village of Red Devil, later told reporters he heard some of his competitors talking about quitting about halfway to Nome.

The musher said he was camped out in a cabin near Galena when a few other mushers came inside during the middle of the night and said they wanted to talk to him. They all were getting cold, as the temperatures had dipped to the 50-below-zero mark, and wanted to quit the race. But they wanted the decision to be unanimous, they told him.

Wilmarth was not a quitter. He did not want to be a part of that conversation.

Joe Redington Sr., his son and others cut the Iditarod Trail from Knik to Nome prior to the 1973 race.

"I told them, 'I'm going to go to Nome,'" he told *Associated Press* writer Mary Pemberton in 2001.

The 31-year-old hurried outside, hooked up his dog team and headed down the Yukon River.

The determined musher, who snared beaver for food along the trail, said people along the Yukon did not want to share food or fish with him.

"Those guys on the Yukon wouldn't give me any food," he said in a newspaper interview later. "They were rooting for their own guys."

Wilmarth crossed the finish line first and collected $12,000 in prize money. It took him 20 days, 49 minutes and 41 seconds to travel the old winter trail that mushers hadn't used for almost 45 years.

He had assembled his team a few months prior to the race, rounding up dogs from villages on the Kuskokwim River. He said

Anchorage Museum at Rasmuson Center, Redington Family Collection. AMRC-b2006-023-3522

Joe Redington Sr., holding the trophy, and Orvile Lake, holding the microphone, congratulate Dick Wilmarth, center, winner of the 1973 Iditarod race in Nome.

he traded his .22-caliber rifle for a snowmachine and then traded the snowmachine for five dogs.

Along the trail he and his friend, renowned sprint dog musher George Attla, hopped onto snowshoes to clear a path for the dog teams after Finger Lake, where there was no trail. Attla followed Wilmarth into Nome to clench fourth place in the historic race.

John Schultz crossed the finish line more than 12 days after Wilmarth. About one-third of the 34 starters dropped out along the way.

Alternating every year between the southern route and the northern route, the current trails cross the Alaska Range, Kuskokwim Mountains, Nulato Hills and more than 200 miles along the mighty Yukon River. Once the mushers take off from Knik, they leave civilization behind and only have small towns and villages such as Skwentna, Nikolai, Ophir and Unalakleet to break the monotony of traveling in bone-chilling cold until they reach the historic gold rush town of Nome, perched on the shores of the Bering Sea.

By the early 1980s, the prize money had doubled and the trail time had dropped almost in half.

SOME LOW POINTS

33

CORDOVA BURNS

Fire plagued many towns in Alaska when wooden structures were heated and illuminated by woodstoves and lanterns. One errant spark or flame could spell disaster. And such was the fate for one quaint little town in Prince William Sound in the early 1960s.

Cordova had seen and survived several fires since its difficult birth in the early 1900s when the discovery of copper led to a railroad connecting it to the Kennecott copper mines. And it lived through a boisterous childhood and stormy adolescence when a few fires destroyed several homes and businesses.

By the 1930s, Cordova had matured and settled down into a modern, prosperous town with a stable population, schools, churches, theater, numerous social clubs, two banks, a library and every type of business.

An almost fatal nonfire blow came in 1938 when the Kennecott copper mines closed down. The railroad was abandoned, the rails sold for scrap and ghost towns were left scattered along the 200-mile right of way.

But although betrayed by copper, Cordova had another resource to fall back on – the silver of the sea. So fishing and canning fish, clams and crab provided employment for the people who stayed with the town. The population did decline, but Cordova lived on.

A devastating fire swept through Cordova's business district on May 2, 1963.

Then, on May 2, 1963, it faced one of its greatest challenges. Cordova's residents awoke in the early hours to find a major fire sweeping through their town.

It started in the Club Café in the Van Brocklin Building and quickly spread through the Club Bar and Cordova Commercial Co. on the corner of First and Council streets, according to Cordova historian Dixie Lambert. Then it jumped to the Donohoe Building, which housed the Cordova Airlines office, Hosick's Tavern and the Cordova Beauty Salon.

The fire swept unchecked to the south and consumed everything in its path.

"C.T. Davis & Sons Grocery, Bill and Edna Reid's Little Bar and Myra McDonald's Cordova Drug Store with the Elks Lodge on the second floor fueled the flames," Lambert said.

Cordovans awoke at 4 a.m. that day to the chilling wail of fire sirens rushing through their streets. Then they heard a bombardment of ammunition as shells exploded.

"In a desperate attempt to stop the fire, dynamite was used to blow up Bill's Bar, owned by Bill and Katherine Hall," Lambert said.

Firemen had used the practice of lighting dynamite in burning buildings in the past to stop the spread of fire, but the strategy did not work this time. The six charges of dynamite only added to the confusion.

"The explosion blew out windows all along First Street but did not stop the advancing flames," Lambert said.

Soon more businesses were ablaze, including Cliff Collin's Jewelry, Cordova Bakery, Lucille Discher's Variety Shop, Pete and Lilly Lovseth's Magazine and Notions Store, Eunice Flinn's Mens Wear and Sporting Goods and the Cordova Insurance office rented by Harold Nordman.

"Soon every store from Browning to Council was engulfed in spectacular flames," Lambert said. "The fire continued its relentless

Cordova Commercial burned, as well as Club and Davis' Superfoods on Main Street.

march by jumping up to Mae Jones' apartment house on Second Street."

The fire then raged through Harold Bosner's building, which housed *The Cordova Times*, and on to Karl Barth's hardware store in the Central Building. Service Transfer's warehouse in the alley and the Van Brocklin apartment building on the corner of Council and Second streets also fell victim to the blaze. The only building left standing on that block was the Club Bowl, a concrete block building with a sprinkler system that kept its roof watered.

The fire did not stop until 14 downtown buildings had been destroyed and many more damaged, including City Hall, the fire department, Cordova Cleaners and First Bank of Cordova.

A little farther away, the Harbor House, the Northern Hotel, the Alaskan Hotel and the Cordova Hotel sustained damage, too. The destruction left more than 125 men, women and children homeless.

At the height of the excitement, everyone was too busy to feel the full impact of the catastrophe. Victims even joked with one another as they staggered out of fire-threatened apartments and stores under huge loads of clothing, bedding, furniture, household goods, gill nets, outboard motors and merchandise. They were relieved that no one had been seriously injured and could even see humor as the whole area around the fire began to look like a huge secondhand store.

"Where's the hot dogs?" one humorist shouted as the flames blazed higher.

Cordova residents helped their volunteer firefighters as did crews from the U.S. Coast Guard cutters *Sedge* and *Sorrell*. A Federal Aviation Association fire crew brought their equipment from Mile 13, too.

More help poured into the town when the U.S. Air Force sent a 20,000-gallon pumper, a 7,000-gallon pickup fire truck and a seven-man firefighting team to Cordova on a military air transport service C-124. The Bureau of Land Management sent more equipment and volunteer firefighters from Anchorage on a C-124, as well, and a Civil Defense firefighting jeep from Seward and a shipment of insulin came in on a C-123.

At noon that day, Cordovans gazed at the blackened ruins of what

The fire on May 2, 1963, destroyed most of Main Street Cordova. This photo shows foundations still burning hours later.

had been a thriving downtown – almost the entire business district was gone.

By 12:30 p.m., with the fire under control, reaction set in. The tired, lined faces of Cordova's weary citizens showed that they now realized their loss. They also realized that if they were to survive this blow, they faced the fight of their lives.

"Cordova was declared a disaster area and the Small Business Bureau helped arrange loans to the business people to rebuild," Lambert said.

She added that the American Red Cross and The Salvation Army offered assistance to the displaced residents. The Alaska Railroad sped supplies from Anchorage to Seward and the Alaska Steamship Co. transported them to Cordova on board the steamship *Iliamna* at no charge.

Those from other towns donated clothing and household goods that were flown into Cordova from Kodiak, Juneau and Anchorage. The Alaska Communications System donated telephone equipment, too, which was installed by FAA and Civil Defense personnel.

The disaster only made the people of Cordova stronger. Instead of the death of the "Stout-hearted City," as Alaska's Sen. E.L. "Bob" Bartlett once called Cordova, the disastrous fire meant a rebirth.

Townspeople pitched in, and in a short time they had cleared all the debris and began rebuilding. Within a week, most businessmen were back in business in temporary spaces in buildings that had escaped the inferno.

Harold Bonser, owner of *The Cordova Times*, put his weekly paper out on schedule, although it was mimeographed at the Red Dragon saloon because his press and linotype had been destroyed.

"He kept everyone abreast of the new locations for the downtown businesses and the rebuilding progress," Lambert said.

The pioneer grocery firm of C.T. Davis & Sons began selling groceries out of its concrete block warehouse, which survived the fire. Cordova Airlines started working out of the First Bank of Cordova, across the street from the ruins of its downtown office.

Help poured into the city from all over the state. A chartered plane filled with 27 business, civic and labor leaders flew in from Anchorage the day after the fire and offered their assistance – from banking services to the skilled muscles of organized labor.

State, federal and private agencies also cooperated, but Cordova's citizens didn't sit back expecting others to pull them through. They didn't waste any time feeling sorry for themselves. By their own efforts, they took care of everyone displaced by the fire.

"In fact," local Civil Defense leaders reported, "we had 104 more offers of temporary housing than we needed."

Gov. William A. Egan, in Cordova a few days after the fire, told its residents: "Because of your loss, I wasn't looking forward to this trip, but I find you are already planning ahead. I am pleased you are thinking of the future and not of the past."

With the spirit and enthusiasm of pioneers past, Cordova's citizens knuckled down and rebuilt their town. But this time they used different building materials – concrete block buildings replaced wooden frames.

While the 1963 fire was one of the worst economic disasters to hit Cordova since its birth, Lambert said "the generous spirit and can-do attitude of Cordovans pulled the town through the ordeal."

Another group of Alaskans also had to dig deep and find their can-do attitude four years later when a devastating flood destroyed many of their homes and businesses in the state's Interior.

34

FLOODWATERS FILL FAIRBANKS

Water in the Chena River inched up ever higher during July 1967 when 3.34 inches of rain, instead of the normal 1.84 inches, fell on Fairbanks. The city's 30,000 residents weren't too worried, though. Most were in the midst of the Alaska Purchase Centennial, celebrating the U.S. purchase of Alaska from Russia in 1867.

Besides, people like longtime resident Sandy Vernon often had seen high water in the Chena. She and others had witnessed a few minor floods of the river in the town's 65-year history. Twice in the early 1900s, water and ice from early spring breakups had breached the river's banks and flooded downtown – but that was more than 50 years ago, most thought.

Vernon and her then-husband, Michael Downing, lived in a rental in Hamilton Acres, just off Trainor Gate Road, near Fort Wainwright. Her parents lived on a homestead in North Pole.

"Mom called to tell me the slough water had risen a lot during the day and was becoming turbulent," Vernon said.

Vernon wasn't overly concerned, however. Officials had taken to radio and television the second week of August to warn townspeople about an impending crest of the river, which separates the north and south neighborhoods of Fairbanks. But as days passed, no water spilled over the river's banks.

SOME LOW POINTS

But when 6 inches of rain fell during a period of five days, the river did crest. And on the evening of Aug. 14, it spilled over its banks at 18.6 feet. The massive amount of water drove unprepared residents to their rooftops and eventually forced nearly 7,000 people from their homes as it destroyed basements, furnaces, furniture and precious family belongings overnight.

"As night fell, the water continued to rise," Vernon said, adding that her husband could not get the couple's car out of the driveway before rushing water filled the street. "We began walking in the dark in waist-deep water."

They waded along in pitch-black darkness, passing abandoned cars that blocked roads.

"Underwater headlights made for an eerie sight," Vernon said. "We were hit by debris spinning in the still rising waters."

The couple felt their way by foot along the ties of an Alaska Railroad track bed, not knowing that the water was washing away the gravel underneath the ties.

University of Alaska Fairbanks, Mark C Glunz Collection. UAF-1996-167-30

Sandy Vernon and her husband felt their way through water covering the railroad tracks along Trainor Gate Road near Fort Wainwright. They were unaware that the floodwaters were washing out the railroad embankment, as seen in this photograph taken many days after the water had receeded.

"It was very dark, very cold, very wet and very scary," Vernon recalled. "People's shouts and pleas for help filled the night, blended with cars honking and dogs barking."

Military vehicles from Fort Wainwright and city fire trucks slowly made their way through the city's streets. Officials called out on bullhorns for residents to evacuate immediately.

Vernon and her husband hopped aboard a fire truck and were taken with about a dozen others to the FE Gold Camp on the Steese Highway in the foothills north of Fairbanks. Although no longer in operation and abandoned, the camp once had provided barracks for its employees.

"There were about 50 of us there," Vernon said, most with ugly bruises, scrapes and cuts from their ordeal in the rushing waters. "All frightened and bedraggled. No power, no running water, but dry in those empty old buildings."

She had no clue what had happened to her mother and three young brothers. Vernon knew her father, teenage brother and another

The Fairbanks Fire Department and U.S. Army soldiers, like those seen here, made their way through the floodwaters in Fairbanks to rescue people.

SOME LOW POINTS

Fairbanks businesses and homes flooded in August 1967. The flood put Fairbanks and Nenana under as much as 9 feet of water. Seven people died, and damage was estimated at $200 million, according to the *Anchorage Daily News*.

family had gone moose hunting, but she did not know where they were hunting.

With telephone lines out, CB radio and ham operators became critically important, as they fed messages to the Fairbanks public radio station that continued to broadcast, Vernon said.

"It was from one of those messages that we learned my father, brother and neighbors were reported lost and whereabouts unknown," she said. It took a week for her to learn that all her family members were safe.

The city became a five-mile-wide lake of deep, sludgy water filled with lost property covered with sewage and garbage. The flood knocked out power, communications, water and sewer utilities. It washed away roads, bridges and rails, too, which isolated Fairbanks and made rescue efforts difficult.

Noatak schoolteacher Rod Hilts and his wife, Sunni, were in Fairbanks for the summer helping with the AK67 expo. He said he thought the 7.2 Richter Scale earthquake that rattled the town in June would be the event he'd remember from his summer's labor, but the great flood two months later eclipsed that memory.

Earlier that day, he and others had assisted famed anthropologist Erna Gunter move priceless artifacts from the museum at the Native display village, which had been set up for the centennial celebration, to keep them safe from floodwaters. Once they finished, Hilts headed toward his home on higher ground off Farmer's Loop Road. That's when he heard an announcement on his car radio.

"If you have a boat, or can get to people you know are needing help, do it."

After reaching his apartment, his wife suggested he run up to the neighborhood store and get a few supplies so they'd have food for the next few days. When he got to the store, he found several others, including his good friend, Wally Blasingame, stocking up, as well.

When water began to slowly seep into the lower level of the store, the men lined up on the stairs and helped the storeowner get hundreds of food cases to the main level. Suddenly, everything changed.

"Get out! Get out!" shouted the storeowner," as water rushed into the basement.

All the men made it to safety in time, as the owner yelled for his customers to grab anything they needed on the way out the door and come back after the flood to pay.

Hilts said he knew if the store was flooding, then the little motel nearby would flood, too. Blasingame, his wife and five children were staying at that motel. So Hilts and Blasingame raced to the motel and saw water had risen to the back of the lot. They grabbed the family and drove to Hilts' apartment where they could stay dry.

Once settled, Blasingame suggested they try to find a boat and help with the rescue effort in town. Hilts agreed, and the men headed up the road.

They soon found a flat-bottom riverboat attached to a truck and got permission from a teen to use his dad's boat. It had plenty of gas. The men drove it to the store, unloaded the boat and took off down College Road toward Fairbanks.

Those who found boats fled their homes with whatever belongings they could grab when the Chena River overflowed its banks in August 1967.

The pair made two rescues and got people to higher ground before they finally crossed the raging Chena River into the downtown area. As they headed east on Third Street they came to an Army National Guard "halftrack" that had nosed over into a washed out hole in the street's pavement. As they pulled alongside the vehicle, its driver popped out of the turret and hollered at them.

"Hey! I have the governor and his secretary in here. Can you get them up to the National Guard Armory on 13th street?"

"Yes!" the men yelled back, and then eased the boat close to the halftrack in the swift running current.

Just as Gov. Walter J. Hickel climbed out of the rig and was about to step on its hood, the boat hit the armored vehicle hard. A hole appeared in the wood just below water level and the Chena began spilling slowly into the boat. Hickel stepped back.

"Will it sink?" he asked.

Hilts assured the governor the boat would not sink, as he shoved a bucket in place with this right foot.

The men motored Hickel and his secretary to the armory, plugged the hole in the boat and continued to rescue a few more people before heading back to Farmer's Loop Road.

Several of those caught in the flood in downtown took refuge in the upper floors of the eight-story Northward Building. People with apartments made room and shared dry living spaces with those in need. They pooled food and cooked large meals for the crowd gathered in Fairbanks' only "skyscraper."

Throughout the rest of the city, rescuers piloted riverboats and other small craft as they skimmed across the muddy water looking up and down streets for people and pets. They ferried most of those found to the University of Alaska, which sat on College Hill, safe from the flood.

Earlier that Monday, university officials had contacted Civil Defense authorities in Fairbanks and told them that the university had 300 beds available for refugees in case the Chena flooded. When the river breached its banks that night, it became apparent that more beds would be needed.

University President William R. Wood didn't hesitate to announce that his institution would welcome all who needed shelter. And as soon as the radio station spread the word, "the trickle of refugees toward campus suddenly became a torrent," according to a story about the flood that appeared in the July-August 1967 issue of *Now in the North*.

"They came at first on foot, by bicycle, by pickup truck, car and camper – by about any means that had wheels," the article reported. "Many arrived only with the clothes they wore."

As floodwaters continued to fill the land, more refugees started to arrive by air. Giant Eielson Air Force Base H-21 helicopters and other military and civilian choppers rescued people from their rooftops and brought them to a heli-pad set up on a parking lot south of the Bunnell Building on campus. Others arrived by boats.

"At one point, the foot of College Hill near University Avenue and College Road resembled a marina," the university article said.

Nearly 7,000 refugees eventually filled the university's 17 major buildings, including eight dormitories, classrooms, rec rooms, laboratories, lounges and hallways. Faculty and staff also opened their homes to those in need.

Feeding the masses became quite an operation. The Salvation Army and U.S. Army troops from Fort Wainwright made sure that food, clothing and equipment made it onto the campus.

Others, like Vernon and those at the FE Gold Camp, had to rely on themselves to forage for food. She said her husband and several other men took a dump truck to the nearest grocery store a couple days after they arrived at their dry shelter.

"Because of reported and forcible lootings, some of the men took along their shotguns, truly riding shotgun," she said.

The men used canoes and rafts to float around inside the store and load items. They only picked up canned food, however, due to health risks from the still present floodwaters.

"There were no labels on the cans, which led to some very interesting and creative meals," Vernon said.

University of Alaska Anchorage, Alfred and Mae Bakken slides, UAA-hmc-0589-1-56

Fairbanks flood victims made their way via boats to grocery stores to find food. They grabbed canned goods, not spoiled by polluted water. Meals were interesting, as most of the cans had no labels.

The refugees at UAF fared a bit better. University records show that refugee volunteers joined the university kitchen staff to serve as many as 15,500 meals on one day – 68,000 meals during the week following the initial exodus from the city.

The Commons served as an emergency food distribution center for residents who lived on high ground near the campus; an infirmary was set up on the first floor of Wickersham Hall, one of two girls' dormitories; recreation activities were hosted at the Patty Building Gymnasium; movies were scheduled in the Duckering Auditorium; an outdoor kennel was put in place near the Patty Building for nearly 100 dogs; and the university media department issued a mimeographed daily newspaper both morning and afternoon to keep refugees informed. The masthead read, High Water News, and as floodwaters ebbed, it changed to (Even Lower) High Water News.

The university also distributed information about how to restore water-damaged property – the same instructions given to victims of tidal waves that struck Alaska's coastal towns after the 9.2 megathrust earthquake of 1964.

The staff of the *Fairbanks Daily News-Miner* settled into the offices of the university student paper, the *Polar Star*, to prepare stories for later publication since the newspaper's offices had been flooded. The *Anchorage Daily News* added the *News-Miner* nameplate to its own editions and furnished abbreviated reports from Fairbanks during this time, just as the *News-Miner* had done in 1964 when Anchorage was shut down because of the Good Friday earthquake.

Within days, Fairbanks Mayor Red Boucher, along with his friend William Randolph Hearst and a few other officials, toured the watery neighborhoods by boat to see the damage firsthand. Longtime *Seattle Times* reporter Stanton Patty, covering the flood, said Boucher looked like "George Washington crossing the Delaware," according to June Allen, author of an article titled, "The 1967 Fairbanks Flood," which appeared in *SitNews* on Aug. 7, 2003.

On Thursday, the governor and representatives from federal disaster aid agencies arrived at the campus and met with more than 300 Fairbanks businessmen to discuss recovery plans.

The floodwaters that filled Fairbanks during August 1967 devastated many businesses, including J.C. Penny's.

In the next few days, Anchorage Mayor Elmer Rasmuson and Alaska's U.S. Sen. E.L. "Bob" Bartlett and Rep. Howard Pollack arrived to show their support. All pledged to do all they could to help Fairbanks get back on its feet.

By the end of that first week, refugees began making their way off campus and returning to their homes. When the fall registration began on Sept. 9, the university's role as an evacuation center was but a memory.

Vernon's father and brother appeared after seven days and took the couple back to the home in Hamilton Acres.

"The damage was surreal during our trek home," Vernon said. "Roads washed away, broken abandoned homes and vehicles with debris as far as the eye could see."

A six-foot gated chain-link fence that surrounded their house had captured a mattress, a doghouse, several trashcans and a large barbeque – none of which was their property.

"The house was tipped off its foundation," Vernon said. "It was declared a total loss by the owner's insurance company."

They had to use a sledgehammer to break open the front door, as it and its frame had swollen shut from sitting in water for a week. Water had filled the house to a point just below the kitchen countertops. Long drapes over the windows and clothes hanging in the closet had wicked water to the top of the material. Sheetrock had crumbled throughout the house.

"The smell of decay was overpowering, as silt had seeped into every crevice and aided the rotting process," Vernon said. "We lost everything, including our submerged car."

The extensive destruction from the Fairbanks flood helped inspire Congress to pass a national flood insurance program. And to prevent a disaster of this magnitude from happening again, the Alaska District proposed the Chena River Lakes Flood Control Project. Its primary purpose was to protect Fairbanks and Fort Wainwright from high waters.

The flood of 1967, which killed seven and caused more than $200 million ($1.4 billion in 2015 dollars) in damage, sparked a new

University of Alaska Fairbanks, Mark C Glunz Collection, UAF-1996-167-31

Families, like this one from Fort Wainwright, salvaged what they could from their waterlogged homes. Note the mattress and pillow drying out on the roof.

SOME LOW POINTS

sense of urgency, so Congress reauthorized a previous flood control act passed in 1958. It passed the Flood Control Act of 1968, in accordance with recommendations from the U.S. Army Corps of Engineers. The project included

Fairbanks streets suffered damage from the flood of 1967, too, as seen in this photograph of a huge sink hole.

the Moose Creek Dam and Floodway, the Tanana River Levee and drainage channels within the protected area. Together, they comprised the largest federal civil works program in the state.

The Alaska District joined the Fairbanks North Star Borough in developing the project. And while the Corps obtained the lands needed for the dam and floodway, the borough acquired the lands for the levee and drainage channels. Construction began in 1973, and the Corps completed the $256 million Chena Project in 1979. A key component of the dam and levee system, located about 20 miles east of Fairbanks, was the massive concrete outlet works and floodgates.

During normal fluctuations of the Chena River, the outlet works remain open, allowing the natural flow of water. Fish and boats can travel through the open gates. At high water, however, the Corps can lower the floodgates, directing excess water to the Tanana River.

Experts say a 1967-type flood probably will never happen again, thanks to the Chena River Lakes Flood Control Project.

The National Civic League awarded Fairbanks its coveted All-America City award in 1968 for how it responded and rebuilt following that devastating flood.

35

CONGRESSMEN DISAPPEAR

T he disappearance of Alaska Congressman Nick Begich on Oct. 16, 1972, sparked the most intensive search for an aircraft in Alaska's history. To this day, questions remain about the ill-fated flight of the orange and white twin-engine plane.

Begich, 40, along with U.S. House Majority Leader Hale Boggs, 58, of Louisiana, Begich's 37-year-old aide, Russell L. Brown, and pilot Don E. Jonz, 38, left Anchorage early that day bound for Juneau to attend a Democratic fund-raiser. Begich was up for reelection and Boggs, a close personal friend, was helping him muster votes around the state.

The men were scheduled to catch an early morning flight, but opted to charter a flight so Boggs could get some rest. He was exhausted from campaigning.

Brown picked up Boggs and Begich and they all drove to the Anchorage International Airport, where they met Jonz, a seasoned and respected airman from Fairbanks. They took off from the airport at 9 a.m.

Jonz, who had flown in Alaska since 1957, checked in with the Anchorage tower at 9:12 a.m. The owner-operator of Pan-Alaska Airways Ltd. filed a flight plan for a VFR path, or visual flight rules, that would have taken the party over water to Cordova, then to Yakutat and on to the state capital.

Authorities figured he was close to the Turnagain Arm entrance to the pass at that time, which is the lowest cut in the nearby 5,000- to 7,000-foot mountains of the Chugach Range. He planned to go through the pass at 12:30 p.m. This route flew over some of the most rugged terrain in the world.

No one ever heard from the Cessna 310 again.

Search planes were in the sky within 90 minutes of the Federal Aviation Administration reporting the six-passenger aircraft had failed to land in Juneau. A U.S. Coast Guard C-130 left Juneau, an FAA C-47 began searching around Yakutat and the Rescue Coordination Center at Elmendorf Air Force Base dispatched three planes. Hundreds of boats from Cordova searched around Prince William Sound.

"Figuring who's on board and all, it's going to be one hell of a search," an official at the Rescue Coordination Center told reporter Howard Weaver in a story titled 'Search covers huge area' that appeared in the *Anchorage Daily News* on Oct. 17, 1972.

Alaska Congressman Nick Begich, right, and U.S. House Majority Leader Hale Boggs of Louisiana appeared at a Democratic fund-raiser in Anchorage the night before their plane disappeared.

Searchers knew the plane had a cruising speed of about 200 mph, an altitude ceiling of about 10,000 feet, due to a non-pressurized cabin, and a five-hour gas supply. They assumed it carried an emergency beacon and survival gear, because Jonz had answered in the affirmative when the flight controller asked him that question at 9:12 a.m.

No one spotted anything nor reported hearing any radio beacon signals.

Most planes had to call off their searches later that day due to bad weather. An Air Force HC-130, equipped to locate the Cessna's emergency beacon, was the only plane that searched throughout the night for airplane number N1812H. It flew along the 560-mile path from Anchorage over Whittier and Prince William Sound, south along the gulf coast then over Yakutat, turning east over Cape Spencer and Sisters Island to Juneau.

When one pilot heard about the conditions in Portage Pass on the morning the congressmen disappeared, including milkshake-thick clouds, extreme turbulence, high winds and marble-size rain drops that could lead to extreme icing conditions, he said, "They had pretty much everything against them," in an *Anchorage Daily News* article

A U.S. Air Force Hercules C-130, like the one pictured here in the late-1960s, searched throughout the night looking for Rep. Nick Begich's missing plane.

SOME LOW POINTS

titled, "Begich, Boggs missing," by Allan Frank, that appeared the day after the plane disappeared.

But many people believed Jonz, who had logged more than 10,000 flying hours, was "one of the best drivers there is." They thought he would be able to set the craft down in an emergency and held onto hope that all the men were alive and waiting for rescue somewhere in the wilderness.

The emergency locator transmitter thought to be on board the plane was designed to start operating on impact and had a range of up to 150 miles. Contact must be made on a line-of-sight basis, however. So if the plane had flown into a valley, searchers would need to fly directly over the plane to hear the signal.

"So far, we haven't heard a squeak out of it," National Transportation Safety Board spokesman William Moore told a newspaper reporter.

A Whittier electrician and several other workers claimed they heard a plane pass over at 9:30 a.m. on Oct. 16. People believed with the unusually mild, 45-degree weather and survival gear presumed to be on the airplane that the men could have survived a forced landing somewhere along their route.

But if the plane had gone into the Sound, their chances weren't as good. At the time of the plane's disappearance, average water temperature was 40 degrees Fahrenheit. Survival in the water under those conditions would be about two hours or less, according to experts.

Two days into the search, hopes rose when monitors in Juneau picked up three brief signals from an emergency beacon about 15 miles northwest of the state capital. But extensive searches flown just above the treetops could not locate any sign of an airplane or passengers.

Searchers selflessly flew in hair-raising weather conditions as hundreds of eyes looked for four needles in a 24,000-square-mile haystack. Even the Air Force sent its super secret spy plane, the SR-71 reconnaissance aircraft, to join the search on the fourth day.

Capable of sustaining altitudes in excess of 80,000 feet and flying more than three times the speed of sound (more than 2,000 mph), this

The U.S. Air Force sent its fastest and most spophisticated reconnaissance plane, the SR71, to help search for Congressman Nick Begich. Its secret equipment could survey everything within a 90-degree arc centered along the plane's line of flight. The jet was the successor to the U2 spy plane of the 1950s and early 1960s.

plane could cover 60,000 square miles in an hour and was equipped with infrared cloud-penetrating cameras.

But none of its efforts found the missing plane. Nor did claims from California ham operators that they'd heard distress calls late Monday night. Even three psychics flown to Alaska by Boggs' wife, Lindy, failed to find the men.

"I was torn between feeling that perhaps I was silly and wishing to do everything I could to be helpful to Hale and the others," Lindy Boggs told the *Anchorage Daily News* five years later.

She added that she spoke with her pastor about the first psychic who contacted her with tips about where the plane could be found. She said she was reluctant at first to give the psychic any credence, but the pastor urged her to follow up because "perhaps he's the answer to all the prayers that have been going up. Of course, you should act on it."

But the psychics she brought north did not have any luck finding the plane. Neither did the slew of other psychics, mystics, religious zealots and superannuated military "experts" who claimed to have special knowledge – nor the clairvoyant Kenyan who drew a map showing the Cessna's whereabouts – locate the missing men.

The longest aerial search in Alaska's history finally was called off on Nov. 24 as fresh snowfalls began covering the landscape. During its record-breaking 39 days, searchers traced down 88 leads or sightings, flew more than 3,600 hours and covered more than 325,000 square miles at a cost of nearly $1 million.

"The probability of detecting a fire or an electronic signal or any visual signal in the area has been fully explored," said Air Force Maj. Ken Shelley in an *Anchorage Daily Times* article. "We have at least 99 percent certainty that we would have seen some of those signals."

Civil Air Patrol pilots concluded that the plane was either under heavy snowfall on a glacier or in the water somewhere between Anchorage and Juneau.

"Basically our thoughts have been lumped into the two theories," CAP pilot Dale Jepsen, who logged 50 hours in the air search, told the *Anchorage Daily News* on Nov. 25, 1972. "The plane is probably on a glacier or in the ocean. After crossing and crisscrossing the territory so many times, there aren't many other possibilities left."

He added that most pilots think the plane is between Anchorage and Cordova.

"We doubt the pilot would bypass Cordova without making radio contact," Jepsen said.

Begich won his second-term bid 17 days after his plane disappeared, beating Republican Don Young of Fort Yukon.

Young won the seat in a special election in March 1973, after a District Court jury in Anchorage returned a verdict on Dec. 12, 1972, that Sen. Nick Begich, Russell Brown and pilot Don Jonz were presumed dead. The judge signed the death certificates on Dec. 28.

University of Alaska Fairbanks, William A. Egan papers, UAF-1985-120-131

Nick Begich, seen here with Alaska Gov. William A. Egan during the 1960s, won his bid for a second term as Alaska's lone Congressman even though he still was missing in November 1972.

An Anchorage District Court jury declared Boggs dead on Feb. 7, 1973. Bogg's wife was elected to her husband's seat in Louisiana later that year.

The U.S. Board of Geographic Names approved naming two peaks in the Chugach Mountains, six miles northwest of Whittier, after Begich and Boggs in 1976. Ten years later, the U.S. Forest Service built the Begich, Boggs Visitor Center at the head of Portage Valley, about 50 miles south of Anchorage. A memorial plaque was placed at the old Congressional Cemetery in Washington, D.C., in October 1982 to honor Begich. A plaque for Boggs had been placed there in 1981, resurrecting a practice that had been dormant for more than a century.

NTSB investigators later concluded that, "poor weather conditions not conducive to visual flight procedures was a critical factor in the crash." But they also said the plane would have to be found and examined before the true cause of the accident could be known.

Another mystery also surrounded this incident. Newspapers reported that Jonz's employees had found the emergency locator beacon that was thought to be in the missing Cessna on their boss' desk at his Fairbanks office. They also found all the survival kits known to them untouched in Fairbanks.

Some officials speculated that Jonz picked up survival gear and another locator beacon from friends or stores in Anchorage to use on the flight. But no one came forward to verify that hypothesis.

The official conclusion of the safety board was that the beacon and survival gear were not aboard the plane.

It didn't take long for conspiracy theories to emerge, due to Boggs' involvement in the investigation into the assassination of President John F. Kennedy and his disdain for J. Edgar Hoover of the Federal Bureau of Investigation. And one of the psychics who came to Alaska on Lindy Boggs' dime claimed he really knew where the plane had landed and that Boggs was still alive and being held for millions in ransom. Still others claimed the men had slipped away in the "Alaska Triangle," which covers Anchorage to Juneau to Barrow, where thousands of people have vanished over the years.

The disappearance of that airplane still remains a mystery.

U.S. Congressman Nick Begich

Nicholas J. Begich, of Croatian descent born April 6. 1932, in Eveleth, Minn., had served one term in the U.S. House of Representatives at the time of his disappearance in October 1972. He claimed to have been interested in politics since he was 7 and followed his father to town council meetings.

He also was interested in education. Begich drove to Alaska in 1956, along with wife Pegge Jean Jendro, after he accepted a position as boys' counselor for West Anchorage High School.

The educator later became principal of Ursa Minor Elementary School on Fort Richardson for four years and also served as student personnel director for Anchorage schools. He later was promoted to superintendent of Fort Richardson schools until forced to resign in 1969, because he had become a state senator representing Spenard. A court ruling barred elected officials from holding government jobs.

"I believe the greatest threat to America is the lack of political understanding and the overwhelming bureaucracy which can develop,"

Anchorage Daily Times photo

Nick Begich left behind his wife, Pegge, and six children, from left, Stephanie, Paul (in his mother's lap), Nick, Mark, Nichelle and Tom, seen here in 1968.

the Democrat said in a newspaper article in 1962 prior to winning his first term in the state Legislature.

Begich fought to improve standards for education and for teachers. He also worked on many other issues, including increasing aid to prospectors, placing controls on junkyards, making seatbelts in cars a priority, promoting fisheries and developing power through coal, gas and water.

The energetic senator beat Lowell Thomas Jr. for the seat in 1966, which is when Republicans fought to get the court to rule that legislators could not serve and get paychecks from government jobs at the same time. Don Young and George Homan also lost their jobs when the courts ruled in the Republicans' favor in 1969.

After losing his bid for the U.S. House of Representatives in 1967, Begich won his campaign in 1970. He defeated Frank Murkowski by more than 5,000 votes.

He once said the high point in his career in Washington, D.C., was the passage of the most comprehensive indigenous claims settlement in American history. Members of Congress praised him, as well, and said the subcommittee package he delivered was a tribute to his role as an architect of the House compromise.

"It is the best individual achievement I have ever heard for a freshman congressman," observed one veteran lobbyist, according to a 1976 Alaska Native Foundation article written about the Alaska Native land claims struggle incorporated into the Alaskool website.

The Alaska Native Claims Settlement Act passed both houses of Congress on Dec. 18, 1971, 10 months before the plane in which Begich was traveling disappeared en route from Anchorage to Juneau in October 1972. Begich, 40 at the time, left behind his wife and six children: Nick Jr, Nichelle, Tom, Mark, Stephanie and Paul.

MASS MURDER IN THE NORTH

36

MASSAGE PARLOR MURDERS

Money. Power. Sex. These were the elements involved in a string of killings connected to lucrative massage parlor and nightclub businesses flourishing in Anchorage during the mid-1970s.

Thousands of pipeline workers were arriving in town with wads of cash to spend – and massage parlors sprang up to help them spend it. The seedy storefronts offered relaxation and companionship from long, lonely hours on the North Slope. The Body Shop Massage in Spenard enticed customers with ads like "come on in and get your batteries checked and charged."

Prices posted on rate schedules ranged from $5 for an actual massage to $100 for a "date." Police considered most of the establishments to be fronts for prostitution, and it was common knowledge that anything could be had for a price at a massage parlor, according to newspaper accounts at the time.

The city had a law that mandated masseuses in the parlors be "of good moral character" and have no record of "pimping, pandering, prostitution, solicitation, lewd or lascivious acts with a child, larceny, robbery, assault with a deadly weapon or other similar crimes." But in Spenard, outside the city limits, no such laws existed.

With so much money changing hands, it's not surprising that many wanted a piece of the massage parlors' lucrative pie. Even the

Kim's Massage was one of many establishments that promised pipeline workers a good time in Anchorage during the 1960s and 1970s.

Internal Revenue Service and Alaska politicians tried to figure out ways to share in the wealth.

"Uncle Sam wants his share," a high-ranking official with the IRS said in 1973. He figured the government should tax the moneymaking massage business, which numbered 26 parlors in Anchorage by the mid-1970s.

The Alaska Legislature entertained a bill in 1975 calling for the legalization and regulation of prostitution to get tax revenue. It never passed out of committee.

The Anchorage Assembly appointed a 12-man commission to look at the possibility of legalizing and taxing the massage business. At a final vote, however, the assembly turned down the commission's plan.

Others took less noble routes to get their hands on all that cash – including murder. And while Alaskans saw several murders during the 1970s, none piqued the interest of the public more than what newspapers dubbed the "Massage Parlor Murders."

It began in November 1972 when Ferris Rezk Jr., owner of Cindy's Massage Parlor in Spenard, was found shot to death in his 1968 blue Plymouth a few blocks from the Kit Kat Club. Anchorage police arrested Clarence Wesley Ladd the next day and charged him with first-degree murder.

Ladd had moved to Anchorage that year after spending time in Cordova. He was a regular at the Kit Kat Club and wanted to get into the massage parlor business. He saw how a small grubstake could yield high profits.

Police believed that Ladd had shot the young Rezk, also known as a small-time pimp and heroin dealer, over a deal gone wrong to purchase Cindy's. Newspapers reported Rezk wanted $10,000 for his business, which was rumored to average weekly receipts of $5,000. Ladd had made a down payment of $4,000 after checking out the club at West 29th Avenue, and he later made one $3,000 payment.

The state asserted Ladd murdered Rezk because he did not have the money for that final $3,000 payment. Killing Resk would solve that problem.

A series of murders surrounding Cindy's Massage parlor rocked Anchorage during the early 1970s.

A standing-room-only crowd filled the courtroom when Ladd's trial began in late spring 1973 to hear Rezk's girlfriend and business partner testify. Patricia "Cindy" Bennett told the court that she saw Ladd shoot Rezk because the "organization wanted him dead," according to an article recounting the events featured in the *Anchorage Times* on Dec. 23, 1979.

Attorney Edgar Paul Boyko represented Ladd. Well-known for winning impossible cases, Boyko told the court that Rezk had been targeted by a criminal organization that wanted to set up a protection racket involving all the massage parlors in town. He said a mysterious hit man for the "Organization" had killed Rezk. The gun used in the murder had ended up in Ladd's hands when he struggled with the killer, who then got away.

Boyko grilled prosecution witness John F. "Johnny" Rich Jr. in an effort to give Ladd's defense credibility. He wanted the jurors to think that Rich was a player in the rumored Organization.

Rich, a well-known figure in Anchorage's underworld, had taken over the lease of Cindy's after Rezk's murder. He renamed the parlor New Cindy's Health Spa & Massage. A longtime Anchorage resident with several misdemeanor gambling charges, Rich also owned the 736 Club and Alaska Firearms Distributors.

As a witness for the prosecution, Rich testified that Ladd had come to him for a loan of $3,000 prior to the murder. He said he denied Ladd's request. Rich also said Ladd's girlfriend had called him after the murder to ask what he knew about the Organization.

Boyko cross-examined Rich for four hours in an effort to convince the jury that Rich was a nefarious character. It was an easy sell at the time – many people in Anchorage believed criminals and the Mob were running their town.

The defense strategy worked. After a month-long trial, the 12-woman jury found Ladd innocent.

Within a few months, Rich disappeared. The last time anyone saw him was on Aug. 22 sitting in his brown 1971 Cadillac near Pacific Auction on Old Seward Highway.

A few days after his disappearance, Ladd and attorney Duncan

Courtesy Stephen Cysewski

Many massage parlors and adult entertainment businesses made their way to Anchorage and were well-entrenched in downtown and Spenard during the early 1970s.

Webb appeared at Cindy's and claimed Rich had given them power of attorney to take possession of the parlor and other properties, according to the *Anchorage Times.*

The attempted takeover failed, and police were notified of the dispute.

Then someone shot the wife and son of nightclub owner Jimmy Sumpter while they slept in their Anchorage home on Nov. 26. The house was set afire to cover the murders. Sumpter's 16-year-old daughter escaped out a window and ran to a neighbor's house to get help.

Sumpter, owner of the Kit Kat Club and Sportsman Too, was out of the house picking up receipts from his clubs at the time of the murders. He arrived home in time to see firemen battling the blaze at his house.

Witnesses told police they had seen a car speeding away from the Sumpter home. The next day, authorities questioned a man named Gary Zeiger, whose car matched the description given at the scene.

Zeiger, who recently had been acquitted of murdering a young Anchorage woman, must have given the police some valuable information, because he was offered protective custody after posting bond. Zeiger declined the offer.

The next day his body was found dumped in the Potter Marsh area. He'd been killed with a single shotgun blast to his chest.

Rich's body was found on Dec. 20. Virginia Pinnick, Ladd's girlfriend, led state troopers to a shallow grave in the Jonesville coalmine area about 17 miles north of Palmer on the Glenn Highway. Rich had been shot twice.

The police began to think all these murders were connected. They believed Zeiger had a hand in both the Rich and Sumpter killings, and Zeiger and Pinnick were known associates of Wesley Ladd.

An indictment was handed down for Ladd and his friend, Guy Benny Eugene Ramey, in March 1974. Court records showed that Ramey had taken a flight to Seattle under the name John Rich the night of Rich's disappearance.

Ladd and Ramey were charged with first-degree murder and kidnapping of Rich. Two weeks after his arraignment, Ramey, 19, pleaded guilty to the kidnapping. The judge sentenced him to 10 years in jail, and Ramey agreed to testify against Ladd.

Pinnick was charged with first-degree murder the next month. The secret indictment connected the 19-year-old woman to Rich's killing. Her involvement was explained a few months later during the trial of Ladd's attorney, Webb, who had been charged with being an accessory after the fact and compounding a crime.

Webb's trial, held that July, happened before Ladd's because attorneys for Ladd wanted a change of venue for their client's trial. They requested it be moved to Kodiak, where newspaper coverage may not have tainted the jury pool.

During Webb's trial, prosecutors laid out their theory of what happened to Johnny Rich. They alleged that Ramey, Ladd and Zeiger had kidnapped Rich, driven him to Pinnick's Eagle River cabin and forced him to sign power of attorney papers for Cindy's.

The state asserted that Ladd shot Rich. Then Zeiger shot him again and took Rich's body to that abandoned mine near Palmer and buried it. Ramey boarded a plane for Seattle under the name John Rich in an effort to show that Rich still was alive.

Webb, who earlier had told investigators that Rich signed those documents in front of him and he then had taken Rich to the airport himself, retracted his statement. Webb told the court he'd been forced to tell police that Rich had gone to Seattle to deal with some business affairs. He said he did so because he was afraid for his life.

After closing arguments, the jury retired to weigh the evidence. But members of the jury could not come to an agreement, and Webb's first trial ended in a hung jury. He was convicted the next year, however, and disbarred from practice as an attorney in 1979.

After a two-week trial in Kodiak, a jury found Ladd guilty of the kidnapping and murder of Rich. Superior Court Judge James

University of Alaska Fairbanks, Kay J. Kennedy Aviation Collection, UAF-1991-98-319

Attorney Duncan Webb lied when he told police he dropped Johnny Rich Jr. at the Anchorage airport, seen here in the 1970s, to catch a flight to Seattle. An associate, Gary Zeigler, had impersonated Rich on that flight south.

Anchorage sprawled in 1973 from downtown toward Spenard and the mountains.

Fitzgerald sentenced Ladd to life in prison and called the Rich killing a "planned execution motivated by revenge."

Rich's daughter, Kim, a teen at the time of these murders, later researched this episode in Anchorage's past and wrote a book about it and her life with her father titled "Johnny's Girl." It later was made into a movie.

In the late 1970s, the Anchorage Assembly decided the time had come to crack down on the massage industry. After a hard-fought battle between parlor owners, municipal officials and citizens, a new ordinance passed in 1978. It required massage parlor operators to apply for licenses as physical culture studios.

That ordinance did not help protect the never-ending stream of young women who came north to work in these establishments, however. And soon strippers, topless dancers and prostitutes began disappearing.

37

ANCHORAGE DANCERS BECOME PREY

Young women began disappearing from Anchorage in the late 1970s – many of them strippers at bars and clubs that featured nude dancing. At first, no one paid much attention.

Joints like the Wild Cherry, Booby Trap and Great Alaskan Bush Company flew dancers in and out from the Lower 48 all the time. The businesses needed fresh, firm new bodies to keep their oil-boom clientele happy and spending.

So when women lured north with a promise of making big bucks "dancing" in the clubs were reported missing, many people just figured they'd gone back south.

But when the remains of young women began appearing in remote areas near Anchorage in 1980, authorities realized they had a serial killer in their midst. It would take another three years before they captured him.

Building workers discovered the first body in July 1980 in a shallow grave on Eklutna Lake Road. It contained the half-eaten remains of a young woman. The animal activity and extreme decomposition made identification impossible.

Police created a facial reconstruction that they widely publicized, but no one came forward with her identity. She became known as "Eklutna Annie."

Later that year another body was found at a gravel pit. The body was badly decomposed, but it later was identified as Joanne Messina, a Anchorage topless dancer.

Two years later, off-duty Anchorage police officers John Daily and Audi Holloway made another grisly discovery. They were hunting in the Knik River valley northeast of Anchorage when they came across a boot sticking out of the sand along the riverbank on Sept. 12, 1982, according to Walter Gilmour and Leland E. Hale, authors of "Butcher Baker." Then they saw a partially decomposed bone joint.

The remains were identified as those of 23-year-old topless dancer Sherry Morrow, last seen on Nov. 17, 1981.

The police created a forensic reconstruction of what the unidentified victim, found in a shallow grave on Eklutna Lake Road, looked like. Investigators named her "Eklutna Annie."

Morrow, who worked at the Wild Cherry, had been shot in the back three times.

Police discovered cartridges from a .223 Ruger Mini-14 hunting rifle at the scene. They also noted there were no bullet holes in the clothing of the victim, who was fully dressed in her grave.

Anchorage police had a nagging feeling following the September discovery. They'd been seeing an

Police released this photograph of jewelry found with "Eklutna Annie" in the hopes that someone might be able to identify her.

A never-ending stream of young women arrived in Alaska to "dance" at places like the Kit Kat Club in Anchorage during the 1970s and early '80s. When girls began disappearing, people thought they had just gone back south.

increase in missing persons reports filed, and many of those missing were prostitutes and topless dancers. But officers kept their suspicions to themselves.

"We don't believe we have a mass murderer out there, some psycho knocking off girls," Anchorage police detective Maxine Farrell told a reporter for the *Anchorage Daily News.*

Nine months later an incident occurred that began to unravel the mystery of what the media called "the missing dancers."

A nervous-looking, pockmarked man approached prostitute Cindy Paulson on an Anchorage street corner on June 13, 1983. He stammered and stuttered as he asked about her fees. Once they agreed on a price, she climbed into his car.

Before she knew it, the red-haired man had a gun to her head. He then slapped handcuffs on her wrists and drove her to a large, blue-gray ranch-style house in Muldoon. He forced her inside, dragged her down to his basement den and chained her naked to a pillar.

Robert Hansen dragged women to his trophy room, seen here in the basement of his home in Muldoon, and tortured them.

The small man with horn-rimmed glasses spent hours raping and torturing the girl. He finally tired and fell asleep on his couch.

Upon awaking, he unchained her, made her dress and then re-cuffed her. He shoved her into the back seat of his car, covered her with a blanket and drove to the Merrill Field airport, according to police reports.

He told her they were going to fly up to his cabin in the wilderness. He said he had taken lots of girls up there "for fun."

The man pulled up to a stop by a small plane, got out and began unloading things from the trunk.

The girl waited for the right moment when his back was turned. She then jumped out of the car and ran as fast as she could toward the lights on Fifth Avenue.

"Stop or I'll kill you!" shouted her captor as he chased after her with a gun.

She kept running. When she reached the roadway she saw

headlights from a truck coming toward her. She frantically waved with the cuffs dangling from her wrists.

Robert Yount, 36, slammed on his breaks. Paulson hopped in.

Paulson's detailed account to the police of her ordeal was backed up by a medical examination and the shackle marks around her neck and wrists. She gave investigators a description of her stuttering assailant, as well as his house, car and plane.

Officers took her to Merrill Field, where Paulson pointed out a blue-and-white Piper Super Cub, tail number N3089Z. It did not take long for the police to learn the plane belonged to Robert C. Hansen, a married 40-year-old baker. Within two hours of Paulson's escape, police knocked on Hansen's door on Old Harbor Road.

He looked exactly like Paulson had described.

Hansen appeared stunned when the police told him of the allegations against him and willingly went with the officers to the police station. During questioning, he remained cooperative. Although he claimed that Paulson probably just wanted to shake him down for money. He said he thought her story was absurd.

"You can't rape a prostitute, can you?" he said, according to authors Walter Gilmour and Leland E. Hale in their book, "Butcher Baker."

He went on to tell the police that his family was on vacation in Europe, but he could provide an alibi. He said he was with friends John Sumrall and John Henning at the time of the attack on Paulson. Both men later backed up Hansen's story.

Hansen also signed waivers to let authorities search his house, car and airplane.

During the searches, the police believed Paulson had been at Hansen's house and in his car and plane as they found her details to be accurate. But they did not know when she had been with Hansen. It all came down to a "he says, she says" between a respected Anchorage businessman and a prostitute with a criminal record. And when Paulson refused to take a lie detector test, the police dropped the investigation.

Anchorage Daily News photo
Investigators carefully sifted through sand and tundra in an effort to dig up evidence in the murders of several prostitutes and topless dancers in the early 1980s.

Three months after Paulson's abduction and attack, a third shallow grave was found along the banks of the Knik River. Topless dancer and prostitute Paula Goulding, 17, had been murdered exactly like Morrow and been redressed after death. An autopsy revealed she had been shot with a .223-caliber bullet.

Now local police knew they had a serial killer on the loose. They delved into Hansen's background and personal life and learned many things about the Anchorage baker.

Born on Feb. 15, 1939, in Iowa, he moved to Alaska in 1967. He and his second wife had two children, appeared to have a happy marriage and were active members of the Lutheran Church. He also had many prominent friends in the community.

His bakery at Ninth Avenue and Ingra Street also appeared to be successful, as he had earned enough money to purchase a Super Cub to help him pursue another passion: hunting.

Hansen was well known in Alaska hunting circles and held records for animals he bagged, including a big-horned Dall sheep with a bow and arrow. In 1969, 1970 and 1971 he had four animals entered into Pope & Young's trophy hunting world-record books.

Police also learned that along with burning a school bus garage when he was younger, and a few thefts later on, Hansen had been accused of raping several prostitutes since arriving in Anchorage. But people kept vouching for him, saying what an upstanding citizen he was and a good person who would never stoop to that, according to newspaper accounts.

Then in 1977, Hansen stole a chainsaw and was sentenced to five years in prison. That's when a prison psychiatrist diagnosed Hansen with bipolar-affective disorder and asked the court to order him to take Lithium to control mood swings. The order never was enforced. Hansen got out of prison after serving only one year of his five-year sentence.

By now Anchorage law officers were thinking Hansen looked good for the murders. They contacted the FBI, which assigned legendary Special Agent John Douglas to the case.

Douglas surmised the killer targeted prostitutes and topless dancers because most were transients who went unnoticed, according to his 1996 book, "Mind Hunter: Inside the FBI's Elite Serial Crime Unit."

Anchorage investigators shared information about Hansen with the profiler, who took note of Hansen's short stature, speech impediment and pockmarked face. Douglas felt the baker had been ridiculed for years and developed low self-esteem, which would have prompted him to move to an isolated area like Alaska. Douglas also said the abuse of prostitutes was possibly a way of getting back at women who had made fun of or rejected him.

The FBI profiler also offered his opinion that perhaps Hansen had turned his love of hunting

Robert Hansen, seen here with a goat he killed in 1969, was an avid hunter.

toward more interesting prey, and he believed the baker was probably a "saver" and would have kept souvenirs from his kills.

The Paulson case was reopened in an effort to get more evidence, and Douglas suggested the police question Hansen's two friends again to see if they would still provide an alibi for him.

When Sumrall and Henning were presented with possible perjury charges, both men changed their story and told investigators they were not with Hansen that evening. They had lied to help Hansen out with what they thought was an embarrassing domestic situation, according to Gilmour and Hale. The men then told police that Hansen was committing insurance fraud. He'd reported a burglary of valuable property from his home, but he actually was hiding those items.

The men's statements and the FBI profile allowed the police to obtain search warrants for Hansen's house and plane. Authorities then arrested Hansen at his bakery on Oct. 27, 1983. They took him to the Anchorage state trooper station and sat him down in an interrogation room that had been staged per FBI suggestions. Maps of the Knik River were pinned on the walls. Pictures of gravesites and victims lined the desk along with files and folders that were marked with names of Hansen's family, friends and acquaintances.

The troopers let him sit alone for a while as they observed his reactions through a

Investigators uncovered a secret hiding place in the attic of serial killer Robert Hansen. Along with the murder weapon, it held jewelry of his victims, an aerial map with markers of graves and several IDs.

two-way mirror. Then Sgts. Glenn Flothe and Darryl Galyan began their interrogation, which lasted five hours.

While the troopers were grilling Hansen, another team of officers searched his house. They eventually found a hidden space in the attic rafters that contained guns, jewelry, newspaper clippings and various ID cards, some belonging to the missing women, according to Michael Newton in his book, "Hunting Humans: An Encyclopedia of Modern Serial Killers." They also found a Ruger Mini-14 hunting rifle and an aviation map dotted with 20 asterisks – two of which corresponded with sites where bodies had been found earlier.

A third marked the spot where another body, that of 24-year-old Joanne Messina, had been found in July 1980. Investigators later learned she had last been seen with a man who stammered and had a pockmarked face.

Hansen denied any involvement in the murders.

On Nov. 3, 1983, an Anchorage grand jury returned four indictments against Hansen: first-degree assault and kidnapping of Paulson; five counts of misconduct in possession of a handgun; theft in the second-degree; and theft by deception in insurance fraud.

Anchorage Times photo

Robert Hansen was arrested in the murders of four women after ballistics evidence proved that cartridges found at the crime scenes matched his rifle.

When the ballistics reports came back on Nov. 20 that confirmed Hansen's rifle was the weapon that killed Sherry Morrow and Paula Goulding, Hansen was charged with first-degree murder. He confessed at that point.

Hansen said the asterisks on the map marked the gravesites of prostitutes he murdered. He told police that he did not murder every woman he raped and then flew to the wilderness, however. If the girls complied and didn't give him any trouble, he flew them home with a warning to not tell the cops what he had done.

But if they resisted his wishes, he forced them to strip at gunpoint and then made them run. It was like "going after a trophy Dall sheep or a grizzly bear," he told investigators.

"As long as ... she would go along with what I wanted out there, OK. We'd go home and that was it," Hansen said in his confession.

"And what if they didn't comply?" an investigator asked.

"They ... they stayed," Hansen said.

The mass murderer said he usually gave the women a head start. Then he hunted them. Once in a while he let a victim think she had escaped. But then he would track her down and make her run again. He continued his cat and mouse game until she was too cold and tired to run anymore.

He'd then shoot her and dress the body. This ritual satisfied his need for control and it was his "trophy," police surmised.

He claimed he killed 17 women and raped another 30. The baker told police that his first victim was Joanne Messina. He said he killed her in July 1980 and then became violently ill.

A few weeks later, he picked up another prostitute. When she said "no" to his request, he chased her down Eklutna Lake Road and stabbed her to death. He said he found that experience thrilling.

From that point on he indulged his fantasy of hunting and killing women. He targeted strippers and prostitutes because they were harder to track and less likely to be missed.

He sent his family on a trip to Europe the summer of 1983. With them gone, he began bringing women to his house. He even ran ads in a local singles newspaper that sought women to "join me in finding what's around the next bend, over the next hill," according to Newton in his book, "Hunting Humans."

At the end of the interview, Hanson was given a large aerial map of the region. He identified 15 gravesites – 12 of which were unknown to investigators. Hansen boarded a military helicopter with investigators the next day and helped them locate the gravesites.

Police said he joyfully pointed out the graves, sometimes dropping to his knees and digging through the snow with his bare hands to help officers get to them.

On Feb. 18, 1984, Hansen pleaded guilty to four counts of first-degree murder in the cases of Joanna Messina,

Mass murderer Robert Hansen marked circles on an aerial map, provided by the police, to show where he had buried the women he had killed.

who disappeared from a Seward campground May 19, 1980; "Eklutna Annie," an unidentified woman he had picked up on an Anchorage street in 1979 and whose body was found near Eklutna Lake in July 1980; Sherry Morrow, 23, last seen on Nov. 7, 1981, when her boyfriend brought her to work at the Wild Cherry; and Paula Golding, who disappeared from her job at the Great Alaskan Bush Company on April 25, 1983.

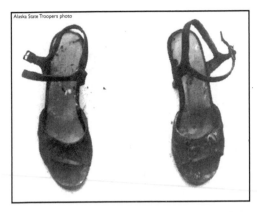

Invesigators found this pair of shoes in one of the graves they found on sandbars near Knik.

Nine days later, prosecutor Frank Rothschild addressed the court prior to sentencing.

"Your honor, before you sits a monster, an extreme aberration of a human being, a man who has walked among us for 17 years ... selling us doughnuts, Danish and coffee, all with a pleasant smile," Rothschild said, according to court records.

"His crimes numb the mind. Hearing him tell of his crimes saps the body of energy, saps the spirit."

Superior Court Judge Ralph Moody sentenced the 45-year-old killer to 461 years plus life without the possibility of parole.

The legal system decided not to prosecute him for the remaining murders, even though he pleaded guilty to them. He never was going to get out of jail and was called "the most prolific mass murderer in modern Alaska history."

In May 2014, due to poor health, Hansen was transferred from the Spring Creek Correctional Center in Seward to the Anchorage Correctional Center, where he could receive medical treatment. The 75-year-old, nicknamed the Butcher Baker, died at Alaska Regional Hospital on Aug. 21, 2014.

His family never knew about his double life, and his wife, Darla, divorced him and left the state two years after his guilty plea.

The Hansen case is the first known killing spree where many of the victims were flown into the wilderness, freed and then hunted down. It also set a legal precedent in 1983 when psychological profiling was used as the main basis for issuing search warrants on Hansen's property, according to Bernard DuClos, author of "Fair Game."

38

THE MAIL DAY MURDERS

When McCarthy's residents awoke on March 1, 1983, they had no way of knowing that six of them would not live to see another sunrise. Most were looking forward to that Tuesday morning – it was mail day.

Anyone who has ever lived in rural Alaska knows the importance of mail day. That's when everyone gathers at the airstrip or postmaster's to visit while waiting for the mail plane to land.

Visiting was the center of their social life. Once a thriving community with about 1,000 people when the Kennecott copper mines were operating decades ago, the 50-mile radius around McCarthy and Kennicott only numbered a couple dozen in the early 1980s.

Members of the community, located about 230 miles east of Anchorage in the middle of the Wrangell-St. Elias National Park and Preserve, generally gathered at Hegland's house to enjoy tea, snacks and conversation while waiting for the mail to arrive.

Les, 64, and Flo Hegland, 58, had lived there since 1967. They'd built an addition onto their front porch to store neighbors' packages and groceries that arrived each week and were considered the community's unofficial postmasters.

The couple's two-way radio was the only one powerful enough to reach the world outside the immediate area – without it McCarthy was cut off from civilization. And that's the way most residents liked

Tourists began showing up in the summers to tour the closed Kennecott mine buildings and area during the mid-1950s, as seen in this photo of people checking out McCarthy. But only a handful of people stayed during the winters, as in 1983.

it. They loved going without commercial electricity, running water and telephones.

"Around here, there are so few of us that we know each other by our boot tracks," McCarthy resident Nancy Gilbert later told a reporter with *The Philadelphia Enquirer.*

Construction worker Christopher Richards, 29, saw Louis Hastings walking toward his red millworker's cabin in Kennicott around 8:30 that morning. He called out to the 39-year-old newcomer to come in for a cup of coffee and then went back to preparing his breakfast. Hastings, who lived in Anchorage, often came to work on a cabin he'd bought several months earlier. The two men were the only people living in Kennicott.

When Richards turned to greet Hastings, he felt something strike his right cheek and shatter his glasses. He ducked. Then he felt something hit the top of his head. He spun around and saw a rifle.

The men struggled for control of the weapon as Richards screamed for Hastings to stop.

"Look, you're already dead," came Hastings' reply. "If you'll just quit fighting, I'll make it easy for you," he added, according to newspaper accounts of the event.

Richards did not give up. Instead he grabbed a knife from near his sink and stabbed his attacker in the chest and again in his right leg. He then escaped into the deep snow in his socks, T-shirt and lightweight slacks.

He managed to make it to a neighbor's unoccupied cabin about three-quarters of a mile away while Hastings kept shooting at him, once nicking him in his right arm. At the cabin, Richards donned a parka, boots and snowshoes and then headed to the Nash's cabin.

Once there, Tim, 38, and Amy Nash, 25, tended to Richards' wounds as he filled them in on the shooter. The newlyweds told Richards they had seen Hastings heading toward McCarthy about 20 minutes before Richards arrived at their place.

The couple jumped on their snowmachine, and towing Richards in a sled behind them, raced to the runway to warn those who would be waiting for the mail plane. They met Gary Green, a local pilot and guide, on the north end of the airstrip. After discussing the shooting incident, Tim Nash decided to go check on the Heglands while Green warmed up his plane to fly Richards to get medical attention at Glennallen, about a 45-minute flight.

As Green taxied over to Richards to load the wounded man in the plane, he saw Tim Nash running back down the airstrip toward him. Nash told Green he'd smelled gunpowder at the Heglands' and saw a huge amount of blood. Then, from the kitchen, he saw Hastings on the back porch. Nash said he fired a shotgun blast at Hastings, but it struck a doorjamb.

Hastings returned fire and hit Nash in the right leg.

The group decided that Green needed to get Richards to medical help and that the Nashes would stay and warn everyone to stay away from the airfield. When Green took off,

University of Alaska Fairbanks, Bruce Haldeman Collection, UAF-2003-139-157

Christopher Richards was the only other person living in Kennicott when Louis Hastings went on his rampage.

he saw the Nashs walking toward each other on the runway. He then contacted the pilot of the incoming mail plane and told him not to land at McCarthy. Next, he radioed the Alaska State Troopers.

Back on the ground, Hastings made his way to the airstrip and crawled up a big mound of plowed snow across from the young couple. He took aim and fired about 10 rounds at them. After the pair fell, he walked toward them and fired another two shots. When Hastings got close to their bodies, he fired two more rounds into their heads. He then dragged them to deeper snow to hide their bodies.

Harley King, 61, soon arrived on his snowmachine pulling Donna Byram, 29, standing on a sled behind. Byram was going to fly out that day on the mail plane.

Byram saw Hastings walking over a snowbank and then noticed blood in the snow. She wondered why anyone would butcher an animal there.

Hastings opened fire as the snowmachine approached the Nashs' bodies.

Byram saw bullets hit King and his snowmachine. Then she felt a bullet hit her upper right arm.

King sped away from Hastings, but lost control of his machine as a bullet had broken his leg. Both King and Byram were thrown toward the path leading to the Hegland's.

Byram tried to load King back on his snowmachine as Hastings made his way toward them.

King told her he couldn't move and she needed to save herself.

As she raced up the path toward the Hegland's, Byram heard two shots and knew King must be dead.

She saw the Hegland's door had been kicked in and decided to hide near their greenhouse. Moments later, she heard Hastings coming up the path. Then she heard him call out.

"One not dead. One not dead."

She stayed as quiet as she could, listening to Hasting's footsteps as he searched for her. Then abruptly he stopped, got on King's snowmachine and sped away.

Soon an unmarked police helicopter flew over McCarthy and state troopers spotted Hastings heading west on McCarthy Road, 20 miles from the town. When they landed, Hastings gave up and did not resist arrest.

University of Alaska Fairbanks, Regina Knill Cope Collection, UAF-1991-156-6

McCarthy was named for prospector James McCarthy, and nearby Kennicott Glacier was named for early explorer Robert Kennicott.

Instead, he tried to convince the officers that his name was Chris Richards and that Lou Hastings had "gone beserk" and was "shooting up McCarthy."

His ruse did not work. Troopers knew the real Richards was receiving medical treatment at Faith Hospital in Glennallen, 100 miles northwest. They also had a good description of the real Hastings: a large, balding, soft-spoken man who wore glasses and had a shaggy red beard.

With Hastings in custody, troopers made their way to McCarthy. They found three dead at the airstrip and then walked up the path to the Hegland's home. There they found Byram scared but alive.

They also found three bodies in the bedroom inside the home, stacked "like cordwood," according to one trooper. The Heglands and Maxine Edwards, a 52-year-old homesteader who had crossed the frozen Kennicott River that morning to visit her friends, had all sustained multiple gunshot wounds. Troopers also found a silencer on the nightstand.

"There was a lot of shooting that went on inside that house," Capt. Jim Landsberry told reporters. "There were a lot of bullets sprayed around."

While Alaskans were shocked to learn about the massacre of six people and wounding of two others, they may have been more shocked when investigators unearthed the reason for the killings. Hastings, a freelance computer programmer who came to Alaska from

Louis Hastings surrendered without incident to Alaska State Troopers the same day he killed six people in March 1983.

California in 1980, wanted to destroy the trans-Alaska oil pipeline.

He had fled the overdeveloped West Coast in search of clean, uncluttered wilderness. But instead he found Alaska booming with development and blamed the pipeline for that condition.

Hastings "was disturbed by the population growth and influx of money into the state and determined that the best way to interrupt this was to destroy the pipeline and thus cut off Alaska's wealth and consequent growth," according to a psychiatric report later made public.

The madman's plan included killing all those who lived in McCarthy and then hijacking the mail plane. He planned to fly the plane to Glennallen, land it and then rig the plane to take off with no one at the controls.

The next step was to commandeer a fuel truck, drive to a pipeline pump station nearby and ram the truck into the pipeline while he shot at the pipe. He figured the truck would burst into flames, and he would die and be burned beyond recognition. Which is what he wanted, because he did not want his family to know that he was a murderer who committed suicide. He thought everyone would assume an unknown killer had murdered him, along with all the people in McCarthy, and then destroyed the pipeline.

During a psychiatric hearing, Hastings' public defender told the court Hasting thought he was doing a good thing.

"... Mr. Hastings thought he was going to be the savior of the Alaska wilderness," John Salemi said.

Newspapers reported that the prosecutor in Hastings' case

thought the mass murderer was quite smart. Hastings was "a very bright guy, a nerdy academic whose wig is on probably a little too tight," he said in a 1997 interview.

In July 1984, Superior Court Judge Ralph Moody sentenced Hastings to 634 years in prison following the mass murderer's plea of no contest.

"I don't think I have any choice but to insure you never walk again as a free man," Moody said when he rejected a plea to have Hastings declared insane at the time of the killings.

Richards never fully recovered emotionally from Hastings' attack.

"I basically considered him to be a quiet, serious guy," Richards later told the *Juneau Empire*. "I considered him a friend."

The summer after the attack, Richards told reporters he could not understand why Hastings used a silencer on his gun.

"Why would you put a silencer on to kill the only other person in a ghost town?"

The attack left Richards with double vision, a plastic eye socket and many unanswered questions.

While many people claimed he was a hero on that horrible day and saved many lives by escaping and telling others about the attack, Richards was tormented with guilt and depression. He started drinking heavily. But he remained in his little cabin at the Kennicott mill site with no electricity and hauling water in plastic jugs.

On Dec. 19, 2001, his cabin went up in flames. Residents from McCarthy hurried to the scene after spotting a red glow. When they saw his white husky mix whining outside the cabin door, they knew Richards was inside. But there was nothing they could do. The cabin burned to the ground.

All the Alaska State Troopers found were a few bone fragments in the ruins.

"Everyone told me Chris had been leading a tormented life," Sgt. Carl Erickson told the *Anchorage Daily News*. The state trooper said no foul play was suspected.

But several people who knew Richards, said Hastings had finally claimed a seventh life.

39

MASSACRE AT MANLEY

Evil arrived in the "grass-mowingest town in Alaska" on May 14, 1984. A brown Dodge sedan loaded with guns, trunks of clothes and an aluminum canoe strapped on top rolled into Manley Hot Springs that Monday.

The driver headed down to the banks of the Tanana River, about three miles southwest of town, and parked. A scraggly drifter stepped out and surveyed the wilderness. He decided this was a good spot to set up camp and settled near an abandoned salmon processing plant.

People began disappearing four days later.

Before Michael Alan Silka, 25, arrived in Manley, life in the small village was easygoing with warm summers, almost constant sunlight and little rain. It was a perfect place for gardening and growing lush lawns.

Most of the 80 or so residents had lived there anywhere from a few months to 50 years. Most were self-employed as fishermen, miners, trappers and builders. The privately owned hot springs served as a perfect spot for a warm, relaxing bath.

Villagers, who regularly traveled back and forth to Fairbanks for supplies, were used to seeing strangers like Silka come to town. After all, the bumpy and dusty road that spurred off the Elliott Highway ended at the old gold rush town on the Tanana River, about 160 miles west of Fairbanks.

The few residents of Manley were used to people traveling to the end of the Elliott Highway, about 160 miles west of Fairbanks, to enjoy the hot springs near their small community. This photo is circa 1913, six years after a miner named Frank Manley built the Hot Spring Resort Hotel.

"We get quite a few weird people that come through just because we're at the end of the road," resident Liza Verment told a reporter for the *Anchorage Times* later that May. They called those who wandered into town each spring "end-of-roaders."

Residents of Manley welcomed strangers into their town, and they considered themselves lucky, as everyone got along so well.

"We don't have the feuding that so many other Interior villages seem to have," 25-year resident Chuck Dart said in an *Anchorage Times* interview. "People here have their spats, but there are no long-term feuds."

But the atmosphere in their little village, where the post office and general store are about the only businesses open year-round, changed dramatically after Silka arrived in town.

Those who spoke to him described Silka, who stood about 5 feet 8 inches tall, as a man preoccupied with staking out a homestead near Lake Minchumina where a federal homesteading program had opened land. He also appeared obsessed with getting a permanent fund dividend check.

Although Silka chatted with several townspeople, he did not share information about his past. He did not tell them his name, or that there was a warrant out for his arrest in his hometown of Hoffman Estates, Ill., for weapons-related offenses. He did not share that he had compiled a record of arrests for assaults on a police officer, vandalism and burglary. Nor did Silka, who had been in Alaska only a month or so, tell them he was suspected of murdering Roger Culp in Fairbanks before he drove to their quaint little town.

Silka had rented a cabin next to Culp in a remote part of Fairbanks in April. Witnesses told police they had seen Silka and Culp enter Silka's cabin together on April 28, the last day anyone ever saw Culp.

When Alaska State Troopers received a report of a disturbance, they found bloodstains and empty ammunition shells outside Silka's cabin. They questioned Silka, who told them he had butchered a moose.

Two weeks later, authorities received a missing persons report on Culp, 34. They returned to Silka's cabin, but he had vanished. They retested the blood on the ground – it was human. They pegged Silka as the prime suspect in Culp's disappearance and figured he'd dumped the man's remains into the Tanana River. Troopers issued an all-points bulletin for his arrest. But public notices didn't get printed until May 21, according to trooper spokesman Paul Edscorn.

No, Silka did not talk about his past with the people of Manley. Instead he spent his days hanging around his makeshift camp. Many had seen the Dodge that he slept in, a gasoline can cut in half with a screen laid over it that he used as a stove, and his 17-foot motorized aluminum canoe that he intended to launch when the ice fully cleared from the channel.

Theresa Coner, a woman who had left Portland, Ore., a month earlier "to get away from all the crazies," was one of the first people to encounter Silka when she went down to watch the ice break and roll out of the river.

She assumed Silka was doing the same. But he was doing more.

"He was messing around with a knife, the longest Bowie knife I've ever seen," Coner later told an *Anchorage Times* reporter. "He seemed really lost, a loner type."

Others said they saw him walking around barefooted and in shorts, talking to himself but not making any sense.

University of Alaska Fairbanks, Walter and Lillian Phillips Collection, UAF-1985-72-68

Residents of Manley often went down to the boat launch area to watch the ice break up each spring.

Sabrenia Gurtler, who had hunted and trapped in Manley for a decade, had a weird experience with the drifter, too. She said she rode her bike down to the river on Wednesday, May 16, to watch the ice. Silka startled her as he emerged from the bushes wearing only a small towel.

The scruffy stranger tried to persuade her to stay by saying there was a bear nearby. But Gurtler had not seen any claw marks in the soft soil, nor had her dog barked any warnings, so she told Silka she would take her chances with the bear and pedaled the three miles back to town, according to an article in the *Anchorage Times*.

Thursday morning, the unemployed transient bought 10 gallons of gas, some Spam and a can of beans from Bob Lee, owner of the Manley Roadhouse. He paid with a $50 bill, perhaps a clue to why Culp disappeared.

That afternoon, people of Manley began to disappear.

Vietnam veteran Larry Joe McVey, 38, and Dale Madjeski, 24, headed to the boat launch around 3 p.m. to put their boat in the water to go fishing. McVey, a trapper who had lived in the fishing and mining community for about 10 years, and his wife, Alice, divided their time between Manley and their trapping camp across the river.

Madjeski, who worked in a local fish camp since moving to Manley about a year before Silka arrived in town, and his wife, Kristen, spent the winter at Baker Creek, just upriver from Manley.

Albert Haden, 27, followed close behind the two men that day. Haden, a trapper who had lived in Manley with his parents since he was a teen, told builder Bill Dade that he was going to the Tanana to look for an old radiator hose among some abandoned cars near the riverbank.

Other villagers noticed Lyman Klein, a 36-year-old ham radio operator, along with his pregnant wife, Joyce, 30, and their 2-year-old son, Marshall, riding their four-wheel, all-terrain vehicle toward the landing around the same time. They liked to go down and watch the broken ice roll out of the river.

Liller Burke watched her husband, Fred "Weed" Burke, leave his fish camp on the Kantishna River between 2:45 p.m. and 3:45 p.m. on his first spring trip down the river. It took about an hour via riverboat to make the trip to the Manley boat launch. Burke, a 30-year-old fisherman and trapper, planned to go ashore to replace the clutch and pressure plates in his Ford pickup. He told his family he'd be home that night.

Fishermen, like Fred Burke, put their boats in the water after the Tanana River ice went out each May.

No one knows exactly what happened after 3

p.m. that Thursday. But no one who went to the boat launch ever returned.

Due to the independent nature of Manley's residents, people didn't realize at first that six of their neighbors had not come back from the river. But many people were becoming concerned by Friday afternoon.

Alice McVey and Kristen Madjeski thought their husbands may have motored two miles west across the half-mile stretch of river to feed six sled dogs at McVey's fish camp. They later learned the dogs had not been fed.

When the men did not return by 5 p.m., Albert Hagen Sr. drove to the landing and noticed Silka's canoe was gone. Residents who encountered Silka earlier had noticed that his canoe looked ill-suited to the river's 8 mph current and his 3-1/2 horsepower engine needed repair.

Hagen Sr. returned two hours later and saw McVey's boat partially beached.

Manley schoolteacher Damaris Morvedt, a close friend of the Kleins, went down to the river to see if she could spot them. She found their four-wheeler behind a shed at the landing and wrote them a message.

"We are concerned about you. Please stop at my house no matter what time and get me up. I want to know for sure!"

Morvedt attached her note to the vehicle.

"It took a little while for people to realize the river landing was the common denominator for all the missing people," Vermet later told the *Anchorage Times*.

Once it dawned on them, more concerned residents went down to the boat launch to look for their missing friends. That's when they spotted a lot of blood-splattered muck and empty ammunition shells alongside Silka's camp.

They immediately suspected that Silka was involved in the disappearances. They called the Alaska State Troopers around 11 p.m., filled them in on the missing people and gave them the license

plate number on Silka's car.

The Special Emergency Reaction Team of the Alaska State Troopers mobilized immediately. The team, specially trained to conduct manhunts and take charge in situations involving hostages, dressed in military fatigues and protective vests. They grabbed communications equipment and heavy-duty firepower.

They then flew two Bell Jet Ranger helicopters to Manley to assist other troopers and Fish and Wildlife Protection officers who

Alaska State Troopers, armed with high-powered rifles, searched for a suspected murderer via helicopter near Manley on May 19, 1984.

already were there working the ground, searching in small planes and running boats along the Tanana.

By 2 a.m. Saturday, troopers were nestled among logs and debris near the landing. They hoped Silka would come back for his car.

"We just sat there and I tried to imagine what it was like ... a 2-year-old kid," investigator Jim McCann later recalled. "We knew he was ours if he came back."

Other troopers scanned hundreds of square miles of wilderness by air.

"One complication we encountered was the recent opening of the spring bear season," Alaska State Trooper Lt. Jeff Hall later said.

MASS MURDER IN THE NORTH

"The normally empty area was full of hunters, all of whom had to be identified and cleared."

Police spent the day landing near hunting camps, verifying identities, and flying up rivers and streams looking for Silka's canoe.

Around 2 p.m. two Fish and Wildlife Protection officers spotted Silka on the Zitziana River, a tributary of the Tanana, about 25 air miles southwest of Manley. They relayed his position to the troopers, who then flew the helicopters to Silka's location.

The left-side doors of the chopper had been removed. Trooper Troy Duncan sat in the left rear seat, his feet on the skid, facing outward. Trooper Hall sat in the left front. Both were armed with high-powered M-16 rifles that held 20-round magazines loaded with tracer rounds, according to an account written by Hall for *Tactical Life*.

The troopers planned to put a sniper on the ground upriver from Silka, according to Hall. Then as Silka approached the sniper, the helicopters would converge and Silka would be surrounded and surrender.

Silka had other ideas.

As the choppers approached around 4 p.m., the second helicopter veered off to check a man standing on the bank of the river. The troopers spotted the canoe tethered behind Burke's riverboat, which was tied to a tree in a slough. Troopers then saw Silka bend over, reach for something and duck behind some trees.

Before the helicopter could react and rise out of harm's way, Silka swung his Ruger, single-shot 30.06 toward the troopers. Silka, Hall and Duncan all fired simultaneously, according to Hall.

Silka fired again, hitting Duncan in the neck. The three-year veteran of the Fairbanks troopers' post died instantly.

Alaska State Trooper Troy Duncan was the third state trooper to die in the line of duty following Alaska statehood.

Investigators towed a boat carrying the bullet-riddled body of mass murderer Michael Alan Silka toward Manley Hot Springs on May 20, 1984.

Hall fired eight or nine bursts. Those bullets found their mark in Silka's legs, body and head. He also died instantly.

Many Manley residents gathered at the roadhouse on Saturday to console each other and share bits and pieces of rumor and fact. And that is where they got the official word that Alaska State Troopers were on the scene and Silka was dead.

"They hadn't made any statements until then," Vermet said. "Rumors were really flying."

Police explained that Silka had been armed with several rifles and pistols. He also had a riverboat belonging to Burke, who troopers believed had been heading for Manley Hot Springs when Silka killed him at the boat landing.

"Silka opened fire from a hidden position, and we returned the fire," said Capt. Donald Lawrence, a commander who had been sitting in the right rear of the helicopter in which Duncan had been killed. Lawrence was hit by bullet fragments and needed treatment for minor wounds to his face.

Following the murders, the people of Manley Hot Springs reminisced about their missing neighbors. They said the seven people were like most people in small Interior Alaska towns. They wanted to be left alone to enjoy the wilderness and to live their lives in peace.

The townspeople also recalled Silka's odd behavior.

"He acted real crazy," said Patricia Lee, who operated the Manley Roadhouse with her husband, in a *Chicago Daily Herald* interview four days after the murders. "He talked about how he could smell clams through the dirt. When I met him, I felt uneasy, but I kept telling myself that was silly."

Another resident said Silka seemed OK.

"... but then he couldn't stop messing around with that knife," Teresa Conger told the *Herald*. "He had a huge knife he just kept sharpening and sharpening. He was just obsessed with that."

Gwen Evans, who worked at the Manley lodge, said she saw Silka regularly and thought he was strange.

"I talked to him three times the day before and got no response," Evans told a reporter in December 1984. "He just was staring off into space. But, in God's name, I didn't know his mind was that far off."

Others said no one tried to get information from him about his past, because that was not something the people of Manley did.

Troopers carry the body of Michael Alan Silka, 25, ashore at Manley Hot Springs on Sunday, May 20, 1984.

Anchorage Times photo

The residents of Manley learned that Michael Alan Silka, seen here in a mug shot taken earlier in his life, had a troubled past and was wanted for questioning in the April murder of his neighbor in Fairbanks.

"A lot of people move here for reasons they don't want to talk about, and you don't want to appear nosy or pry," a Manley resident told the *Anchorage Times* the day after the murders were discovered. "They have a right to their private business."

Some speculate that Madjeski and McVey were the first to meet up with Silka. Perhaps the drifter killed the men after an argument or for their boat. Hagen may have come along and witnessed the killings, so Silka took care of him, too.

The Kleins may have picked the wrong time to make one of their frequent forays to look at the river. Silka would not want witnesses to his crimes. And Burke may have arrived in time to see Silka dragging dead bodies along the shore and dumping them into the swirling, mud-choked Tanana River.

Silka may have liked Burke's 20-foot boat, with its customized snowmachine windshield and newly painted engine, better than the first men's boat. So he tied his canoe to the back of it and ended up on the Zitziana where the troopers found him.

It appears that Silka headed to Alaska because he wanted to live the life of a woodsman in the wilderness. Those who knew him in Illinois said he always dressed like a hunter and was basically a loner.

After spending a cold night on a sandbar after they ran out of gas, troopers brought Silka's body back to Manley Sunday morning.

They had wrapped it in an orange tarp, put it in Silka's canoe and towed it back with Burke's boat, splattered with Silka's blood from the shootout the previous day.

They also brought back what they found tucked into Burke's boat: five high-powered rifles, two metal ammunition boxes and cardboard boxes full of shells. More boxes of bullets were found in Silka's car, along with traps, camping gear, snowshoes, an archery set, two wolf pelts and other outdoor equipment.

Some Manley residents vented their anger at Silka by destroying his beat-up sedan and then pushing it into the Tanana.

"The boys shot it up, beat it up, tore it up and shoved it in the river," flying service operator Cy Hetherington later told newspaper reporters. "I think it may have helped. It got some of it out of their systems."

Manley resident Frank Gurtler told the *Anchorage Times* that there no longer was any sign of the vehicle in the river.

"When they first pushed it in there was a little corner sticking up, but now there's nothing," Gurtler said. "That river rolls things up in a ball, turns them around and carries them off. They'll never see that car again."

The same goes for the bodies Silka apparently dragged to the river.

Authorities spent days searching the mucky bottom of the silt-choked Tanana

Anchorage Times photo

Searchers dragged the bottom of the Tanana River with hooks like these in an effort to find the bodies of missing Manley Hot Springs residents.

River for the missing people. Residents and some people from other areas joined the effort with boats, grappling hooks and gaffs. They found no trace of the seven presumed killed by Silka.

Many believed the bodies would never be found.

Then during mid- and late June, the river gave up four of the victims: Lyman Klein, Dale Madajski, Larry Joe McVey and Fred Burke. All had died from gunshots to their heads.

By the end of the year, Joyce Klein, her 2-year-old son, Marshall, and Albert Hagen Jr. were still missing, as was Roger Culp of Fairbanks.

Controversy swirled when Silka was buried with military honors at the National Cemetery in Sitka. Established in 1867, following Alaska's purchase from Russia, it is the oldest national cemetery west of the Mississippi River.

The military stood by its decision, stating that Silka had served honorably in the U.S. Army and that was the only criteria for a military burial, which had been requested by his father. Silka had been honorably discharged from the Army in 1981, following a four-year hitch – part of which he spent as a helicopter mechanic at Fort Wainwright near Fairbanks.

"Anyone honorably discharged from any of the military branches, including the Coast Guard, is eligible, regardless of whether they're Black or White, man or woman, Jew or Gentile," cemetery director Marv Krause told a reporter for the *Anchorage Times* on June 9, 1984.

"We do not have an area for paupers or for anyone like Mr. Silka, accused of what he has done," Krause added.

State Trooper Duncan was posthumously honored with the Medal of Valor, given a memorial service in Fairbanks and then buried near his mother in Texas.

Six Mass Murders in Five Years

The Manley Hot Springs massacre was the sixth time in less than five years that mass murder hit an Alaska community. It began, some say, with Robert C. Hansen, Anchorage bakery owner, who admitted killing 17 women over a several year span until police arrested him in 1983. Hansen was sentenced to 461 years in prison.

On Aug. 29, 1979, the second string of murders started when a woman disappeared in the Fairbanks area. She later was found dead. Five more victims followed. After four years investigating the deaths, police narrowed their list of suspects to U.S. Air Force enlisted man Thomas Richard Bunday. He had been assigned to Eielson Air Force Base, and then was transferred to Texas.

He admitted to Alaska State Troopers that he had killed five of the six women. But before he could be tried, he drove his motorcycle on to a Texas highway and smashed it head-on into a truck. Police suspected it was a suicide.

The next murders occurred on May 3, 1982. Charles Meach, a mental patient on a work-release program from Alaska Psychiatric Institute in Anchorage, shot four teens at Russian Jack Springs Park – two girls and two boys.

Alaska Department of Health and Social Services photo

ALASKA PSYCHIATRIC INSTITUTE

Charles Meach was receiving treatment at the Alaska Psychiatric Institute in Anchorage when he murdered four teens on May 3, 1982.

Meach was receiving treatment at API following an innocent by reason of insanity verdict in the beating death of an Anchorage grocery store clerk in 1973. The court sentenced Meach to serve 396 years for killing the teens.

On Sept. 7, 1982, only four months after the Russian Jack Springs Park murders, a 58-foot purse seine fishing boat from Blaine, Wash., burst into flames a short distance from the dock at Craig in Southeast Alaska. When Alaska State Troopers stepped inside the *Investor*, they discovered the remains of at least seven people. Mark and Irene Coulthurst, their two children and an uncertain number of their crew had been shot. Investigators believed some of the bodies had been consumed in the fire and never were located.

Witnesses told the troopers they had seen a young man leave the blazing boat. Police investigated this case for two years and then arrested a former crewmember, John Kenneth Peel.

The first trial, held in Ketchikan in 1986, ended in a hung jury. The second trial, held in Juneau in 1988, resulted in an acquittal of murder and arson charges. Those murders remain unsolved.

The investigation and trials of Peel cost the state of Alaska nearly $3 million, according to a *SitNews* article about the murders. Peel, who sued the state for $175 million for wrongful prosecution, agreed to a $900,000 settlement in 1997.

Then came Louis Hastings, an unemployed computer programmer, who bought a cabin in Kennicott, nestled in the Wrangell Mountains southeast of Glennallen. He seriously wounded the only other person living in Kennicott, then moved on to nearby McCarthy and killed six of that old mining community's residents on March 1, 1983. He was sentenced to 634 years in prison.

Following Michael Alan Silka's massacre of seven people at Manley Hot Springs' boat launch on May 17, 1984, Alaskans ended their first 25 years of statehood wondering if sanity and peace would ever return to their beloved state.

25 Years In The News

40

1960s: In The News

University of Alaska Fairbanks, Cecil H. Kornegay Photographs, UAF-1999-204-102

1960: Fort Wainwright

Ladd Air Force Base was transferred to the U.S. Army in 1960 and renamed Fort Wainwright. This photo shows the main street with the base hospital and headquarters to the right, as well as barracks and housing for civilian workers down the street.

1961: Survival story tops news

The survival story of postal clerk William C. Waters, a Kentucky tourist lost for 69 days in the subarctic wilderness northeast of Fairbanks was the No. 1 story for 1961. Waters, 42, parked his car off the highway near Circle June 20 to hike into a small lake several miles away. When two moose hunters finally found him sitting along a creek many miles north on Aug. 27, about 100 pounds lighter and nearly starved, Waters became the subject of widespread national and international publicity.

University of Alaska Fairbanks, Woodrow Johansen Papers, UAF-2007-64-679

1961: Oil leases awarded

At the beginning of 1961, Alaska Gov. William A. Egan told legislators he expected the state would receive $2.5 million from its oil industry during the year, according to an Anchorage Daily Times yearend wrap-up that December. While some lawmakers thought the estimate overly optimistic, the state received $22 million from two competitive oil leases earlier that year.

Gov. Egan and his wife, Neva, are seen here with Standard Oil Co. executive Jack Crooker at the opening of the Kenai oil line from Soldotna and Swanson River field to Nikiski Beach on Oct. 11, 1960.

1962: Japanese ship seized

Gov. William A. Egan's dramatic seizure of two Japanese catcher boats and the 1772-ton herring fleet mother ship, the Banshu Manu, off Uganik Bay in Shelikof Strait in mid-April made the No. 1 news story of 1962. This international herring story with its arrested captains dominated front pages and newscasts for days throughout the United States and Japan.

1962: Sitka spruce

Although many people thought the Sitka spruce (picea sitchensis) became the official tree of Alaska at statehood, the Alaska Legislature did not pass legislation making it so until Feb. 28, 1962. Gov. William A. Egan signed the legislation into law shortly thereafter with Mrs. Urban Nelson, representing the Alaska Garden Association and Reps. Dora M. Sweeney of Juneau and Grace Johnson of Nome looking on.

Alaska State Library, Dora M. Sweeney ASL-P421-574

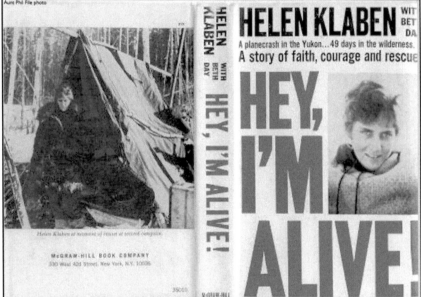

Aunt Phil File photo

1963: Crash victims survive more than a month in the wilderness

The No. 1 story for 1963 was the amazing survival of 21-year-old Helen Klaben and Ralph Flores, a 42-year-old Mexican-born pilot from California, after their plane crashed in the Canadian wilderness near Watson Lake while flying from Fairbanks to California. The pair survived 49 days in sub-zero temperatures with a tarpaulin as their only shelter and melted snow and a few biscuits their sustenance. A passing pilot finally spotted the huge SOS that Flores had stamped into the snow. Flores lost 51 pounds, Klaben lost 45 and had the toes of her right food amputated due to frostbite. She wrote about the experience in 1964 in "Hey, I'm Alive," which later was made into a movie.

1966: St. Michael's Cathedral burns

While the Great Earthquake and reconstruction dominated the news in 1964 and 1965, the burning of St. Michael's topped the news in 1966.

"The Heart went out of Sitka on the icy morning of Jan. 2, 1966, when fire destroyed the beloved St. Michael's Cathedral," reported the Seattle Times. "The 119-year-old Russian Orthodox church, a favorite landmark with Alaskans and tourists of all faiths, was a link to the past ... to the time when Sitka was the elegant capital of Russian America ... and later, in 1867, when Czarist Russia transferred Alaska to the United States atop Castle Hill in Sitka."

1966: Beatles land in Anchorage

On June 27, 1966, the Beatles touched down at the Anchorage International Airport at 1:45 p.m. to refuel their DC-8 jet, which was winging them to Japan for a concert. When a mechanical problem was detected, authorities whisked away the famous group of young musicians to the town's swankiest hotel, The Anchorage Westward (now the Hilton), to rest while mechanics repaired their plane.

It didn't take long for Anchorage youth to hear the news. A large crowd gathered in the alley near the hotel and began chanting their love for their teen idols.

The group did not respond to their adoring fans, and remained in their suite on the 10th floor until they boarded a bus at 1 a.m. to return to the airport. From lower right, Paul McCartney, George Harrison, Ringo Starr and John Lennon.

"Anchorage, Alaska, was like a cowboy town to us," Ringo later recalled. "It was really like a backwater. My only great memory of Alaska is that at the airport they have a huge, magnificent white bear in a glass case."

1967: State Motto

The state motto, "North to the Future," became official on Oct. 1, 1967, by an act passed by the Alaska Legislature, which also directed that the motto be put on automobile license plates.

1968: Wien jet crashes near Iliamna

A Wien Consolidated Airlines Fairchild F-27B, similar to the one seen in this photo near Fairbanks, crashed near Iliamna on Dec. 2, 1968. All 39 passengers and crew on board were killed.

Flight 55 departed Anchorage International Airport at 8:46 a.m. While preparing its approach to Iliamna, the aircraft encountered extreme turbulence at 11,500 feet. Witnesses reported hearing an explosion and seeing a fireball in the sky descend in a steep spiral toward the ground. The plane crashed into Foxy's Lake, Pedro Bay, an area described as a frozen marshland surrounded by mountains.

Rescue-recovery efforts were hampered by winds gusting to 55 mph and temperatures dipping to 11 degrees below zero. A U.S. Air Force helicopter did reach the scene but could not stay due to the weather conditions. The pilot reported no survivors and said the airplane was so disfigured it was not recognizable as an aircraft.

National Transportation Safety Board investigated this accident for nearly two years. It concluded that the probable cause was an in-flight structural failure caused by an encounter with severe to extreme turbulence, which had not been forecast nor known to the flight crew. The experts also said a number of fatigue cracks had previously formed on the aircraft wings and maintenance had been lacking in the company.

1968: Jade becomes state gem

The Alaska Legislature made the state's abundant dark-green jade, seen here on pallets in Fairbanks, Alaska's official gem in 1968. Jade, called the Stone of Heaven by the Chinese, was present when delegates signed Alaska's Constitution at the University of Alaska Fairbanks in 1956. A jade lamp adorned with gold and silver trim provided light for the ceremony.

Anchorage Museum at Rasmuson Center, Wien Collection, AMRC-b85-27-561

University of Alaska Fairbanks, William A. Egan papers, UAF-1985-120-127

1968: Statesman dies

Edward Lewis "Bob" Barlett, who served as Alaska's Territorial Delegate to Congress for 14 years and as the state's senior senator for another eight, died at age 64 on Dec. 11, 1968. He authored or co-authored more than 900 bills with a remarkably high rate of passage, a record of legislative success that alone qualifies him for honor.

His more exclusive distinction is one few members of Congress can claim. He helped create the state that he represented. Bartlett is seen here getting ready to present Alaska's first elected governor, William A. Egan, the first 49-star flag to fly over the U.S. Capitol on July 4, 1959.

1968: Sen. Ted Stevens

Alaska Gov. Walter J. Hickel appointed Anchorage attorney Ted Stevens to the U.S. Senate on Dec. 24, 1968, to fill the seat left vacant when E. L. "Bob" Bartlett died in office on Dec. 11. Stevens is pictured here with his wife, Ann, as Vice President Spiro Agnew performed the swearing-in ceremony.

Anchorage Daily News photo

1969: Hickel becomes Secretary of Interior

U.S. President Richard M. Nixon appointed Alaska Gov. Walter J. Hickel, cutting cake in this photograph, to become the nation's new Department of the Interior Secretary. He took that post on Jan. 24, 1969.

Seated is Keith Harvey Miller, Hickel's Secretary of State, who became Alaska's new governor when Hickel accepted the national post.

Anchorage Museum at Rasmuson Center, Steve McCutcheon Collection, AMRC-AMRC-B1990-014-S-Pol-16-61

NASA photo

1969: Alaskans receive first live feed from satellite

Alaskans had a front-row seat to watch astronaut Neil Armstrong plant the first footsteps on the moon on July 20, 1969, when the first live satellite telecast came to Anchorage.

Legendary Alaska broadcast pioneer August G. "Augie" Hiebert birthed television in Alaska with KTVA, which first signed on the air on Dec. 11, 1953. Two years later, Hiebert founded the state's second television station, KTVF in Fairbanks. His television stations aired programming on tape-delayed basis via videotaped recordings of network programs flown to Alaska from Seattle.

The "father of Alaska television" worked behind the scenes with the U.S. military and the Alaska congressional delegation to bring a live satellite feed of the historic moments of that lunar mission. The signal came through loud and clear, and Alaskans joined the rest of the world in watching the big adventure as it happened.

Following that historic step, Alaska leapt forward with satellites providing television, long-distance telephones and other high-speed communications of the day.

www.Senate.gov photo

1969: Gravel dreams up Dome City

Alaska Democrat Mike Gravel, who defeated U.S. Sen. Ernest Gruening in the 1968 primary and Republican Elmer Rasmuson in the general election, proposed a never-built "Denali City" development above the Tokositna River in 1969.

As he envisioned it, the $800-million, climate-controlled Teflon-domed city across the Knik Arm from Anchorage would have contained malls, condos, a golf course, hotels and a conference center. It would have boasted year-round 72-degree temperatures and a stunning view of Denali, America's highest peak. Gravel sought federal funds for his dream, which never materialized.

41

1970s: In The News

Anchorage Museum at Rasmuson Center, Steve McCutcheon Collection, AMRC-AMRC-B1990-014-5-Pol-16-4

1970: Hickel fired

On Nov. 25, 1970, U.S. President Richard M. Nixon fired Interior Secretary Walter J. Hickel.

Hickel returned to Alaska and turned his attention to his business affairs and state politics.

1971: Alaskans watch 1971 NFC championship game live

Television broadcasting pioneer Augie Hiebert, seen here on the left with Jeff Bowman, broke new ground on Jan. 3, 1971, when he treated Alaskans to their first-ever live satellite broadcast of a professional football game from the U.S. mainland. Alaskans watching KTVA Channel 11 saw the Dallas Cowboys beat the San Francisco 49ers by a score of 17 to 10 in that 1971 National Football Conference championship game.

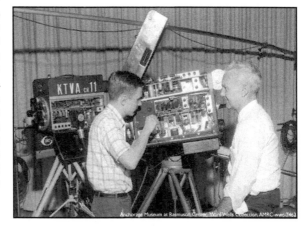

Anchorage Museum at Rasmuson Center, Ward Wells Collection, AMRC-wwc-7462

Anchorage Daily News photo

1971: Alaska Airlines jet crashes near Juneau

On Sept. 4, 1971, an Alaska Airlines Boeing 727 jet, carrying 111 people, crashed into the 2,500-foot level of a mountain ridge only 8 minutes away from Juneau while the craft was preparing to land. It was the worst accident in U.S. aviation history involving a single plane.

With wreckage spread over a two-mile area, it took nearly a week to recover the bodies of those on board Flight 1866 from a rain-soaked, wind-whipped mountain 20 miles west of Juneau in the Chilkat Range, according to newspaper accounts. This photo shows searchers combing through the wreckage.

National Transportation Safety Board investigators later determined misleading navigational information – bent radio beams – caused the pilot, Capt. Richard Adams, to descend prematurely. The final report, released in January 1973, criticized the Federal Aviation Administration for not requiring the use of "double check" navigational aids.

Alaska Airlines paid out about $20 million in wrongful death claims.

1972: Actor Steve McQueen arrested

Famous Hollywood legend Steve McQueen was arrested in 1972 after he repeatedly sped up and down Fourth Avenue in Anchorage doing "brodies" in an Oldsmobile Toronado. A field sobriety test, where his attempt to walk a straight line ended with him somersaulting instead, showed him to be intoxicated.

McQueen reportedly said: "There ain't a two-bit cop in this one-horse town that's going to arrest me." This mug shot shows he was wrong. He later was convicted in absentia for reckless driving, but not for drunk driving.

Anchorage Daily News photo

SCRC I   AJ 19261
*STEVE T MCQUEEN
DOB 03 24 30   MALE

1972: Benny Benson dies

John Ben "Benny" Benson, the Aleut who designed the Alaska state flag in 1926, died in a Kodiak hospital at the age of 58 on July 2, 1972. His design, which he created for an American Legion contest for schoolchildren, consists of eight gold stars on a field of blue that represent the Big Dipper and the North Star.

"The blue field is for the Alaska sky and the forget-me-not, an Alaska flower," Benson said at the time of winning the contest. "The North Star is for the future state of Alaska, the most northerly of the Union. The Dipper is for the Great Bear – symbolizing strength."

1973: Limited Entry instated

The Alaska salmon fisheries limited entry program became law in 1973, prompted by a decreasing supply of salmon due to overfishing and the expansion of canneries in Alaska.

1974: Ernest Gruening dies

After a long and illustrious career serving Alaska as a politician and statesman, Ernest Gruening died on June 26, 1974, at the age of 87. He served as Alaska's territorial governor, an activist for statehood and U.S. senator. Gruening also was one of the first to fight for the rights and wellbeing of Alaska's Native people. His ashes were scattered on a mountaintop above Juneau.

1975: Wien Air Alaska crashes near Gambell

Thirty-one people were on board a Wien Air Alaska Fairchild F-27, similar to the one seen in this photograph in Juneau, when it slammed into the side of Seuvokuk Mountain near Gambell on St. Lawrence Island on Aug. 30, 1975. Ten died, but 21 lived through the flaming crash – most lived due to the heroic efforts of then-Alaska State Trooper Gilbert Pelawook, according to an article in the Anchorage Daily Times.

Pelawook, a passenger in the plane, was heading back to Gambell were he was stationed. He later said he saw the plane pass a new housing development in Gambell and knew they were in trouble.

"I knew where we were heading (into the mountain)," he later told a Times reporter. "I tightened up my (seat) belt and got ready."

The trooper blacked out on impact. When he came to, he found himself hanging upside down and the plane was on fire.

"I looked around and everyone looked dead," he said, so he unhooked his seatbelt and left the plane.

Then he heard crying and moaning coming from inside the craft. Pelawook turned around and went back inside the cabin.

"I did what I was supposed to do," he said, adding that his training at the Alaska State Trooper Academy in Sitka and emergency medical technician course helped him do what needed to be done.

He found some passengers dead, so he left them and searched for the living. He shielded himself with a piece of wreckage as he dragged victims from the blaze. Then he finally got burned when the metal shield melted on his hands and leg.

Anchorage Museum at Rasmuson Center, Wien Collection, AMRC-b85-27-1304

The National Transportation and Safety Board determined fog was heavy that day, below minimum approach criteria, and the crew failed to follow instrument approach procedures. The airplane collided with the mountain on a missed approach to landing after multiple missed approaches.

Anchorage Museum at Rasmuson Center, Ward Wells Collection, AMRC-wws-1663-5

1975: Alaska aviation legend dies

"Going by airplane was better than beating yourself to death on a pair of snowshoes," Alaska aviator Don Sheldon told James Greiner, author of Sheldon's 1974 biography titled "Wager With The Wind."

Sheldon, who died of cancer at 53 on Jan. 25, 1975, became well known across Alaska for his dramatic flights and rescues. He was regarded as the authority of flying around Denali and supported most of the climbing efforts of the mountain before his death. Sheldon built the Talkeetna Air Service into an internationally known entity among mountaineers.

The bush pilot, seen here on Denali in 1955, was buried in the shadow of the mountain he loved.

1976: Voters create fund

Alaska voters approved an amendment, which was signed by Gov. Jay Hammond who is seated in this photo, to the Alaska Constitution. It created a publicly owned state investment fund that would receive at least 25 percent of all state oil revenues and related income in 1976. That evenutally became the source for the Permanent Fund dividend.

Alaska Permanent Fund Corporation photo

University of Alaska Fairbanks, Kay J. Kennedy Aviation Collection, UAF-1991-98-682

1976: Molly Hootch case

The suit of Tobeluk v. Lind, known by most as the Molly Hootch case, was settled in 1976. A detailed decree provided for the establishment of a high school program in all 126 villages covered by the litigation, unless people in the village decided against a local program. Prior to this, children who wanted to go to high school had no choice but to leave their villages, like these teens from Shungnak on their way to a boarding school in Oregon.

1977: University changes name

Alaska Methodist University, chartered in 1957, was restructured and became Alaska Pacific University in 1977.

Construction on the university, seen here in 1962, began when the cornerstone was laid on Sunday, July 12, 1959. When the first students enrolled in classes in 1960, campus facilities were limited and consisted only of Grant Hall — the academic and student center — and Gould Hall, the student residence.

University of Alaska Anchorage, Christine M. McClain Papers, UAA-hmc-0370-series15a-4-88

Alaska State Archive, Exxon Valdez Oil Spill, ASA-RG348-SR612-AS17959-1940

1977: 200-mile fishing limit

A 200-mile fishing limit law went into effect in March 1977. Foreign fishing vessels could now fish within 200 miles of the United States, but they had to get American licenses and had quota limits for various species. The U.S. Coast Guard kept watch on the seas.

1977: Noel Wien dies

Famous aviator Noel Wien, second from left, died on June 18, 1977, of a heart attack at age 78. Other Wien employees in the photo, from left, are Ray Petersen, Wien, Merle K. Smith, Frank Whaley and John Cross.

Wien made a name for himself in Alaska as one of the Last Frontier's first flyboys. He started commercial aviation in the territory by taking paid customers aloft on "joy rides" in June 1924. The next month, he

University of Alaska Fairbanks, Kay J. Kennedy Aviation Collection, UAF-1991-98-888

made the first flight between Anchorage and Fairbanks. Wien followed the Alaska Railroad tracks and completed that run in three hours, 45 minutes.

He and his brother, Ralph, cofounded Wien Airways, which merged with Northern Consolidated in 1968 and became Wien Air Alaska. They grew their airline into Alaska's largest intrastate air carrier.

Alaska State Library, Alaska Office of the Governor, ASL-P213-4-009

1978: Bush pilot wins second term as governor

The gubernatorial election of 1978 that found its way through the courts became the state's top story in 1978. Republican Jay Hammond, a bush pilot and fisherman from Naknek, won a second four-year term – but not before two losers in the Aug. 22 primaries made some noise.

Republican Walter J. Hickel and Democrat Ed Merdes charged that nominations of Hammond and Democrat Chancy Croft were filled with irregularities and misconduct by election officials. Superior Court Judge Ralph Moody ordered a new election, but that ruling was overturned on appeal to the state Supreme Court, according to newspaper articles at the time.

Hammond beat Croft and Hickel, who waged a last-minute write-in campaign.

1978: D-2 Lands hot topic

The Alaska Native Claims Settlement Act required the Secretary of the Interior to withdraw as many as 80 million acres of federally owned land in Alaska for inclusion in four national conservation systems: parks, forests, wildlife refuges and wild and scenic river areas.

Alaska State Library, Pipeline Impact Collection, ASL-P17-9127

Congressman Morris Udall, seated center, held what became known as D-2 lands hearings across Alaska. This photo was taken during hearings at the University of Alaska Fairbanks.

As Congress haggled over the wording of an Alaska lands bill, Interior Secretary Cecil Andrus withdrew 110 million acres of Alaska land for federal study. President Jimmy Carter soon designated 56 million of those acres as national monuments under the Antiquities Act.

1978: Ann Stevens dies in airplane crash

Ann Stevens, wife of Alaska's U.S. Sen. Ted Stevens, died in an airplane accident on Dec. 4, 1978. She was one of the best-loved women in politics. From Barrow to Bethel, Fairbanks to Wrangell, everyone knew her.

The chartered twin-engine Learjet in which she was flying with six others was just touching down at the Anchorage International Airport that windy afternoon when a gust of wind must have caught it. The aircraft flipped over and skidded on its back, breaking into three parts, according to newspaper accounts.

Four other Alaskans died in the crash, too, including Anchorage attorney Joseph Rudd, Clarence Kramer of Sitka, pilot Richard Sykes of Anchorage, owner of Inlet Marine, and co-pilot Richard Church, also of Anchorage. Sen. Stevens and Tony Motley were injured.

The National Transportation Safety Board report issued later said the Learjet encountered strong, gusting crosswinds during the landing attempt, which caused the aircraft to roll abruptly and unexpectedly. The loss of control resulted from inappropriate pilot techniques in his attempt to regain control of the plane.

Board member Francis H. McAdams disagreed with his colleagues, and said the pilot was in a vulnerable position "to be struck by strong horizontal gusts compounded by wind shear." He added that the board did not know everything about the accident, "and we're pontificating that the pilot techniques were at fault."

1979: Old Believers become U.S. citizens

Eighty-six Russian Old Believers who found refuge and religious freedom in Alaska in the late 1960s became U.S. citizens on Monday, April 30, 1979, on the Kenai Peninsula. The men, women and children, all dressed in their brilliant peasant clothes like the children in this photograph taken in front of their church, renounced allegiance to any foreign nation in the Anchor Point school gymnasium.

Another 55 members of the religious sect had become citizens in July 1975.

"We are grateful to be accepted in the United States after our liberties were denied in all countries where we've been before," Pavel Fefelov said in an Anchorage Daily News article that day. Old Believers, who originally left the Soviet Union and fled to Manchuria after the Russian Revolution in 1920, eventually came to Alaska and carved out a life in the village they call Nikolaevsk. Russian is spoken in the home, but English is spoken in school.

Old Believers separated from the Russian Orthodox Church after 1666, as a protest against church reforms. The group stressed a strict and private lifestyle that forbade television, radio, musical instruments, tobacco, strong liquor, shaving and birth control.

1979: Progress brings high prices

For Bush Alaska, the 1970s brought changes like improved airstrips, new high schools, clinics and city buildings. It also brought rural Alaska face-to-face with the price of progress.

Electric bills, fuel oil bills and telephone bills added up in communities that historically relied on subsistence lifestyles. A Selawik resident told a reporter at the time that no one had told the villagers that long-distance charges were in addition to installation and monthly fees for phone service. They were shocked when bills of $200 and more showed up at the local post office.

Alaska Athabascan Chief Peter John of Minto is seen using a phone in this photograph.

42

1980s: In The News

Anchorage Daily News photo

1980: *Prinsendam* burns and sinks

An engine room fire quickly spread on the 427-foot cruise ship *Prinsendam* in early October 1980. The crew called for help from the Gulf of Alaska on Oct. 5, and the U.S. Coast Guard, Air Force and several oil tankers from Valdez responded.

The rescuers found most of the 350 passengers and 200 crewmembers had evacuated to lifeboats by the time they arrived on the scene. But with time and fuel running out, helicopters picked people from the lifeboats and hoisted them on board the tankers. Some were taken to Valdez and some to Yakutat and then flown to Sitka.

All passengers and crew were rescued, and only a few had injuries. The *Prinsendam* burned and then sank in 9,000 feet of water while under tow to Sitka.

1980: ANILCA passed

Congress passed the Alaska National Interest Lands Conservation Act on Nov. 12, 1980, and President Jimmy Carter signed it into law on Dec. 2 that year. The act provided varying degrees of special protection to more than 150 million acres of land in Alaska, doubling the size of the country's national park and refuge system and tripling the amount of land designated as wilderness, such as on Admiralty Island seen below.

Specifically, it provided more than 43 million acres of new national parklands, the addition of more than 53 million acres to the National Wildlife Refuge system and 25 wild and scenic rivers, with another 12 to be studied. It also created Misty Fjords and Admiralty Island national monuments in Southeast along with the Steese National Conservation Area and White Mountains National Recreation Area to be managed by the Bureau of Land Management. And it added more than 56 million acres to the Wilderness Preservation System and added more than 3 million acres to Tongass and Chugach national forests.

It was called the most significant land conservation measure in the history of the nation.

1980: Proposed PFD payment brings lawsuit

Alaska Legislators enacted the first Alaska Permanent Fund dividend that was made up of 10 percent of all state oil revenue. They also established rules to give a Permanent Fund dividend payment to every adult Alaska resident – $50 for every year of residency since 1959.

Payment to residents was put on hold, however, after Anchorage attorneys Ron and Patricia Zobel challenged the constitutionality of the program. The couple filed a lawsuit against the State of Alaska.

The Zobels were widely vilified in public and even received death threats during the next several years. Their case provided the first live coverage of a court proceeding in Alaska's history.

1981: William Sheffied elected governor

Democrat William "Bill" Sheffield, seen here with his lieutenant governor, Stephen McAlpine, was elected Alaska's governor in 1981. He served one term from 1982 until 1986.

1982: First PFD checks issued

The U.S. Supreme Court ruled in favor of the Zobels in 1982, saying prior legislation was unconstitutional. So the state Legislature passed a law authorizing equal dividend payments to all six-month residents.

The first Permanent Fund dividend checks were distributed on June 14, 1982, in the amount of $1,000 to all Alaskans who had resided in Alaska for six months. The Legislature paid it with surplus oil revenues, not with Permanent Fund income. The residency requirement for eligibility was changed to 12 months in 1990.

25 YEARS IN THE NEWS

1982: Pope celebrates mass on Anchorage Park Strip

Alaskans packed the Delaney Park Strip to celebrate mass with Pope John Paul II on his visit to Anchorage Feb. 26, 1981. When he returned to Alaska three years later, he told the people that he remembered a little girl, Molly Marie Jordan of Palmer, who had welcomed him on his first trip to the Last Frontier with a bouquet of forget-me-nots and then died of cystic fibrosis 10 months after meeting him.

"Shortly afterward, that little girl was called home to her Heavenly Father. But her loving gesture is not forgotten and her memory is held in blessing.

"I found in what she did at the time a living truth about the people of the vast Alaskan territory – that in your thoughts and your prayers you remember the Pope."

Anchorage Daily News photo

University of Alaska Fairbanks, Alaska Earthquake Archives, UAF-1972-153-105

1983: Time zones changed

Time zones shifted to include all Alaska, except western-most Aleutian Islands, to one zone called Alaska Standard Time in 1983. It made most Alaska time one hour earlier than Pacific Standard Time, which helped businesses and the military communicate most of the day within and outside of the state.

1983: Crab season cancelled

The once-abundant crab population, as seen in this photograph taken in Kodiak in the 1970s, became so low that most commercial seasons had to be cancelled in Alaska in 1983.

Anchorage Museum at Rasmuson Center
Wien Collection, AMRC-b85-27-1354

1984: Respected Native leader dies

Alaska Native leader Frank Peratrovich died on Jan. 4, 1984, at the age of 88. He was one of the first Natives elected to the territorial Legislature, one of two Natives on the Alaska Statehood Committee and the only Native at the Constitutional Convention in 1955-56.

Peratrovich, who came from the small Tlingit community of Klawock in Southeast, was the second Native to become president of the Alaska Senate following statehood. He succeeded William Beltz of Nome.

"He didn't talk very often, but when he did, he had something to say and everyone listened," Anchorage photographer Steve McCutcheon later said. Peratrovich was a living historical bridge from the old ways to the modern times.

1984: Gov. William A. Egan dies

Alaska's first elected sourdough governor, William A. Egan, died in Anchorage on May 6, 1984. Seen in this photograph giving a speech at the Anchorage Westward Hotel in the

1970s, Egan had been diagnosed with lung cancer the month before he died at age 69.

Many saw Egan, a Democrat, as a man who was frugal with state dollars, considered statewide interests, crusaded for airfields across bush Alaska and pushed for the state's highway and ferry systems.

He set up the executive and judicial branches of government, created a state education department, encouraged offshore leasing and nurtured the fishing industry – all in his first terms as governor from 1959-1966. He was beat by Walter J. Hickel in 1966, but elected again in 1970. He then lost to Republican Jay Hammond by 287 votes in 1974.

1984: Alaska population booms

Alaska's population reached 500,000 by its 25th Anniversary in 1984. More than 50,000 arrived the year before, and most of those new residents settled in Anchorage, as seen in this photo of a large crowd downtown. Although the Matanuska-Susitna Borough was listed as the fastest-growing area of Alaska with a 71 percent increase since 1980, according to the Alaska Department of Community and Regional Affairs.

1984: State looks at natural gas line

An estimated 26 trillion cubic feet of natural gas at Prudhoe, like that on the Kenai Peninsula seen here, and 5 trillion cubic feet at Kuparuk still awaited construction of a natural gas line to deliver it to market. Costs estimated at $43 billion to build the line in 1984 (compared to $8 billion that built the oil pipeline in the 1970s) kept the project on the back burner. That $43 billion in 1984 translates to about $98 billion in 2015 dollars.

1984: Alaska celebrates 25 years of statehood

Alaskans celebrated the state's 25th anniversary throughout 1984, including at a banquet in the Wood Center at the University of Alaska Fairbanks that January. A wall-size reproduction of the stamp that commemorated the special year is shown at the head of the table.

1984: State buys Alaska Railroad

The state purchased the Alaska Railroad from the U.S. government for more than $22 million in 1984.

1984: Russians seize Homer ship

The five-man crew of the 115-foot Homer-based supply ship *Frieda-K* thought they were in American waters when they decided to take a side trip to Little Diomede Island to buy some souvenir T-shirts in September 1984, according to an article in the Anchorage Daily News. However, the crew of a Russian military ship thought they were in foreign waters and arrested them.

The Russian soldiers took the Homer seamen to an abandoned military barracks in the Siberian city of Provideniya. The Alaskans later said the communist soldiers ate their candy and smashed their emergency locator transmitter, but refused to accept the biblical literature the men tried to give them.

Eight days later, the Homer men were handed over to the U.S. Coast Guard by a Soviet warship in a mid-ocean rendezvous west of Nome. Released were Tabb and Tate Thoms, Mark Halpin, Charles Burrall and Tony Miller. Burrall later wrote a book about the ordeal titled "Captured By The Russians."

1984: Plaque placed at Lincoln Memorial

Alaska and Hawaii finally joined the other 48 states on the Lincoln Memorial in Washington, D.C., in December 1984. The names were recognized in a 3-by-6-foot granite plaque inlaid into a stone landing on the stairs leading up to the memorial. The inscription explained that Alaska and Hawaii were not states when the memorial was completed in 1922, which is why their names and dates of admission to the union were not listed along the frieze that rings the memorial.

ABOUT THE AUTHORS

This book contains a collection of Alaska history stories written by my aunt, Phyllis Downing Carlson, as well as stories written by me that came from tidbits found among the notes and rare books I inherited when she died in 1993.

Born in 1909, Aunt Phil moved to Alaska in 1914 and lived the history so richly described in her work. She grew up in Cordova, where her father worked on building the railroad to the Kennecott copper mines; he then served as the conductor aboard the Copper River and Northwestern Railroad. Phyllis graduated with a class of seven from Cordova High School in 1928, then studied journalism at the University of Washington and earned a teacher's certificate from Central College of Education in Ellensburg, Wash.

Aunt Phil landed her first job, which paid a whopping $150 a month, at Cooper Landing on the Kenai Peninsula. The new teacher kept the Yukon stove stoked in the little log schoolhouse and worked around cases of milk and staples stored for the winter.

After three years in the isolated community of 30, a widowed father of three of her pupils put an end to her single days. Carl Carlson moved her to the village of Tyonek, across Cook Inlet from Anchorage, and Phil again taught school in 1935 while Carl ran the village sawmill and served as postmaster.

Phyllis Downing Carlson, who arrived in Cordova, Alaska, in 1914 at the age of 5, lived and loved the history about which she wrote.

University of Alaska Anchorage, National Geographic Society Katmai Expeditions Collection, UAA-hmc-0186-volume6-H138

Above: As a child, Alaska historian Phyllis Downing Carlson skipped down these dirt streets in Cordova, pictured here in 1919.

Below: Aunt Phil taught school in the Native village of Tyonek in 1935. The village looked much like this photograph taken in 1898. She befriended Chief Simeon Chickalusion and was invited back to a potlatch when the village relocated after the earthquake of 1964.

University of Alaska Anchorage, Edwin Forbes Glenn Collection, UAA-hmc-0116-series3a-32-1

The young bride met Tyonek Chief Simeon Chickalusion, who spoke English, Russian and his Native tongue. She later wrote an article, titled "The Tribe That Kept Its Head," about the chief and residents of Tyonek that ranked as one of the best articles submitted in a 1967 *Writer's Digest* contest. Years later, the village invited her back to a potlatch to share stories of the chief with the village young people.

The Carlsons moved to Anchorage in 1939, where Carl helped build Fort Richardson. The couple pitched a tent at Fifth Avenue and Denali Street and started framing a house over the tent. When they completed their home, they took down the tent and dragged it out the front door.

After World War II, the couple moved to Cordova, where Aunt Phil honed her journalism skills. She produced her own radio show, "Woman to Woman," and conducted countless interviews that eventually led her to research Cordova's history through the local newspaper's archives. "Oh, I had a wonderful time," she later recalled. "They had a real storehouse."

Her popular radio show led to the compilation of entertaining articles about Alaska, and for more than 40 years, Aunt Phil researched and wrote award-winning pieces as she moved about the state. Her stories appeared in a multitude of publications, including *Alaskana, Alaska Journal, Alaska Sportsman, The Anchorage Times* and *Our Alaska.*

She settled back in Anchorage from Kodiak after the Good Friday earthquake of 1964, and spent so much time researching and talking with librarians at the Z.J. Loussac Public Library, they hired her.

People said she didn't need to use the card catalog, because she knew the location of every volume.

"I don't remember faces," she said. "But I remember what I looked up for people."

The Alaska Press Women chose Aunt Phil for its Woman of Achievement Award in 1988. The organization cited her as an authority on Alaska history, recognized throughout the state by writers, researchers and politicians alike.

As a retiree, she served on a variety of boards, including

the Anchorage Bicentennial Commission, Historical Landmarks Preservation Commission, State Historical Society and Alaska Press Women.

When she passed away in 1993, her treasured tales landed in my hands. As providence would have it, I, too, am a writer and lover of Alaska history. And since Aunt Phil was one of my favorite relatives, I feel it a privilege to perpetuate her work.

My Alaska roots stem from both sides of my family. My father, Richard Allie Downing – Aunt Phil's younger brother – was born in Cordova in 1916. Not only was his father a part of the railroad history there, but his grandfather, John Couch Downing, had witnessed the staking of gold claims around the area many years before when he sailed as the captain of the *Excelsior,* the famous steamship that carried news of the riches found in the Klondike back to San Francisco in July 1897.

Seward Community Library, SCL-1-798

My mother's grandfather, Robert Burns Mathison, arrived in Hope from Texas in 1898 and helped establish that little mining town. He pulled a small fortune out of Resurrection Creek and Chickaloon River and built a sawmill and mercantile. His son, Robert Lewis Mathison, married my grandmother, Inez Lee Brown, who traveled to the small community to work for her uncle, Charlie Shields, after being widowed in Kansas.

Robert L. Mathison, left, maternal grandfather of Laurel Downing Bill, and his brother, Charles, walk away from the Pacific Coast Trading Company and U.S. Mineral Surveyor and Assaying Office in Seward around 1906. The brothers, who mined with their father, Robert Burns Mathison, prospected around the gold-rush town of Hope.

From that union came my mother, Hazel Isobel, and her identical twin, Hope Alisabeth, born at the Anchorage railroad hospital in 1920. The twins spent

ABOUT THE AUTHORS

summers in Hope and winters in Seward, where they graduated high school in 1938.

My folks met at the University of Alaska Fairbanks, married in 1941, and settled in Fairbanks to raise their family. I was the fourth of their children born at old St. Joseph's Hospital, in 1951, following brothers Richard Ellsworth and Michael Woodrow and sister Meredith Lee.

I grew up between that gold-rush town and Juneau, where we moved after my father became the first commissioner of Public Works when Alaska became a state in 1959. That's where my younger sister, Deborah Lynn, was born in 1965 – shortly after my mother christened the *Taku*, the Alaska Marine Highway System's second ferry.

In 1973, I married and then spent 22 years in King Salmon with my fisheries biologist husband, Donald Bill. I worked for the Bristol Bay Telephone Cooperative Inc. and raised two children, Kimberly and Ryan, and a foster daughter, Amie Morgan.

When the children graduated from Bristol Bay High School, and Don retired from the Alaska Department of Fish and Game, we moved to Anchorage. I went back to school in 1999, at the tender age of 48, and learned that I had a passion for writing. I earned a bachelor's degree in journalism in May 2003 from the University of Alaska Anchorage and have spent the past few years writing my own award-winning articles for various Alaska newspapers and magazines while working on this labor of love.

Condensed versions of articles in Aunt Phil's Trunk appeared in *The Anchorage Chronicle*, a weekly newspaper published by Alaska Newspapers Inc. from July 2002 until the paper closed its doors on Dec. 31, 2004. *The Senior Voice*, a monthly Alaska newspaper, picked up the column in February 2005.

I truly hope you enjoy this volume packed with stories from Alaska's first 25 years as a state that came from extensive research, just like the rest of the books in the *Aunt Phil's Trunk* Alaska history series.

– Laurel Downing Bill

BIBLIOGRAPHY

Allen, Lawrence J. *The Trans-Alaska Pipeline. Vol 1: The Beginning,* Scribe Publishing Co., Seattle, WA: 1975.

Allen, Lawrence J. *The Trans-Alaska Pipeline. Vol 2: South to Valdez,* Scribe Publishing Co., Seattle, WA: 1976.

Alyeska Pipeline Service Co. *Alyeska: A 30-Year Journey.* Alyeska Pipeline Service Co., 2007.

Alyeska Pipeline Service Co. *The Facts: Trans Alaska Pipeline System,* 2007

Andrews, C.L. *The Story of Alaska.* The Caxton Printers, Ltd., Caldwell, OH: 1944.

Arnold, David F. *The Fisherman's Frontier: People and Salmon in Southeast Alaska,* University of Washington, Seattle, WA: 2008.

Atwood, Evangeline and DeArmond, Robert N. *Who's Who in Alaskan Politics,* Binford & Mort, Portland, OR: 1977.

Berger, Justice T. R. *Village Journey, The Report of the Alaska Native Review Commission,* Farrar, Straus, and Giroux New York, NY: 1985.

Borneman, Walter R. *Alaska: A Narrative History.* Harper-Collins, New York City, NY: 2003.

Catton, Theodore. *Inhabited Wilderness: Indians, Eskimos, and National Parks in Alaska,* University of New Mexico Press, 1997.

Clifton, L.J. and Gallaway, B.J. *History of Trans Alaska Pipeline System,* Feb. 15, 2001.

Coate, Peter. *Trans-Alaska Pipeline Controversy: Technology, Conservation, and the Frontier,* Lehigh University Press, Bethlehem, PA: 1991.

Cohen, Stan. *Highway on the Sea,* Pictoral Histories Publishing Co., Missoula, MT: 1995.

Cole, Dermot. *Amazing Pipeline Stories.* Epicenter Press, Kenmore, WA: 1997.

Cole, Terrence. *Fighting for the Forty-Ninth Star: C.W. Sneadden and the Crusade for Alaska Statehood,* UA Foundation, Anchorage, AK: 2010.

Cox, D.C. and Pararas-Carayannis, George. *A Catalog of Tsunamis in Alaska.* World Data Center A- Tsunami Report, No. 2, 1969.

Dobler, Bruce. *The Last Rush North.* Little, Brown and Co., Boston, MA: 1976

Douglas, John and Mark Olshaker. *Mind Hunter: Inside the FBI's Elite Serial Crime Unit.* Pocket Books, New York, NY: 1996.

DuClos, Bernard. *Fair Game.* CreateSpace Independent Publishing Platform, 2013.

Fineberg, Richard A. *A Pipeline in Peril: A Status Report on the Trans-Alaska Pipeline.* Alaska Forum for Environmental Responsibility, Ester, AK: 1996.

Gilmore, Walter and Hale, Leland E. *Butcher, Baker,* Penguin Books, New York, NY: 1991.

Gruening, Ernest. *An Alaskan Reader*, Meredith Press, New York, NY: 1966.

Gruening, Ernest. *The Battle for Alaska Statehood*. University of Alaska Press, Fairbanks, AK: 1967.

Gruening, Ernest. *The State of Alaska*. Random House, New York City, NY: 1954.

Hanrahan, John and Gruenstein, Peter. *Lost Frontier: The Marketing of Alaska*, W.W. Norton, New York City, NY: 1977.

Haycox, Stephen and Mary Mangusso, eds. *An Alaska Anthology: Interpreting the Past*, University of Washington Press, Seattle, WA: 1996.

Haycox, Stephen. *Alaska – An American Colony*, University of Washington Press,Seattle, WA: 2002.

Haycox, Stephen. *Frigid Embrace. Politics, Economics and Environment in Alaska*. Oregon State Universty Press, Corvallis, OR: 2002.

Hilscher, Herb. *The Heritage of Alaska*, National Bank of Alaska, Anchorage, AK: 1971.

Hinckley, Ted C. *The Americanization of Alaska*, 1867-1897. Pacific Books, Palo Alto, CA: 1972.

Hulley, Clarence C. *Alaska Past and Present*, Binfords & Mort, Portland, OR: 1953.

Kaye, Roger. *Last Great Wilderness: The Campaign to Establish the Arctic National Wildlife Refuge,* University of Alaska Press, AK: 2006.

Kohlhoff, D. *When the Wind Was a River*. Seattle, University of Washington Press, Seattle, WA: 1995.

Kollin, Susan. *Nature's State: Imagining Alaska as the Last Frontier*. University of North Carolina Press, Chapel Hill, NC: 2001.

Kruse, John A. *Fairbanks Community Survey*. Fairbanks Institute of Social and Economic Research: 1976.

McBeath, Jerry et al. *The Political Economy of Oil in Alaska: Multinationals vs. the State*, Lynne Rienner Publishers, Boulder, CO: 2008.

McGinniss, Joe. *Going to Extremes*. Alfred A. Knopf, New York City, NY: 1980.

McGrath, Ed. *Inside the Alaska Pipeline*. Celestial Arts, Millbrae, CA: 1977.

McPhee, John. *Coming Into the Country,* Farrar, Straus and Giroux, New York City, NY: 1976.

Mead, Robert Douglas. *Journeys Down the Line: Building the Trans-Alaska Pipeline*. Doubleday, New York City, NY: 1978.

Mitchell, Donald Craig. *Sold American: The Story of Alaska Natives and Their Land, 1867–1959,* University Press of New England, Hanover, NH: 1997.

Naske, Claus M. and Ludwig J. Rowinski. *Anchorage, A Pictorial History*, Donning, Norfolk, VA: 1981.

Naske, Claus M. and Slotnick, Herman E. *Alaska: A History of the 49th State,* University of Oklahoma Press, Norman, OK: 1987.

Newton, Michael. *Hunting Humans: An Encyclopedia of Modern Serial Killers.* Breakout Productions, Port Townsend, WA: 1990.

O'Neill, D. *The Firecracker Boys,* Saint Martin's Press, New York, NY: 1994.

Rich, Kim. *Johnny's Girl,* William Morrow and Co. Inc., New York, NY: 1993.

Ritter, H. *Alaska's History: The People, Land, and Events of the North Country,* Alaska Northwest Books, Anchorage, AK: 1993.

Romer, John and Elizabeth. *The Seven Wonders of the World: A History of the Modern Imagination,* Henry Holt and Co., New York City, NY: 1995.

Kizzia, Tom. *Pilgrim's Wilderness,* Crown Publishers, eBook: 2014.

Roscow, James P. *800 Miles to Valdez: The Building of the Alaska Pipeline,* Prentice-Hall Inc., Englewood Cliffs, NJ: 1977.

Ross, Ken. *Pioneering Conservation in Alaska,* University Press of Colorado, CO: 2006.

Smelcer, John. *The Day That Cries Forever,* Todd Communications, Anchorage, AK: 2006.

Strohmeyer, J. *Extreme Conditions: Big Oil and the Transformation of Alaska,* Simon and Schuster, New York, NY: 1993.

Wharton, David. *They Don't Speak Russian in Sitka: A New Look at the History of Southern Alaska,* Markgraf Publications Group, Menlo Park, CA: 1991.

Wickware, Potter. *Crazy Money: Nine Months on the Trans-Alaska Pipeline,* Random House, New York City, NY: 1979.

Tower, Elizabeth A. *Alaska's Homegrown Governor,* Elizabeth A. Tower, Anchorage, AK: 2003.

Tower, Elizabeth A. *Anchorage City History Series,* Epicenter Press, Seattle, WA: 1999.

Magazines/Periodicals
Alaska History Magazine, Project Chariot, Fall 1989
Alaska Magazine, 50 Years of Statehood series, 2008
Alicia Patterson Fund Newsletter, Tundra Times: Survival Story, July 15, 1972
Business Week, Alaska tries to break the ice, Nov. 4, 1967
Election News, Vol. 3, No. 3, November 1999
Forbes Magazine, Nov. 25, 1969
Harper's Magazine, Politicians, Natives & Oil, by Lewis Lapham, May 1970
International Business, Alaska: America's Frozen Assets, Jan.-Feb. 1978
Life Magazine, April 1964
National Geographic, April 1969
The Alaska Call, In six decades, a bare trickle; then ..., June 1959
The Alaska Call, July 1959
The Alaska Call, Alaska Development in Brief, August 1959
The Alaska Call, September 1959
The Alaska Call, Who Owns Alaska's Land, May 1959
The Alaska Call, Project Chariot, by Charles Keim, February 1960

The Alaska Call, Fish Lake Goes Aristocrat, by T.A. Moyer, March 1960
The Economist, Alaska After The Flood, Aug. 26, 1967
The Greatlander, Sept. 27, 1972
The Kiplinger Magazine, Changing Times, March 1967
Time Magazine, June 1975
We Alaskans Magazine, Nuclear Excavation, by Dan O'Neill, December 1989

Alaska Newspapers

Alaska Dispatch News, 59ers, the original 'Alaska or bust' caravan, March 8, 2012
Alaska Dispatch News, Wind-toppled flagpole holds surprise from past, Sept. 5, 2012
Anchorage Daily News, various, April 24, 1961 through Dec. 31, 1984
Anchorage Daily News, A 'Billion Dollar' Week, Sept. 13, 1969
Anchorage Daily News, Alaska's Land, Dec. 23, 1970
Anchorage Daily News, Jay Hammond Open Letter to AEC, Nov. 6, 1971
Anchorage Daily News, Alaska Native Land Claims, Several-part series, Robert D. Arnold,
    Alaska Native Foundation, August 1978-January 1979
Anchorage Daily News, The Flag Unfurled, Jan. 3, 1984
Anchorage Daily News, '64 Quake: In harm's way, by David Hulen, March 3, 1989
Anchorage Daily News, Feds tap $3 million to clean up nuke site, Feb. 10, 1993
Anchorage Daily News, Survivor of McCarthy massacre killed in fatal fire, by Tom Kizzia,
    Jan. 2, 2002
Anchorage Daily Times, various, May 21, 1958 through Dec. 31, 1975 (then paper changed
its name to Anchorge Times)
Anchorage Times, various, Jan. 1, 1976 through Dec. 31, 1984
Anchorage Daily Times, Blessed People, Blessed Land, Jan. 3, 1964
Anchorage Daily Times, Dinner Honors Atwood, April 1, 1967
Anchorage Daily Times, Alaska Revisited, Aug. 12, 1967
Anchorage Daily Times, Special on the 1960s, Jan. 2, 1970
Anchorage Daily Times, The Pole That A Gag Built, November 1970
Anchorage Daily Times, A Look Back, Jan. 5, 1975
Anchorage Times, Statues immortalize 2 statesmen, Nov. 25, 1984
Anchorage Times, Disjointed government perplexed early governor, Dec. 12, 1984
Associated Press dispatch July 13, 1897
Associated Press, Dec. 26, 1964
Associated Press, National Survey, Feb. 7, 1966
Associated Press, Top News Stories, Dec. 27, 1966
Associated Press, Alaska, Ten Years Later, Jan. 3, 1969
Associated Press, Twas Big Bear, Jan. 2, 1970
Associated Press, Dec. 1, 1972
Associated Press, State tributes mount for Bill Egan, May 7, 1984
Associated Press, First Iditarod Winner, March 11, 2001
Fairbanks Daily News-Miner, Insane Patients To Go Outside, Dec. 17, 1908
Fairbanks Daily News-Miner, March 22, 1960
Fairbanks Daily News-Miner, Historic Flag Day, June 14, 1960
Fairbanks Daily News-Miner Aug. 12, 1961
Fairbanks Daily News-Miner, 16th Annual Progress Edition, March 18, 1965
Fairbanks Daily News-Miner, Jan. 27, 1966
Fairbanks Daily News-Miner, M/V Queen of Prince Rupert, March 17, 1966
Fairbanks Daily News-Miner, State tributes mount for Bill Egan, May 7, 1984
Homer Tribune, Bringing home 'Betty' by Naomi Klouda, 2009
Homer Tribune, '64 earthquake provides cautionary tale, by Naomi Klouda, Oct. 4, 2011
Juneau Empire, July 31, 1961
Juneau Empire, News of the Gold Camp, Robert DeArmond, 1980
Juneau Empire, Massacre survivors try to forget McCarthy's fateful day, Aug. 3, 1998
Juneau Empire, The original capital creep, April 13, 2013

Juneau Empire, Reconsider the ferry system, Albert Judson, Nov. 7, 2014
SitNews, Alaska's First Legislature, 1913, June Allen, Jan. 18, 2003
SitNews, The 1967 Fairbanks Flood, June Allen, Aug. 7, 2003
SitNews, William A. Egan Day, June Allen, Oct. 8, 2003
SitNews, The Grand Ships of the Alaska Marine Highway System, Dave Kiffer, July 8, 2006
SitNews, A Look Back at Alaska's Worst Unsolved Mass Murder, Dave Kiffer, Sept. 6, 2006
SitNews, We're Off On The Road To Alaska's Captial!, Dave Kiffer, Aug. 31. 2009
SitNews, Alaska's Deepwater Highway, June Allen, May 1, 2013
Southeast Alaska Empire, Jan. 3, 1969
The Arctic Sounder, Alaska or bust, by Ross Coe, Feb. 24, 2012
Tundra Times, Oct. 1, 1962
Wrangell Sentinel, Jan. 30, 1963

Various Outside Newspapers
Beatrice Daily Sun, Sept. 1, 2012
Chicago Daily Herald, May 21, 1984
Copley New Service, May 6, 1979
Los Angeles Times, Earthquake by Amy Hubbard, March 27, 2014
New York Post, Jan. 14, 1969
Philadelphia Daily News, Alaskan gets 634 years, July 28, 1984
Spokane Daily Chronicle, April 16, 1964, WSU Graduate, Family, See Changes in Kodiak,
    by Evelyn Bullock
The Boston Globe, 6 slain in shootings, March 3, 1983
The De Kalb Daily Chronicle, De Kalb, Illinois, Oct. 4, 1967
The De Kalb Daily Chronicle, De Kalb, Illinois, Oct. 5, 1967
The Miami Herald, He told me I was a dead man, March 4, 1983
The New York Times, Push to Move Alaska's Capital, May 28, 2002
The Philadelphia Enquirer, Slayings of six stagger a proud Alaskan outpost, March 9, 1983
The Saturday Evening Post, Can Alaska Survive as a State? By Robert Schulman,
    Oct. 5, 1963
The Seattle Times, April 3, 1965
The Seattle Times, July 14, 1968
The Seattle Times, July 15, 1968
The Seattle Times, July 16, 1968
The Seattle Times, July 17, 1968
The Seattle Times, Alaska Comes of Age, Dec. 29, 1968
The Seattle Times, For Sitka, a new St. Michael's, Jan. 1, 1970
The Washington Post, Oct. 20, 1968
The Washington Post, Sept. 23, 1969
Tulsa Tribune, What a Tulsa Editor Found In 49th State, Aug. 30, 1960
Wall Street Journal, July 27, 1961
Wall Street Journal, March 24, 1960
Wall Street Journal, March 25, 1960
Wall Street Journal, March 28, 1960

Miscellaneous Government Sources
The Alaska Committee, A Brief History of Capital-Move Measures PD Alaska Department
    of Economic Development, Arctic Oil Sparks Interest In Alaska, March 1969
Alaska Department of Natural Resources, Title: Land Ownership in Alaska, Fact Sheet,
    March 2000
Kodiak City Hall, Emergency Bulletin No. 10, April 5, 1964
National Science Foundation Grant, Chronology of Physical Events of the Alaskan
    Earthquake, Genie Chance, 1966
U.S. Army Center of Military History (CMH Pub 72-6)

U.S. Army, JBER 50 Years since 1964 earthquake catastrophe: Military integral to recovery, Commentary by Chris McCann, JBER Public Affairs, March 24, 2014

U.S. Army JBER, Operation Helping Hand, The Armed Forces React to Earthquake Disaster, document prepared by Headquarters, Alaskan Command

U.S. Department of the Interior, National Park Service. Elmendorf Air Force Base Volume I, 1999

U.S. Department of the Interior, History of Trans Alaska Pipelie System

U.S. Department of Health & Human Services, Voices of Our Elders, Boarding School: Cultural Trauma & Diaspora, , UAF Unity in the Arts Fall 2001

U.S. Fish and Wildlife Service, Project Chariot, by Douglas L. Vandegraft, May 6, 1993

U.S. Geological Survey, Alaska's Good Friday Earthquake, March 27, 1964, Preliminary Geologic Evaluation, Circ. 491

U.S. Geological Survey, Effects of the Earthquake of March 27, 1964 at Whittler, Alaska, Prof. Paper 542-B

U.S. Geological Survey, Effects of the Earthquake of March 27, 1964 at Seward, Alaska, Prof. Paper 542-E

U.S. Geological Survey, Effects of the Earthquake of March 27, 1964 at Kodiak and Other Communities on the Kodiak Islands, Prof. Paper 542-F

U.S. Geological Survey, Geologic Effects of the March 1964 Earthquake and Associated Seismic Sea Wave on Kodiak and Nearby Islands, Alaska, Prof. Paper 543-D

U.S. Coast and Geoetic Survey, Preliminary Report: Prince William Sound, Alaskan Earthquake, March-April 1964

U.S. Coast and Geodetic Survey,The Prince William Sound, Alaska, Earthquake of 1964 and Aftershocks, v. 1, Operational Phases, No. 10-3

Miscellaneous Publications

Jamison, H.C. "Harry," speech to Alaska Geological Society Technical Conference, April 19, 2008

Lenzner, Terry F. The Management, Planning and Construction of the Trans-Alaska Pipeline System, Report to the Alaska Pipeline Commission, Washington, D.C.

Looking Back 50 Years of AMHS serivce in Southeast, Greg Knight and Rachel Coblentz, April 18, 2013, Vol. 111, No. 16

Petroleum News, Harnessing A Giant, 40 years at Prudhoe Bay, Special Publication, 2008

Railway Age Weekly, January 1965

Tactical Life, Firefight at Manley, by Jeff Hall, Dec. 10, 2010

This Date in Native History, Earthquake Devastates Chenega, by Alysa Landry, March 27, 2014

University of Alaska Fairbanks, Now in the North, July-August 1967

Personal Interviews/Letters/Speeches

Virginia Lacy, Cordova historian
Don Davore, Talkeetna homesteader
Doug Beckstead, JBER historian
Letter from past Anchorage Mayor, George Byer, Dec. 4, 1970
Letter from Kenaitze Indian Tribe member Alexander Wilson, 1968
Letter from Virginia Lacy, Cordova
Ron Hilts, Seldovia
Sandy Vernon, Johns Creek, Georgia
Wanda Showalter, Kenai letters, 2014
Dixie Lambert, Cordova historian

Television Programs

KTUU - 50 Years of Statehood series, 2009
National Geographic Channel. World's Toughest Fixes: Alaska Oil Pipeline. Season 2, Episode 10, Aug. 20, 2009

Public Broadcasting System, The American Experience: The Alaska Pipeline. Davis, Mark. Season 18, Episode 11, April 24, 2006

Web sources

http://www.nativevillageofportlions.org/, retrieved March 3, 2015

http://afognak.org , Our History, Native Village of Afognak, retrieved March 2, 2015

http://akhistorycourge.org, Governing Alaska, retrieved Jan. 4, 2015

http://www.akhistorycourse.org/articles/article.php?artID=350, A Struggle for Land, retrieved March 30, 2015

http://alaskahistoricalsociety.org, Personal Memories of a Statewide Disaster: Ouzinkie in 1964, by Anjuli Grantham, retrieved March 2, 2015

http://www.alaskool.org/projects/landclaims/LandClaims_Unit4_Ch20.htm, retrieved April 6, 2015

http://arcticcircle.uconn.edu/VirtualClassroom/Chariot/vandegraft.html, Project Chariot: Nuclear Legacy of Capt. Thompson, Douglas L. Vandegraft, U.S. Fish Wildlife Service, retrieved April 3, 2015

http://chenegamios.com, Chenega History, A Story of Endurance, retrieved March 1, 2015

http://indiancountrytodaymedianetwork.com, Native History: Earthquake Devastates Native Village of Chenega, by Alysa Landry, retrieved March 1, 2015

http://maps.thefullwiki.org/Construction of the Trans-Alaska Pipeline System, retrieved March 29, 2015

http://valdezalaska.org, 1964 Good Friday Earthquake, retrieved March 5, 2015

http://www.akhistorycourse.org/articles, The Struggle For Land, Juneau Empire, retrieved April 3, 2015

http://www.akresource.org, Trans Alaska Pipeline System Facts, retrieved March 28, 2015

http://www.alaska.edu/uajourney/history-and-trivia/public-service-an-added-d/part-1/, retrieved March 14, 2015

http://www.dot.state.ak, Alaska Department of Transportation & Public Facilities, retrieved Feb. 18, 2015

http://www.explorenorth.com, Ouzinkie, Alaska – a Community Guide, retrieved March 2, 2015

http://www.kodiak.org, Discover Kodiak, 1964 Earthquake/Tsunami, retrieved March 2, 2015

http://www.ktuu.com, Survivor Recounts How Kaguyak Was Lost Forever, retrieved March 2, 2015

http://www.morningsidehospital.com, retrieved Feb. 22, 2015

http://www.pgs.org, The Alaska Pipeline, American Experience, retrieved March 29, 2015

https://www.metlakatla.com/communityOrigins.php, retrieved March 20, 2015

http:/www./Influx.uoregon.edu,The End of the Road, Kevin Coughlin, retrieved May 28, 2015

http://www.scientology.org, retrieved Feb. 22, 2015

http://www.sitnews.us/JuneAllen/AlaskaJade/100504_jade_mountain.html, retrieved Dec. 5, 2012

http://www.usace.army.mil/About/History/HistoricalVignettes/ReliefandRecovery/047 AlaskaEarthquake.aspx, retrieved March 4, 2015

http://www.aoc.gov Bob Bartlett Statue, retrieved Jan. 23, 2015

http://www.wikipedia.org/wiki/Alaska Mental Health Enabling Act, retrieved Feb. 22, 2015

INDEX

59ers, 199–209

A
Afognak Village, 172–175
Alaska Constitutional Convention, 15–16, 30
Alaska Mental Health Enabling Act, 79, 86
Alaska National Interest Lands Conservation Act (ANILCA), 419
Alaska Native Allotment Act of 1906, 240
Alaska Native Claims Settlement Act, 240, 245, 415
Alaska Pacific University, 414
Alaska Permanent Fund, 413, 420
Alaska Psychiatric Institute, 79–86, 147
Alaska Railroad, 126–129, 424
Alaska Statehood Bill, 16–17
Alyeska Pipeline Service Co., 281–282, 286–288, 297–298, 307, 309
Anchorage, 47–55, 359–378
    impact of earthquake on, 95–112
Annabel the elephant, 318–321
ARCO, 254–256, 264–266, 268
Aunt Phil. see Carlson, Phyllis Downing

B
Bartlett, Edward Lewis "Bob," 70, 84, 406
Beatles, 404
Begich, Nick, 350–358
Benson, Benny, 411
Bill, Laurel Downing, 67, 71
Blue Canoes. see Marine Highway System
Boggs, Hale, 350–358
Brown, Russell L., 350–358

C
Carlson, Phyllis Downing, 90–91, 425–429
Cessna 310 airplane, 350–358
Chance, Genie, 94–104, 113, 141, 153
Chenega Village and Chenega people, 152–155
Chilkat ferry, 66, 70–71, 73
Civil Code, 26
Coe, Henry Waldo, 79, 83
Cordova
    fire, 332–337
    iceworm, 313–317
    impact of earthquake on, 156–159
court system, 41

D

Deadhorse, 262–267
Diamond, Anthony J., 14
Downing, Hazel, 69, 71
Downing, Richard, 64, 67, 73

E

earthquake. see Good Friday Earthquake
economy, 58–63
Egan, Governor William A., 59, 68–69, 107
    death of, 422
    first state legislature, 37, 42–43, 46
    inauguration of Alaska Marine Highway System, 12–22, 64
    opening of Kenai oil line, 402
    visit to Valdez after earthquake, 148, 150
Eisenhower, Dwight D., 17–18, 43
Eklutna Annie, 367–368
elephant, 318–321

F

Fairbanks, 338–349
ferry system. see Marine Highway System
firetruck, 322–326
first territorial legislature, 27–30, 318–321
flag, 43–44, 47–57
Flores, Ralph, 403
Fort Wainwright, 401

G

Good Friday Earthquake, 87–198
    Anchorage, 95–112
    Chenega, 152-155
    Cordova, 156-159
    Homer, 160
    Kaguyak, 180–182
    Kenai-Soldotna, 162–163
    Kodiak, 164
    Old Harbor, 175–177
    Ouzinkie, 177–179
    Portage, 117–125
    rebuilding after earthquake, 183–198
    Seldovia, 161
    Seward, 130–140
    Valdez, 141–151
    Whittier, 113–116
Gravel, Mike, 408
Gruening, Ernest, 411

PREVIEW OTHER VOLUMES
AUNT PHIL'S TRUNK

PREVIEW OF VOLUME ONE

Aunt Phil's Trunk Volume One, released in 2006, features the early days in Alaska's past when Native people settled the land, Russians explored and exploited the fur trade and prospectors flooded into the country in search of gold. Includes a few hundred historical photos.

Rock carvings dot landscape

Alaska's petroglyphs, Greek for rock carving, are among many enigmas of science. Because their true meanings are elusive, they remain a mysterious link to a people who inhabited Alaska a long time ago.

Massacre at Nulato

Russians had traded peacefully with the Natives of Nulato, but one day in 1851 that all changed when the Koyukon Indians came to town. Red Shirt, seen here, may have led the raid.

Gold found near Juneau

The stack on the right shows around $22 million in gold dug out near Juneau between 1885-1904. The cube on the left represents what America paid Russia for Alaska in 1867, $7.2 million.

University of Washington, Eric A. Hegg Collection, HEG457

Tent cities sprout up

Following discoveries of gold in the Klondike region, tent cities, such as Dawson seen here, sprang up on the boggy flats in the wilderness.

Gold seekers head north

Thousands of prospectors streamed north and climbed the Chilkoot Trail, seen here, in the hopes of reaching their fortunes of gold.

University of Washington, Alaska and Western Canada Collection, AWC442

Flame of the Yukon

Kathleen Eloisa Rockwell, also known as Klondike Kate, whirled her way across dancehall stages in the Yukon, delighting her audiences with her moves and fancy costumes. She and other dancehall beauties helped lonely miners cope in the wilderness.

University of Alaska Fairbanks, Barrett Willoughby Collection, UAF 1972-116-335

Nuggets in Nome

By July 1, 1900, Nome was a busy frontier town with a population of around 20,000. It also boasted more than 60 saloons, dozens of criminals, a few hundred prostitutes and dishonest officials.

University of Washington, Eric A. Hegg Collection, HEG270

PREVIEW OF VOLUME TWO

Aunt Phil's Trunk Volume Two, released in 2007, features entertaining stories that include the birth of Fairbanks, the lawless years following the Klondike Gold Rush and how the Iditarod Trail was blazed. This volume, also filled with more than 350 historical photographs that showcase life in Alaska from 1900 to 1912, will keep you spellbound!

Fairbanks springs up on the tundra

After Felix Pedro discovered gold in the Interior in 1902, hordes of prospectors rushed into Alaska's interior. One savvy merchant, who set up his trading store along the banks of the Chena River, helped put the town of Fairbanks - pictured above - on the map.

And all the gold that came out of the region was just too tempting for outlaws to resist. One in particular, the Blue Parka bandit, proved daring and bold - until he robbed an Episcopal preacher.

Aunt Phil File photo

Alaska's first law officer

Alaska's first law officer in the Interior knew a thing or two about the criminal element. Frank Canton, appointed deputy marshal for Circle in February 1898, had served with distinction as a peace officer in Wyoming and Oklahoma Territory. He'd also escaped from prison while serving time for a litany of offenses, including murder.

NOAA photo

NOAA photo

Many of those hardy gunslingers and prospectors who made Tombstone a household word in the late 1800s, landed in Alaska and the Yukon after the demise of the Arizona city. Among them were lawman and gunslinger Wyatt Earp, pictured on the left, and John Clum, right, who set up Alaska's postal system in the late 1890s.

Gold discovered in the Iditarod region

Anchorage Museum at Rasmuson Center, John Urban Collection, AMRC-b64-1-171

On Christmas Day 1908, two men discovered gold along the Haiditarod River, a tributary of the Innoko. Soon a new settlement called Iditarod became the largest town in Alaska, boasting more than 4,000 people and sporting newspapers, hotels, electricity and telephone service. Soon teams of men and dogs had blazed a trail from Seward to Nome to haul gold and supplies.

University of Alaska Fairbanks Museum Classification UA91-017-001

Cordova's sourdough preacher-painter

Paul Eustace Ziegler's work aptly captures the epic struggle of sourdough days, portraying that historic period when pioneer men and women conquered a rugged wilderness and opened the Alaska Frontier.

Massive volcanic eruption 1912

June 6, 1912, the earth exploded. People living within several hundred miles in Southwest Alaska were given a taste of what hellfire and brimstone of Biblical teachings might be like when a volcano erupted.

University of Alaska Fairbanks, Amelia Elkinton Collection, UAF-1974-175-399

PREVIEW OF VOLUME THREE

Aunt Phil's Trunk Volume Three, released in 2008, highlights Alaska's early days as a territory of the United States. From the building of the Alaska Railroad, to new-fangled automobiles, to those amazing flying machines of the 1920s, this book – with more than 350 historical photographs – is filled to the brim with adventures of the era between 1912 and 1935.

Railroad spurs Anchorage

The U.S. government sparked a stampede of hard-working railway workers to Cook Inlet when it chose to build a railroad from Seward to the coal fields of the Matanuska Valley in 1915.

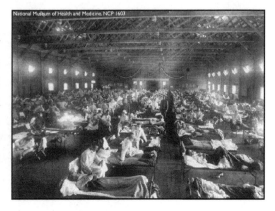

Flu epidemic hits Alaska

Soldiers coming home from World War I brought back more than battlefield memories. The flu epidemic of 1918 devastated many Alaska villages.

First car blazes trail

On July 29, 1913, one of Alaska's trail-blazers started a historic journey – the first automobile trip over the wagon trail from Fairbanks to Valdez. Robert Sheldon, who had never seen an automobile, also built the first car in Alaska.

Airplanes change Alaska forever

Airplanes, which changed Alaska forever, started dotting the skies of the North Country in the early 1920s. Brig. Gen. William Mitchell had a hand in bringing the magnificent flying machines to Alaska. His Black Wolf Squadron, made up of four De Havilland DH-4B aircraft, took off from New York on July 15, 1920, to "demonstrate that we could establish an airway to Alaska and Asia." They made the 4,500-mile trip in 55 flying hours.

Anchorage Museum at Rasmuson Center, General Photograph File, AMRC-b96-17-16

Diphtheria outbreak hits Nome

Alaskans and their dog teams came to the rescue to race vials of life-saving serum from Anchorage to Nome following an outbreak of diphtheria in 1925. Together, the teams covered the route in 127-1/2 hours, which was considered a world record.

Natives gain recognition

Alaska Natives marked a milestone in the mid-1930s, when the federal government recognized their right to locally govern their affairs by tribal governments.

Alaska State Library, Dr. Daniel S. Neuman Collection, ASL-P307-0104

Minnesota Department of Transportation photo

Black fog over Barrow

Wiley Post and Will Rogers crashed and died in 1935. A typewriter recovered in the wreckage had Rogers' unfinished last "piece for the papers," and the final word he'd typed was "death."

PREVIEW OF VOLUME FOUR

Aunt Phil's Trunk Volume Four, released in 2009, shares the highs and lows during the World War II years in Alaska's history. Follow the GIs north as they build the Alaska-Canada Highway, drive the Japanese from the Aleutian Chain and turn Anchorage into a metropolis. This volume also shines a spotlight on the Cold War, the Natives' struggle for equality and the march toward statehood. As with the other volumes in the series, this book has about 350 historical photographs to complement the entertaining stories from 1935 to 1960.

University of Alaska Fairbanks, Kay J. Kennedy Aviation Collection, UAF-1991-98-851

Secret mission with Russia

America and the Soviet Union had a secret pact during World War II. Soviet pilots landed at Ladd Field in Fairbanks on Sept. 24, 1942, to begin training for their missions between Alaska and Russia.

Alcan Highway built in record time

Thousands of GIs with the U.S. Army Corps of Engineers, along with more than 6,000 civilians, laid 1,400 miles of primitive road through the wilderness of Canada and Alaska in record time. Built in less than nine months, the rough trail and its 133 bridges were a great accomplishment, especially considering the extreme temperatures and conditions.

Alaska State Library, Alaska Highway Construction, ASL-P193-044

Alaska State Library, Aleutian/Pribilof Project Collection, ASL-P233-v150

Japanese bomb Aleutians

Dutch Harbor families awoke early on June 3, 1942, unaware that their world was about to explode. But soon the drone of Japanese Zeros cracked the silence of the dawn. By 5:45 a.m., more than a dozen bombers and fighters were screaming over their town.

Japanese ousted from Attu

On May 11, 1943, U.S. troops headed for Attu Island in the military's first-ever amphibious landing. A campaign that was expected to last a few days, stretched into weeks, and it wasn't until May 29 that the American pincers finally closed. Before the battle was over, there would be 549 American and 2,351 Japanese dead.

School Curriculum Now Available

More books from
Aunt Phil's Trunk!

Aunt Phil's Trunk of Trivia **$9.95**

If you love Alaska trivia and you love solving easy to medium puzzles of all kinds from word searches to crosswords to sudokus, then these books are for you. While you challenge your mind, you'll expand your knowledge of Alaska history because each puzzle involves a bit of Alaska lore.

The Spell of the Yukon **$14.95**

This recreation of Robert Service's first published works (in 1907) is sure to please any Alaska history buff. It includes classics like "The Shooting of Dan McGrew" and "The Cremation of Sam McGee," along with a short biography about the bard, who was known as the Voice of the Yukon.

*** **Curriculum Available!** ***

The Call of the Wild **$19.95**
and Other Northland Stories

Written after Jack London returned from the Klondike, this tale of adventure in the frigid north introduced the rest of the world to Alaska in the early 1900s. Several more stories that London wrote about the northland also are included in this collection. Alaska Author Laurel Downing Bill wrote a short biography about London in the back of the book.

*** **Curriculum Available!** ***

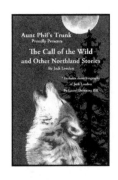

Sourdough Cookery **$14.95**

More than 100 heart-healthy recipes, including mouth-watering cakes, cookies, breads and more. And if you order through www.auntphilstrunk.com, you will receive a FREE packet of sourdough starter from the 1896 gold fields of Hope, Alaska!

Alaska Children's Books

Raven's Friends $9.95
Alaska Animals Far and Wide

Raven's Friends, Alaska Animals Far and Wide, released June 2012, is written and illustrated by Kim Sherry. Children ages 3-8 will love this book as they follow its narrator, Raven, through 32 pages filled with colorful illustrations and poems that share facts about animals that call Alaska home.

Raven's Friends $9.95
Tails Along Alaska Trails

Raven's Friends, Tails Along Alaska Trails, released June 2013, is written and illustrated by Kim Sherry. Children ages 3-8 will love this book as they learn new things about animals that travel along Alaska trails. These 32 pages are filled with colorful illustrations and poems.

The Dragline Kid $9.95

The Dragline Kid and Her Golden Wish, released July 2014, is written by Alaska author Lisa Augustine and illustrated by artist Melody Trone. Children ages 3-8 will delight in this story of a little girl who dreams of finding a gold nugget in Alaska's wilderness.

Muckluck, Alaska $14.95

From Grannie Annie, to Olav the town marshal, to Mrs. Eversall and her cow "Bossy," these pages are filled to the brim with humorous and poignant fictional stories set in 1930-1940s Alaska.

NEW in 2018!

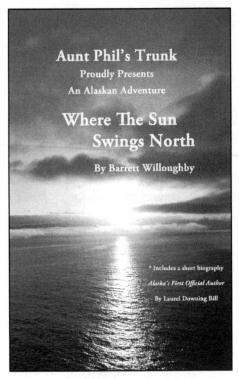

Aunt Phil's Trunk
Proudly Presents
An Alaskan Adventure

Where The Sun
Swings North

By Barrett Willoughby

* Includes a short biography
Alaska's First Official Author
By Laurel Downing Bill

$19.95

Published in 1922, Where The Sun Swings North is the first novel written by Florence Barrett Willoughby, who many call Alaska's first official author.

This tale of adventure is a fictionalized account of her family's real-life experience when stranded on Middleton Island in the Gulf of Alaska for 10 months in 1896-1897 when Willoughby was 10 years old. They may have had few provisions, but they had an intense will to live.

The cast of characters in this story includes a heroine and her Irish husband, a younger lady pure of heart, a drunkard and a diabolical trader who wants the Irishman's wife for his own. Add to this group the elements of Alaska's wild land and unpredictable weather and you've got a tale of adventure you won't soon forget.

***** Includes short biography of Barrett Willoughby
compiled by Alaska author Laurel Downing Bill *****

Coming Christmas 2018!

The Spoilers
By Rex Beach

Aunt Phil's Trunk
Proudly Presents

The Spoilers

By Rex Beach

The Man Behind the Words
By Laurel Downing Bill

Nome 1900

NEW YORK KITCHEN

Rex Ellingwood Beach was in the right place at the right time to get material for his 1906 bestselling story, *The Spoilers*. When he arrived in the new gold rush settlement of Nome in 1900, he found gangs roaming the streets, buildings being set on fire to provide distraction for looters and gold claims being jumped and rejumped multiple times.

He also witnessed the bold attempt by "senator maker" Alexander McKenzie, a Republican political boss, and crooked North Dakota federal judge Arthur H. Noyes, to steal gold from the best placer mines and the tireless attempts of the prospectors to reclaim those mines.

Beach's successful fictional account of the drama that unfolded before his eyes was made into a motion picture five times between 1923 and 1955.

This book also contains a biography of Beach, titled "The Man Behind The Words," written by Alaska author Laurel Downing Bill.